LEGACIES OF THE SUBLIME

SUNY series, Studies in the Long Nineteenth Century
Pamela K. Gilbert, editor

LEGACIES OF THE SUBLIME

Literature, Aesthetics, and Freedom from Kant to Joyce

CHRISTOPHER KITSON

Published by State University of New York Press, Albany

© 2019 State University of New York

All rights reserved

No part of this book may be used or reproduced in any manner whatsoever without written permission. No part of this book may be stored in a retrieval system or transmitted in any form or by any means including electronic, electrostatic, magnetic tape, mechanical, photocopying, recording, or otherwise without the prior permission in writing of the publisher.

For information, contact State University of New York Press, Albany, NY
www.sunypress.edu

Library of Congress Cataloging-in-Publication Data

Names: Kitson, Christopher, 1987– author.
Title: Legacies of the sublime : literature, aesthetics, and freedom from Kant to Joyce / Christopher Kitson.
Description: Albany : State University of New York Press, 2019. | Series: SUNY series, studies in the long nineteenth century | Includes bibliographical references and index.
Identifiers: LCCN 2018027699 | ISBN 9781438474175 (hardcover : alk. paper) |
  ISBN 9781438474199 (e-book) | ISBN 9781438474182 (pbk. : alk. paper)
Subjects: LCSH: Sublime, The, in literature. | Aesthetics in literature. | Sublime, The. | Kant, Immanuel, 1724-1804—Influence.
Classification: LCC PN56.S7416 K58 2019 | DDC 801/.93—dc23 LC record available at https://lccn.loc.gov/2018027699

10 9 8 7 6 5 4 3 2 1

Contents

Acknowledgments — vii
Abbreviations — ix

Chapter 1.
Fear and Freedom: The Legacies of the Sublime — 1

Chapter 2.
"The Awakening of a Manchester":
The Communist Manifesto, *Chartism*, Industrial Spectacle,
and the Communist Subject — 19

Chapter 3.
Orders of Magnitude: *The Time Machine*, Deep Time,
and Wells's Mathematical Sublime — 55

Chapter 4.
Details and Detonators: *The Secret Agent*, Schopenhauer,
Nietzsche, and the Ironizing of the Sublime — 95

Chapter 5.
Journeys through Nighttown: "Circe," "The 'Uncanny,'"
and the Inhabited Subject — 135

Conclusion
The Sublime beyond the Uncanny — 179

Notes — 185
Works Cited — 191
Index — 201

Acknowledgments

I would like to thank my colleagues at the School of English at the Queen's University of Belfast, who provided the environment in which this book could be nurtured, shaped, and realized. In particular, I am grateful to Daniel Roberts, Moyra Haslett, David Dwan, Leon Litvack, Joanne Burns, Joanne Davies, Patricia McCann, Mark McGahon, Charlie Small and John Heaney for their help, advice, and support. Thanks are also due to Andy Smith of Sheffield University, who provided me with a judicious eye and very useful direction. My greatest debt of all, however, is to Brian Caraher, whose diligent help and very many erudite and thoughtful conversations have more than anything else made this book it what it is.

The final stages of work were completed at the Institute for Advanced Studies in the Humanities at the University of Edinburgh, to whom I would like to express my deep gratitude for the time, resources, funding, and stimulating environment they provided. This book would also simply not exist without the generous assistance of the Arts and Humanities Research Council, who provided me with a doctoral studentship.

I am grateful also to the staff and readers at SUNY Press for the care with which they guided this book into production.

More personally, I would like to thank my family and friends. My parents have been invaluable in their support all through the time I was working on this book. Most of all, my deepest thanks go to my wife Felicity, who has been by my side through everything.

Abbreviations

A	*Anticipations*
CJ	*Critique of the Power of Judgment*
CLJC	*Collected Letters of Joseph Conrad*
DF	*The Discovery of the Future*
FLT	*First and Last Things*
MECW	*Marx Engels Collected Works*
MEW	*Karl Marx Friedrich Engels Werke*
OED	*Oxford English Dictionary Online*
PP	*Practical Philosophy*
SA	*The Secret Agent*
SE	*The Complete Standard Edition of the Works of Sigmund Freud*
SR	*Sartor Resartus*
TM	*The Time Machine*
U	*Ulysses*
WWR	*The World as Will and Representation*

CHAPTER 1

Fear and Freedom

The Legacies of the Sublime

When Immanuel Kant included the "Analytic of the Sublime" in his 1790 *Critique of Judgment*, he stood in a tradition of aesthetic speculation reaching back over a century. The sublime had been a staple of philosophy and criticism ever since Boileau's 1674 translation of Longinus. The category was discussed by authors from Addison, Burke, and Kames to Herder and Mendelssohn. It had been brought to bear on topics from art to ethics, history, and theology, and along the way it articulated much about how eighteenth-century subjects thought, felt, and understood themselves. Yet in the period after the third *Critique*, the sublime lost its ubiquitous place. By the middle and late nineteenth century, it became rare as an explicit topic of discussion. This remained the case until the closing decades of the twentieth century, when the category was resurrected by postmodern theorists with literary critics and, more recently, analytic philosophers following them. With this, the sublime has once again become a mainstay of scholarly rumination, the subject of copious debate about its nature and relevance to the experience of modern life.

This view of the sublime's uneven history, its career encompassing ubiquity, dissolution and a long dormant period as well as a sudden and seemingly unbidden return to prominence, leaves some important questions unanswered. Did the sublime really disappear without trace in the early nineteenth century? If so, why was it taken up again so readily in the late twentieth? If the postmoderns did not pull the sublime from oblivion, or invent a new one from whole cloth, what was its status in the later nineteenth and early twentieth centuries? In fact the view of the sublime as a phenomenon relevant only to two isolated historical moments, while it is an important starting point, is incomplete. It masks a deeper story of how talk about this idea has come to define modern culture in profound ways. Appreciating this involves considering the sublime not only as part of the eighteenth-century or postmodern zeitgeist, but as a category which shaped the debates and influenced the imaginations of those throughout the intervening period. The legacy of the eighteenth-century sublime is a pervasive way of thinking about the modern subject in philosophy and literature and it is in the ostensible gap of the late nineteenth and early twentieth centuries that this more deeply felt influence shows itself.

The Romantic Threshold

Scholarship about the fate of the sublime in the nineteenth century has recently tended towards a fuller view of its influence. The key issue is the sublime's strangely ambivalent relationship to romanticism. The great majority of the major texts on the sublime were written well before the close of the eighteenth century: Addison's writings in the *Spectator* (1712–1714), Burke's *Enquiry* (1759), and Kames's *Elements of Criticism* (1765) are examples (Ashfield and de Bolla). High romantic authors such as Wordsworth and Coleridge do indeed write on the sublime, but they tend not to give the term quite the prominence it has for, say, Burke. Yet for all this, the sublime is largely held to be a crucial concept for understanding the culture of romanticism. Critical works such as Thomas Weiskel's *The Romantic Sublime* and Frances Ferguson's *Solitude and the Sublime* successfully apply the concept to romantic texts. These studies follow Samuel Monk's influential study *The Sublime*, which advances the thesis that the eighteenth-century sublime was a crucial element in the large-scale cultural shift from the Augustan to the romantic. In all, there appears to be something of a paradoxical relationship between the sublime and romantic culture. This is summed up by James Kirwan in his *Sublimity*: "[t]he period that saw the sublime fading from aesthetics also saw the appearance of those very works that we are now most likely to think of as illustrative of the sublime" (Kirwan 126). There seems to be a mismatch between the sublime's importance in the cultural climate, which is held to increase as romanticism develops, and its presence as a subject of explicit discussion, which at the same time wanes. The sublime as a culturally inflected construct clearly undergoes change in the transition from the mid-eighteenth century to the romantic period; it is no longer the favored category of critics and aestheticians that it once was. Yet it is far from clear that this change is a simple decline.

Kirwan considers the lack of theorizing about the sublime and its increasing cultural prominence to be in fact aspects of the same process. For him, the early nineteenth century sees the sublime shift between discourses. He talks about an "inverse ratio between the interest of aesthetics and the interest of taste with regard to the sublime," which leads him to conclude that "the 'decline' of the sublime in the nineteenth century is, then, a phenomenon confined entirely to the discipline of aesthetics" (Kirwan 127; 128). Yet even localized within the province of aesthetics, things are not so simple as a decline. There is instead an inclusion of what had been called the sublime into broader categories such that it is no longer treated as a separate and clearly delineated entity. Other categories, such as beauty, art, or imagination, take on aspects of the sublime's role and are inevitably altered in the process. Thus "as the significance of the aesthetic (or more usually Art) per se becomes equivalent to one notion of the significance of the sublime, so the sublime slips into a minor role" (126). The changes of the early nineteenth century, on this view, see the presence of the sublime become more implicit but also more wide-ranging.

Peter de Bolla's work on the sublime can usefully flesh out the processes which Kirwan identifies. In *The Discourse of the Sublime*, de Bolla distinguishes ways in which categories can be located in their discursive context. They can take the form either of what he calls a discourse on something or a discourse of something. A discourse on something is "to be taken as a discrete discourse, a discourse which is to be read in a highly specific way, within a very well defined context" (de Bolla 9). Such discourses are marked out by their explicit commitments and positioning; they are "discourses which say 'read me like this'" (10). There is also a discourse of something, which "does not [. . .] demand that it be read as a discrete discourse on something" (10). A discourse of something is instead characterized by its wide distribution, that it is "made up of a number of discrete discourses" (10). Thus the discourse of politics, for example, will be located "in a wide range of discursive situations—this is clear from our own sense of the political" (10). To put it in de Bolla's terms, then, what the early nineteenth century witnesses is a marked shrinking of the discourse on the sublime, a decline in the amount of texts which are explicitly and self-consciously part of a definite practice of inquiry into the sublime. It does not follow from this, though, that the discourse of the sublime likewise shrinks. In fact, given the processes that Kirwan identifies, with the sublime becoming more ubiquitous in culture outside of aesthetics and being absorbed into other aesthetic categories, it seems that the sublime became even more present. The discourse of the sublime grows as the discourse on the sublime shrinks. This view is extremely useful in allowing the sublime to be studied across time. De Bolla identifies the political economy of the 1840s as a legacy of the sublime even though his focus is tightly on the period of the Seven Years' War—something taken up in the next chapter. This view, moreover, is implicit in the several recent studies which locate the sublime in various particular discursive contexts throughout the nineteenth century, such as Vybarr Creggan-Reid's study of the discourse on time, Ann Colley's of travel writing, and Stephen Hancock's of the domestic novel.

Whilst this book is similarly interested in the post-romantic developments of the sublime, it hews somewhat closer to de Bolla's work than that of Creggan-Reid, Colley, or Hancock.[1] Unlike these authors, I do not restrict my analysis to one specific and discrete discourse. This is because, like de Bolla's, this book attempts to give an account of the sublime's relevance to a particular tradition of subjectivity and, as de Bolla notes, "categories such as the subject are more likely to be stretched across a vast array of discrete discourses rather than inhering within any one," so the areas in which these preoccupations interact with subjectivity occur in a great range of texts (de Bolla 8). De Bolla's project is to show the role of the sublime in producing "the autonomous subject, a conceptualization of human subjectivity based on the self-determination of the subject and the uniqueness of every individual" (8). He does this by showing how structural features of discourses lead to specific ways of conceiving the subject. In particular, he argues that the discourses on the national debt and the sublime led to "a conceptualization of the subject as the excess or overplus of discourse itself; as the remainder, that which cannot be appropriated or included within the present discursive network of control" (6). That is, the subject is underdetermined by legislating discourses, and this means it can be understood as self-determining. This book's account takes after this thesis. It, too, seeks to show how the sublime associates an excess with the subject's potential independence.

Kant and the Sublime Tradition

One particular philosophical articulation of this structure has an unmatched influence. This articulation appears at the very threshold of romanticism and makes a powerful intervention in the discourse on the sublime just as it was starting this process of diffusion. Because of this, it profoundly shaped the development of the sublime into the nineteenth century and beyond. This account is that given in Kant's

Critique of Judgment. In the *Critique*'s "Analytic of the Sublime," Kant inaugurates a way of staging the sublime so that it connotes human autonomy with reference to nature. This reworking of the sublime tradition was so useful in articulating important parts of the post-Kantian intellectual climate that it became very widely influential. In Kant's account, the subject is confronted with an object which presents itself as a threat to either the subject's physical being or its cognitive processes. Contemplating this object causes an ambivalent response. This ambivalence is then taken to speak of an underdetermination of the subject by the object, since the threatening object should naturally determine only a negative response. The excess represented by the positive element of the ambivalent feeling reveals the subject's capacity to judge things outside of what nature determines. This structure bears a similarity to the generation of autonomous subjectivity that de Bolla finds in mid-century British discourse of the sublime. De Bolla's "discursive network of control" instead becomes, in the context of Kant's moral philosophy, the heteronomy of the subject's natural being. The "Analytic" can thus be placed in the context of the broader sublime tradition and can be read as a complex encounter between that tradition and the themes of Kantian philosophy.

As the description above suggests, central to Kant's account of the sublime is its status as an ambivalent feeling. The sublime is for him a "negative pleasure," and he states that "the object is taken up as sublime with a pleasure that is possible only by means of a displeasure" (*CJ* 129; 143). In this, Kant is squarely in the sublime tradition. Affective ambivalence was a commonplace of commentary on the sublime. There is some suggestion of it in Longinus's rhetorical treatise where the effects of the sublime are distinguished from the "merely persuasive and pleasant" (Longinus 143). The theme was picked up and given prominence in the eighteenth century by John Dennis. In his 1704 *The Grounds of Criticism in Poetry*, Dennis claims that "enthusiastic terror contributes extremely to the sublime" (Ashfield and de Bolla 37). In describing his crossing of the Alps, he dwells upon the ambivalence of the experience: "The sense of all this produc'd different motions in me, viz. a delightful Horrour, a terrible Joy, and at the same time, that I was infinitely pleas'd, I trembled" (Dennis 1943; 380). The conceptual chiasmus of "a delightful Horrour, a terrible Joy" emphasizes that the feeling is intensely ambivalent. The eighteenth-century author on the sublime who gives most prominence to the theme is Burke, who develops his theory of pain and pleasure as independent of one another in order to account for the sublime's unique ambivalent relationship to them (Burke 30–31).

Kant is just as forthright as Burke on the sublime's ambivalent affect. As with Burke's theory, Kant's dynamic sublime is impossible without a feeling of fear. He says "that which we strive to resist is an evil, and, if we find our capacity to be no match for it, an object of fear" (CJ 144). Thus "nature can count as a power, thus as dynamically sublime, only insofar as it is considered an object of fear" (144). The dynamic sublime object, then, is, one which, if we were compelled to try to resist it, we would stand no chance, even being destroyed in the attempt, and is therefore an object that naturally and appropriately evokes fear. The mathematical sublime identifies a different but analogous species of natural negative reaction. Mathematically sublime objects make us fear not for our physical wellbeing but for our cognitive abilities. Kant describes this kind of sublime as "a feeling of displeasure from the inadequacy of the imagination in the aesthetic estimation of magnitude for the estimation by means of reason" (141). The usual role of the imagination in estimating magnitude is thwarted by the sublime object. Displeasure thus comes from a threat to cognitive processes important for navigating objects around us. Kant therefore falls in line with the tradition that takes a negative component to the affect as essential to the sublime. For him, the sublime is occasioned only by those objects which can pose a threat to our ways of interacting with the world either physically or mentally.

For Kant, the negative aspect of the sublime feeling is eminently explicable. If this were all there was to it there would be little to say; it is trivial to assert that threatening objects tend to cause a negative reaction. It is because the experience is ambivalent, not just negative, that the sublime is interesting. The positive aspect of the sublime is what indicates an excess over and above the obvious ways in which natural objects determine our reactions. The discussion of the mathematical sublime goes on to say that it is also "a pleasure that is thereby aroused at the same time from the correspondence of this very judgement of the inadequacy of the greatest sensible faculty in comparison with ideas of reason" (CJ 141). Where an object's size causes us displeasure from the inadequacy of our imagination, there is also a pleasure derived from the exercise of our reason. Drawing together mathematical and dynamic, Kant asserts that the sublime discloses factors over and above the logic of nature:

> For just as we found our own limitation in the immeasurability of nature and the insufficiency of our capacity to adopt a standard proportionate to the aesthetic estimation of the magnitude of its domain, but nevertheless found in our own faculty of reason another,

nonsensible standard which has that very infinity under itself as a unit against which everything in nature is small, and thus found in our own mind a superiority over nature itself even in its immeasurability: likewise the irresistibility of its power certainly makes us, considered as rational beings, recognise our physical powerlessness, but at the same time it reveals a capacity for judging ourselves as independent of it and a superiority over nature on which is grounded a self-preservation of quite another kind than that which can be threatened and endangered by nature outside us, whereby the humanity in our person remains undemeaned even though the human being must submit to that dominion. (CJ 145)

The objects of the sublime expose "the insufficiency of our capacity" and "our physical powerlessness," but the experience of the sublime reveals also an excess on the part of the subject. The positive aspects of the sublime experience are those which are not determined by natural factors, such that we find "a unit against which everything in nature is small," and "a self-preservation of quite another kind than that which can be threatened and endangered by nature." In both cases, the positive aspect of the sublime ambivalence shows "a superiority over nature," a foundation for the self-determination of the subject.

Moral Heroism

The emphasis on autonomy gives away that this interpretation of sublime ambivalence has its roots in Kant's ethical theory. For Kant, the sublime is very close to ethics: "In fact a feeling for the sublime in nature cannot even be conceived without connecting it to a disposition of the mind which is similar to the moral disposition" (CJ 151). This linking of the sublime with ethics is another way in which Kant revises commonplaces of the sublime tradition with reference to his own preoccupations. The discussion of the sublime as having a close relation to the ethical has a long history. De Bolla, for example, notes that "[i]t is often remarked that eighteenth-century theories of the sublime began in ethics" (de Bolla 32). He says of Shaftesbury and Hutcheson that "if either writer can be said to be interested in aesthetics *per se*, that interest is clearly tempered by their profoundly ethical standpoints" (32). The investigation into the aesthetic in general, and the sublime in particular, was for these writers occasioned by the enquiry into the moral feeling, so it is not surprising that the sublime was held by them to be ethically elevating. For Thomas Reid, later in the century, the contemplation of grand objects "inspires magnanimity and a contempt of what is mean" (Reid 494). More broadly, the sublime is in important instances held to help produce a virtuous character. This is the case for Burke's theory. Burke does not associate the sublime with magnanimity; indeed, his sublime is ultimately self-interested, arising as it does from the instinct for self-preservation (Burke 36). Nonetheless, as Tom Furniss and Terry Eagleton point out, Burke's theory also serves to valorize the figure of the virtuous bourgeois laborer (Furniss 2; Eagleton 56). Burke's sublime is, as Eagleton puts it, the "rich man's labour," and is recommended as an important inoculation against the corrupting idleness to which the beautiful can dispose us (56). There is, therefore, a widespread tendency to link the feeling for the sublime to the cultivation of some virtue, however conceived.

The way in which Kant does this is strongly influenced by a related but usually distinct sublime thread. This thread is the heroic sublime. It, too, links particular aspects of character to the feeling of the sublime, but these aspects reside on the objective side rather than the subjective. That is, certain heroic characters come to be presented as objects which themselves inspire a sublime feeling. The powerful and courageous heroes of antiquity and myth are frequently cited. Interest in such characters stretches back to Longinus, who dwells upon how Homer "is accustomed to enter into the greatness of his heroes," and points to the passing of Ajax, Achilles, and Patroclus as evidence in his judgment that *The Odyssey* is only an inferior epilogue to the *Iliad* (Longinus 152–53). This interest continued into the eighteenth century, with James Beattie pointing to Milton's Satan, as well as Achilles and Alexander, to exemplify sublime characters (Beattie 370). John Baillie, too, speaks of the "affections unexceptionably sublime, as heroism, or desire of conquest, as in an Alexander or a Caesar" (Baillie 20). Given the nature of these characters, of course, the heroic sublime could sit somewhat uncomfortably with the moral sublime; the taste for characters known for their cruelty could be difficult to reconcile with a sublime that was held to be morally edifying (Kirwan 47).

Nevertheless, there is an element of the heroic sublime in Kant's theory. His reference to the sublimity of lawfully conducted war hints at some influence by this theme:

> Even war, if it is conducted with order and reverence for the rights of civilians, has something sublime about it, and at the same time makes the mentality of the people who conduct it in this way all the more sublime, the more dangers it has been exposed to and before which it has been able to assert its courage. (*CJ* 146)

Kant here rather unsuccessfully tries to avoid the moral qualms raised by stipulating respect for the "rights of civilians" (146). However, more interesting in this passage is that the discussion of war also touches upon the moral sublime. The sublimity found in war, as Kant here claims, can also foster a positive virtue. It is an opportunity to be courageous. This is significant because the overcoming of inclination, of which courage is a paradigm example, is essential to Kant's conception of the moral agent. Famously, for Kant moral worth is present only in autonomous action—that is, in action that is done out of respect for the demands of rational duty. Any actions to which the agent is inclined are considered heteronomous and so lack this worth. The most vivid depiction of this conception of moral agency can be found in *The Groundwork of the Metaphysics of Morals*. One of Kant's examples concerns a man who is not disposed to benevolence:

> [I]f nature had put little sympathy in the heart of this or that man; if (in other respects an honest man) he is by temperament cold and indifferent to the sufferings of others, perhaps because he himself is provided with the special gift of patience and endurance toward his own sufferings, and presupposes the same in every other and even requires it: if nature had not properly fashioned such a man (who would in truth not be its worst product) for a philanthropist, would he not still find within himself a source from which to give himself a far higher worth than what a mere good-natured temperament might have? By all means! It is just then that the worth of character comes out, which is moral and incomparably the highest, namely that he is beneficent not from inclination but from duty. (PP 54)

It is in acting independently of inclination that worth of character is found. Moreover, inclination is here identified with nature; it is nature which has put little sympathy in the heart of the man, and has endowed him with his unusual patience and strength. The man's moral worth comes from his overcoming of nature in his constitution and his inclinations. This view can be contrasted with, say, an Aristotelian or virtue ethical approach, in which the inclinations themselves are to be aligned with ethical norms. Instead, the demands of morality entail a heroic conflict with nature in its guise as inclination.

In the experience of the dynamic sublime, Kant's subject imagines itself as a moral hero like that described in the *Groundwork*. For an object to be dynamically sublime it must be fearful and, for Kant, judging an object to be fearful involves considering it hypothetically as a threat to us:

> We can, however, consider an object as fearful without being afraid of it, if, namely, we judge it in such a way that we merely think of the case in which we might wish to resist it and think that in that case all resistance would be completely futile. (CJ 144)

Thus, even if we are not directly afraid of something, not afflicted by any immediate inclination away from it, we nonetheless think of a situation in which we would be afraid. Confronted by an object which we could not resist, we would have the strongest possible natural inclination against it. Thus nature, in the form of physical power and in the related form of our inclination to fear that power, would seem impossible to overcome. Yet even as we judge the fearful object to be overwhelming, we find a way in which we could freely resist it. This is argued in the discussion of dynamically sublime objects. These objects

> make our capacity to resist into an insignificant trifle in comparison with their power. But the sight of them only becomes all the more attractive the more fearful it is, as long as we find ourselves in safety, and we gladly call these objects sublime because they elevate the strength of our soul above its usual level, and allow us to discover within ourselves a capacity for resistance of quite another kind, which gives us courage to measure ourselves against the apparent all-powerfulness of nature. (144)

Kant reiterates the point, claiming that nature is judged to be sublime

> because it calls forth our power (which is not part of nature) to regard those things about which we are concerned (goods, health and life) as trivial, and hence to regard its power (to which we are, to be sure, subjected in regard to these things) as not the sort of dominion over ourselves and our authority to which we would bow if it came down to our highest principles and their affirmation or abandonment. (CJ 145)

Thus, these objects, which would otherwise be both irresistible and the cause for terrible fear, become sublime when we regard them from a position of security. This is because they cause us to present a case in which we could, like the moral hero of Kant's early ethics, overcome the very strongest of our natural inclinations. We show courage equal to any hero of antiquity in these cases, as we imagine ourselves heedless of our very lives in the exercise of freedom. Kant has united a moral sense of the sublime, one which discloses us our potential to be moral agents, with a heroic sublime which is inspired by great and courageous feats of will.

So Kant's particular staging of the sublime emerges out of a complex interaction between aspects of the sublime tradition, all guided by the preoccupation with autonomy which dominates his ethics. This means that, despite the many links between Kant's theory and the eighteenth-century tradition of the sublime, the Kantian staging is quite distinctive. Emily Brady sums it up when she states that Kant's theory "stands out from those of his predecessors and contemporaries for its strong metaphysical component," which "links the sublime as a form of aesthetic experience with the sense of freedom possessed by moral beings" (Brady 47). Yet to stop there would understate what is remarkable about the "Analytic." This is because it not only stands out from other theories of the sublime, it also fits somewhat awkwardly even within the *Critique of Judgment* itself. The third *Critique*, according to Kant, was an endeavor to expound in the concept of judgement "the mediating concept between the concepts of nature and the concept of freedom" (CJ 81). The importance of this, as Paul Guyer suggests, is that, whilst Kant does not abandon his view of the "unlimited freedom of the noumenal agent," he qualifies his attitude to how this freedom should express itself (Guyer *Experience of Freedom* 37). Freedom should be expressed within the sensuous world of nature, rather than only occurring in opposition to it:

> What is added is the idea that a feeling engendered by aesthetic response can represent this metaphysical claim to us through our imagination, and that it is apparently quite important that the basis of morality receive such a sensible representation. (37)

This is part of what Guyer calls a "profound ripening in Kant's conception of morality which took place in the last decade of his creativity" (31). In this ripening, Kant came to the view that inclination and moral action are not necessarily opposed, and that the former may aid the latter. The example discussed above from the *Groundwork* can be contrasted with one from *Religion Within the Limits of Reason Alone*. Here Kant describes someone who possesses a "joyous heart" in following duty. A "slavish determination of mind," Kant here says, "can never obtain without a hidden *hatred* of the law, and the joyous heart in following its duty (not complacency in the *acknowledgment* of it) is a sign of the genuineness of virtuous disposition" (Kant in

Guyer *Experience of Freedom* 32). There is no longer here any interest in resisting inclination with gritted teeth. The view put forward is instead that, as Guyer says,

> the nature of one's feelings is not simply to be taken as a given, to be ignored by the free will and overridden when necessary, but that feelings, as part of one's natural being, should and can be modified to help perfect the harmony between one's natural and rational being. (Guyer *Experience of Freedom* 32)

This is the ethical context in which the *Critique of Judgment* should be interpreted. Indeed, the third *Critique*'s talk of mediation between nature and freedom does suggest that it aims to bring natural inclination and moral autonomy into harmony. As Guyer suggests, in the *Critique of Judgment*, Kant "has certainly gone beyond the heroic view of the *Critique of Practical Reason*, on which the free will simply ignores the facts of nature" (46). The "Analytic of the Sublime" is part of this project. It explains a way in which natural objects can induce awareness in the subject of its freedom. Moreover, since this is an aesthetic pleasure, if a mixed one, then a taste for the sublime feeling can be allied to moral action.

Nevertheless, it is striking that the "Analytic of the Sublime" appeals to the previous, heroic view of moral freedom in order to induce this awareness. Unlike the beautiful, the sublime does not foster harmony between the natural and rational being; rather it depends on staging a conflict between them in which reason triumphs. The sublime comes from realizing the free will's ability to overrule even the strongest natural inclinations. The point is not that the *Critique of Judgment* is incoherent. The sublime, of course, does not rely on the actual exercise of such a drastic act of freedom; the subject is merely caused to contemplate it. Nevertheless, this is a significant difference of emphasis between the "Analytic of the Sublime" and the rest of the third *Critique*. Kant's sublime is an idea oddly set apart, drawing its logic and force from earlier iterations of Kant's ethics and from the sublime tradition rather than fitting seamlessly into his later work.

Staging Freedom

Given that Kant's sublime has to some extent a valency of its own even in the text in which it first appears, it is unsurprising that it took on an independent life outside of his philosophy. His striking and distinctive approach to the sublime, and its emphasis on the revelation of freedom, was by no means peripheral to the reception of Kant's aesthetics. This can best be seen in the writings of his contemporary and disciple, Friedrich Schiller. Schiller was an important figure in the reception of Kant, and Kant's aesthetics in particular, serving as a route to Kantian ideas for many teutonophiles. Germaine de Staël's account of Kant's sublime, for instance, was mediated by Schiller (Kirwan 69). Thomas Carlyle, who is treated in the next chapter, had likely only limited familiarity with Kant, but he was far more familiar with Schiller (Ashton 92). Schiller's popularity is significant because he took up and expanded Kant's sublime. Frederick Beiser points out how Schiller's sublime begins from "perfectly Kantian premises," which view the sublime as opposing sensible nature to rational freedom (Beiser, *Schiller* 260). Schiller's essay "Concerning the Sublime" is framed at the outset by the issue of human free will. He begins by stating that "[t]he will is what distinguishes the human race," and then, "[a]ll other things must; the human being is the entity that wills" (Schiller 70). Schiller is, if anything, more explicit than Kant is about the connection between ambivalent affect and moral autonomy. He says that the "feeling of the sublime is a mixed feeling," one that combines "*being in anguish* (at its peak this expresses itself as a shudder) and being happy (something that can escalate to a kind of ecstasy)" (74). Crucially, he states that "[t]his synthesis of two contradictory sensations in a single feeling establishes our moral self-sufficiency in an irrefutable manner" (74). Schiller's account of the sublime here states succinctly that it is the ambivalence, the complexity of the sublime feeling that "establishes" our independence.

Besides being more explicit about it, Schiller also broadens the implications of this logic. This occurs in his discussion of the Laocoön sculpture in his essay "On the Pathetic." Here Schiller takes as his starting point the famous facial expression of Laocoön upon being attacked by serpents. Schiller describes the expression as one which demonstrates Laocoön's suffering and turmoil, but which nonetheless does not show him crying out in pain or panic. Schiller interprets the sculpture according to a variation on the Kantian sublime. The following comment is crucial:

> Whenever the vipers would have taken hold of him, it would have moved and shaken us. The fact, however, that it occurs precisely at that moment when he deserves our respect as a father, the fact that his demise is represented as the immediate result of fulfilling

his paternal duty, as the consequence of the tender concern for his children– this ignites our participation to the utmost. It is now as though he freely chooses to surrender himself to the disaster and his death becomes an action of his will. (Schiller 59)

Schiller emphasizes the troubling negative affect, both for Laocoön and for the "moved and shaken" viewer. However, the emphasis is on the vindication of Laocoön's will. He has chosen to perform his paternal duty even at the cost of his life. He thus demonstrates that the serpents are, as Kant would have it, "not the sort of dominion over ourselves and our authority to which we would bow if it came down to our highest principles and their affirmation or abandonment" (*CJ* 145). Guyer lays out the consequences of this, saying that Schiller transforms "Kant's analysis of the dynamical sublime into an account of the depiction of freedom in the highest forms of art" (Guyer *Modern Aesthetics* 476). Where in Kant's sublime observing natural power ultimately reveals our moral freedom, "in Schiller's account of tragedy it is the will and action of the depicted character that reveal the power of *his* moral being, and perhaps by implication of our own as well" (476). In this way, the Kantian sublime began to develop and transform after the third *Critique*. Schiller maintains Kant's structure of the sublime and its central emphasis on the independence of the subject, but he expands the definition and possibilities of Kant's sublime. For one thing, Schiller applies it to a work of art, whereas Kant insists the sublime is only a response to natural objects. Relatedly, Schiller has a less traditional sense of what can be a sublime object. The serpents that threaten Laocoön are quite different from the ocean storms and starry skies that Kant cites. Both of these developments are consequences of the most important shift represented by Schiller's reinterpretation. This is that he opens the sublime up to being a staging of human freedom. Rather than its being found only in a very specific variety of aesthetic experience that an individual might encounter, the logic of the Kantian sublime can exist within a work of art. The sublime thus becomes a way art can express, and interrogate, human self-determination. Schiller's enthusiastic adoption and revision of the Kantian logic of the sublime reveals that crux in its history when it transformed from being primarily a discrete and self-conscious discourse to being a broadly influential implicit one.

This is the sublime that the next generation of post-Kantian thinkers took up. It is prominent in the thought both of Hegel and Schopenhauer. Hegel's aesthetics have a lesser role for the sublime than do those of Kant or Schiller but, as the next chapter discusses, the influence of the Kantian staging of the sublime is visible in the life or death struggle of the "Lordship and Bondage" section of the *Phenomenology of Spirit*. Schopenhauer's sublime, discussed in the fourth chapter, is largely a development of Kant's. These philosophers were of course themselves immensely influential as figures in the modern development of thought about the self. Charles Taylor talks of the importance of Kant and his followers on this count. He says of Kantian autonomy that it

> has been a powerful, it is not overstated to say revolutionary, force in modern civilization. It seems to offer a prospect of pure self-activity, where my action is determined not by the merely given, the facts of nature (including inner nature), but ultimately by my own agency as a formulator of rational law. This is the point of origin of the stream of modern thought, developing through Fichte, Hegel and Marx, which refuses to accept the merely "positive", what history, or tradition, or nature offers as a guide to value or action, and insists on an autonomous generation of the forms we live by. (Taylor 364)

The figures here mentioned, of course, have great philosophical differences between them. But they, as well as Schopenhauer, Nietzsche, and even Freud, not to mention the literary writers who engaged with their work, all participated in the endeavor of working through a modern subjectivity characterized by self-determination. Among those who followed in this current, then, the sublime was on hand to provide a way of dramatizing and giving shape to their various conceptions of this modern self.

As the breadth of this tradition suggests, the uses of the sublime made by these authors will differ in various ways. Perhaps the biggest axis of difference concerns whether the sublime's staging of the human against nature is given an individual or a collective significance. That is, whether the emphasis is put on the individual's experience of their own freedom or whether it is humanity as a whole's relationship with the natural world that is focused upon. This ambiguity emerged early in the post-Kantian tradition. It is something which Matt Ffytche picks up on in the course of discussing Fichte. He points out that Taylor's locution of "autonomous generation of the forms we live by" raises the question

> does this mean we as individuals, or we collectively, as humankind? To what degree are the forms of our ethical life necessarily shared? If the aspiration of this radical autonomy is "ultimately to a total

liberation," is this of the self or of society? [...] "self-defining subjectivity' appears to suggest a creative individualism; but Taylor also observes that the modern shift to a self-defining subject was bound up with a sense of control over the world—"at first intellectual and then technological"—which seems to imply, at root, collective and social phenomena. (Ffytche 43)

This ambivalence is a real one and is visible in the various uses to which the sublime was put. There are those which engage this collective, social emphasis and those which stay in the realm of the private and individual, although of course the distinction is by no means always clear cut. The former is represented in Carlyle's and Marx's and Engels's concern with social and economic development, and also in the way the sublime tradition interacts with post-Darwinian ways of thinking about humanity's place in nature, as exemplified by Huxley and Wells. The latter tendency is found in the emphases of Schopenhauer and Freud on the deep problems of living an individual life as a human being entangled within nature.

Subjects and Objects

While this introduction has largely been concerned with the philosophical provenance of this inheritance, it remains to stress that it is by no means strictly philosophical. The sublime in the late nineteenth and early twentieth century was characterized precisely by its not being confined to philosophy and aesthetics, but by its presence across many discourses. Indeed, the sublime as I follow it exists inevitably at the threshold between philosophy on one side and literature on the other. This study therefore takes as its material both literary and theoretical texts brought together by common influence and concern. These texts generally present a representative of the sublime object and the subject of the experience. The precise depiction of each of these elements varies greatly. In the *Critique of Judgment*, of course, the object is represented by the traditional accoutrements of the natural sublime, starry skies and waterfalls. Whilst the pull of these eighteenth-century commonplaces remains and periodically resurfaces in altered form, as in Wells, or as a resource of metaphor, as in Conrad's descriptions of the London streets, a greater variety of sublime objects come to the fore. These include Marx's and Engels's industrial landscape as manifestation of bourgeois power and the disturbing dreamscape featured in Joyce's "Circe."

The other side of the equation provides even more interesting variations of the basic structure. As different authors amend and appropriate the sublime subject, it becomes variously embodied and embroidered. It becomes linked with particular positively valued qualities or virtues, something seen in the technocratic bent and scientific thinking of Wells's "New Republicans," and also in the chivalric virtues of Conrad's Assistant Commissioner of Police in *The Secret Agent*. The subject will also often have a class position, as is of course the case for the class-conscious proletarian of *The Communist Manifesto*, and will also be gendered. Indeed, the gendering of the sublime as masculine is a particularly pervasive fact, explicit in Burke and implicit but, as Barbara Claire Freeman points out, still very present in Kant (Freeman 72). This gendering casts a long shadow over those articulations of sublime agency that are governed by this Kantian inheritance. The presentation of the sublime subject as male is ultimately subverted in Joyce's radically plural form of subjectivity.

These literary texts are discussed alongside non-literary works in order to contextualize and clarify the philosophical issues at stake. However, the literary texts do not stand as simple explanations or paraphrases of the ideas in the philosophical ones. The unfolding of this legacy is considerably more complicated than this. Given that the sublime stands at the intersection of aesthetics, philosophy, and literature, the distinctions between the discourses often becomes unstable. For example, the literary flourishes and narrative strategies that Freud uses turn out to be central to his attempt to theorize the uncanny. For their part, the literary texts do not simply embody the discursive ones, but provide critiques, modifications, or expansions of the theories. Conrad's *The Secret Agent*, for example, reflects much of Schopenhauer's aesthetic theory, but Conrad also in some ways goes further than Schopenhauer, with the novel's "ironic treatment" developing consequences only implicit in Schopenhauer's theory. Likewise, the sublime in Wells's early fiction works to expose the tensions in the utopian visions of his later nonfiction. This book, then, examines sites of dialogue between the literary and philosophical or theoretical texts in which the legacies of the sublime persist. The history it documents is of course not exhaustive; it focusses on one, albeit influential, strand of a complex cultural inheritance, and works of necessity by exemplification. Nevertheless, in the chapters that follow, my readings will endeavor to allow the subjects of the modern sublime to step forth, one after another, from their various backgrounds, and in doing so tell some part of the story of the sublime's profound legacy.

CHAPTER 2

"The Awakening of a Manchester"

The Communist Manifesto, Chartism, Industrial Spectacle, and the Communist Subject

The Communist Manifesto is a definitive text of the nineteenth century and of modernity in general. Its cultural impact has been enormous, and the text's literary qualities have had, in a sense, a life of their own. Commentators routinely praise the *Manifesto* in terms far fuller than would be expected of a political pamphlet. This praise largely concerns the *Manifesto*'s evocation of modernity. Jonathan Sperber calls it a "literary masterpiece" (Sperber 203) and Eric Hobsbawm mentions its "dark literary eloquence" (Hobsbawm). Gareth Stedman Jones is confident of the text's canonical status mainly because of its artistic merit: "[T]he *Manifesto* will remain a classic, if only because of its brief but still quite unsurpassed depiction of modern capitalism" (Stedman Jones, "Introduction" 5). The theme of the text's literary pre-eminence is also dwelt upon by Marshall Berman, who claims that Marx praises the bourgeoisie "more powerfully and profoundly than its members have ever known how to praise themselves" (Berman 92). As such, he places this depiction at the heart of his study of modernity and modernisation, *All That Is Solid Melts into Air*, taking this phrase from the *Manifesto* as emblematic of Marx's "melting vision" in its "cosmic scope and visionary grandeur" (89). It is not only cultural critics who have been impressed with the power of the *Manifesto*'s rhetoric. Its influence can be found in the fact that the text more or less invented a genre of writing, having spawned political and artistic manifestos of many persuasions (Puchner 11). In short, what this body of cultural response testifies is that the *Manifesto* is a classic modernist text, one which has found a particularly compelling idiom in which to depict the world of capitalist modernity.

This idiom does not come from nowhere. Rather, deeply involved in the text's depiction of capitalism is an appeal to the sublime, one which has multiple sources. From Thomas Carlyle, Marx and Engels inherit a mode of depicting modern history and industrial development with reference to the sublime. Like Carlyle, they combine the rhetoric of the sublime with the symbolism of historical crisis and with a suggestion of the apocalyptic. But most importantly, like Carlyle they stage a model of human freedom defined by workmanship, by the human ability to alter nature through self-directed activity. Yet, for all the commonalities of concern and imagery taken from Carlyle, the most direct source for the *Manifesto*'s sublime is Hegel's "Lordship and Bondage," itself a reworking of the Kantian staging of the sublime. Hegel's text gives Marx and Engels a means by which to dramatically stage the proletariat as the independent agent of their revolution.

The Spectacle of Capitalism

The section of the *Manifesto* that holds probably the most vivid literary interest is its first, the section entitled "Bourgeois and Proletarians." This section gives an account of the development of human society up to the present day, with special interest given to modern history and the rise of the bourgeoisie. Instead of a detailed chronology it uses instead broad, suggestive strokes to encompass pervasive historical processes in single gestures. The following is representative of its scope:

> From the serfs of the Middle Ages sprang the chartered burghers of the earliest towns. From these burgesses the first elements of the Bourgeoisie were developed.
> The discovery of America, the rounding of the Cape, opened up fresh ground for the rising Bourgeoisie. (*MECW* 6: 485)

The listing of these very wide-ranging phenomena in a few sentences is characteristic of how the *Manifesto* achieves its impression of grand proportion. In the above quotation, for instance, a summary which encompasses a temporal expanse of decades or centuries is followed immediately by another which encompasses an intercontinental spatial one. This sense of scale is encoded in the *Manifesto*'s frequent use of catalogues. Such a strategy is inaugurated in the famous opening lines of the section:

> The history of all hitherto existing society is the history of class struggles.

> Freeman and slave, patrician and plebeian, lord and serf, guild master and journeyman, in a word, oppressor and oppressed, stood in constant opposition to one another. (6: 482)

Here various examples of contending classes are enumerated, then brought under a single category. The catalogue underlines the sheer variety of phenomena which constitute "all hitherto existing society" (6: 482). These phenomena are nevertheless summed up "in a word." Indeed, the construction "in a word" is so used no less than four times in quick succession during the exposition of modern history. Its function is always to introduce a single category which contains a great multiplicity of elements.[1] In this way, the *Manifesto* cultivates its sense of grand proportion by maintaining a tension between potentially endless accumulation and single conceptual statement. At times the verbosity of the rhetoric even seems to undermine the claim to comprehensive summary which the phrase implies: "In one word, for exploitation, veiled by religious and political illusions, [the Bourgeoisie] has substituted naked, shameless, direct, brutal exploitation" (6: 487). The "one word" referred to here is clearly "exploitation," but the catalogue of adjectives which accompany it undermines the sense that such a single word really captures the quality of capitalist exploitation.[2] The general effect of this tension between accumulation and summary is that of a dizzying array of phenomena held, albeit unsteadily, in one view. The section's description of the ways in which the bourgeoisie has revolutionized the world also tends toward this effect. It emphasizes the vastness of its subject matter through treating it as a many-sided phenomenon, which can only with difficulty be glimpsed in its entirety. The section is introduced by another insufficient summarizing statement, the single-sentence paragraph: "The bourgeoisie, historically, has played a most revolutionary part" (6: 486). In the ensuing description no chronology is followed. Instead, various actions or characteristics of the bourgeoisie are picked up and discussed in turn: its sacrifice of all values in favor of free trade, its incessant questing for greater productive power and for fresh markets, its relentless urbanization. The phrase "the bourgeoisie has" becomes a continual refrain, beginning each new paragraph with fresh revolutionary action on their part (*MECW* 6: 486–90). The variety of ways in which the bourgeoisie has revolutionized society seems to render an attempt at a single sequential narrative impossible, such that the development of capitalism is not so much a tale told in the *Manifesto*, but rather a spectacle to be approached from every angle.

These rhetorical strategies reflect the nature of the modern epoch which "Bourgeois and Proletarians" describes. The capitalist era is one in which phenomena of dizzying multiplicity and unprecedented scale have become facts of life. The bourgeoisie requires "a constantly expanding market for its products," which causes it to expand "over the whole surface of the globe" (*MECW* 6: 487). Its crises are crises of overproduction, happening "[b]ecause there is too much civilization, too much means of subsistence, too much industry, too much commerce" (6: 490). Just as the scope of modern history can only with difficulty be contained in one description, so these crises show that "[t]he conditions of bourgeois society are too narrow to comprise the wealth created by them" (6: 490). This capacity to produce multiplicity is figured also as productive power, which is naturally of large scale:

> Meantime the markets kept ever growing, the demand ever rising. Even manufacture no longer sufficed. Thereupon, steam and machinery revolutionised industrial production. The place of manufacture was taken by the giant, Modern Industry. (6: 485)

It is significant that in the above quotation "steam and machinery" become agents in their own right and step forward fantastically personified as a giant.[3] The productive forces of the bourgeoisie are so huge that they defeat attempts to control them:

> Modern bourgeois society with its relations of production, of exchange and of property, a society that has conjured up such gigantic means of production and exchange, is like the sorcerer, who is no longer able to control the powers of the nether world whom he has called up by his spells. (6: 489)

Just as the quantity of wealth produced overflows the structures of the bourgeoisie, so the dynamic force of its industry overpowers them. The extent of this power is described with reference to some of the familiar touchstones of the sublime. The *Manifesto* states that "[the bourgeoisie] has accomplished wonders far surpassing Egyptian pyramids, Roman aqueducts, or Gothic cathedrals" (6: 487). Significantly, it is the grand and venerable architecture beloved of the Romantic sublime that provides the context here. Kant's employment of the pyramids in the *Critique of Judgment* shows clearly the coincidence of preoccupations (*CJ* 136). This architecture, formerly exemplary of the sublime, is now far surpassed. Yet the superlative things that the *Manifesto* puts in their place are only ill-defined "wonders." There is no indication as yet what these wonders may be. The achievements of the bourgeoisie are evoked as obscure but tremendous objects existing beyond the pyramids and cathedrals.⁴ Several paragraphs later, the variety of things that may constitute these wonders are specified. This process itself runs into another exhausting catalogue:

> Subjection of Nature's forces to man, machinery, application of chemistry to industry and agriculture, steam-navigation, railways, electric telegraphs, clearing of whole continents for cultivation, canalization of rivers, whole populations conjured out of the ground—what earlier century had even a presentiment that such productive forces slumbered in the lap of social labour? (*MECW* 6: 489)

It is literally true that industrial capitalism is powerful in terms of capacity for production. However, the rhetoric of the sublime is not limited to expressing this fact. The social implications of rising capitalism are figured using the imagery of wild nature. The bourgeoisie is a flood, it has "drowned the most heavenly ecstasies of religious fervor, of chivalrous enthusiasm, of philistine sentimentalism, in the icy water of egotistical calculation" (6: 487). Compare this imagery with some of Kant's examples in his "Analytic of the Sublime," of "thunder clouds towering up into the heavens, [. . .] volcanoes with their all-destroying violence," and particularly "hurricanes with the devastation they leave behind, the boundless ocean set into a rage, a lofty waterfall on a mighty river, etc." (*CJ* 144). The natural imagery used in the *Manifesto*'s description of modern society sits comfortably alongside that sketched by Kant, with the two also happening to echo one another in their torrential catalogues.

The *Manifesto*'s Terror

Marx and Engels thus adopt in various ways strategies that present their subject matter as a spectacle of great magnitude and power, one which constantly threatens to defeat attempts to control and to represent it. The powers unleashed by modern social conditions are as threatening as a giant, a demon or a flood, things which, as with the objects of Kant's dynamic sublime, "make our capacity to resist into an insignificant trifle in comparison with their might" (*CJ* 144). Yet for all of this, the spectacle is also exciting. The achievements of the bourgeoisie are, after all, "wonders," which surpass ancient monuments (*MECW* 6: 487). Capitalism is clearly potentially threatening, but it is also compelling.

The spectacle therefore articulates the ambivalence of the *Manifesto*'s authors towards the bourgeois epoch itself. For Marx and Engels, capitalism presents human beings with unprecedented positive possibilities as well as grave dangers. On the one hand, capitalism constitutes a monstrous threat to humane values and to the wellbeing of the vast majority of people. The tone of some descriptions suggests outrage at the thoroughness of the social world's disenchantment. The bourgeoisie has "reduced the family relation to a mere money relation" (*MECW* 6: 487). It has "stripped of its halo every occupation hitherto honored and looked up to with reverent awe" and "converted the physician, the lawyer, the priest, the poet into its paid wage-labourers" (6: 487). What Marx and Engels here articulate is of course no unalloyed nostalgia. The fact that the bourgeoisie has "for exploitation, veiled by religious and political illusions [. . .] substituted naked, shameless, direct, brutal exploitation" represents at least a step away from hypocrisy (6: 487). Nevertheless, the shamelessness and brutality of capitalist exploitation is egregious, and this exploitation can be implemented on a much larger scale and much more efficiently than before. More people, moreover, suffer from it, since the "lower strata of the middle class [. . .] sink gradually into the proletariat, partly because their diminutive capital [. . .] is swamped in the competition with the large capitalists" (6: 491–92). Here the flood metaphor is applied directly to the hostile economic conditions in which individuals find themselves. They are unable to resist the resources of the capitalists who "swamp" them, and thereafter they have no choice but to endure exploitation, and with it capitalism's most pervasive threat to human wellbeing, the alienation of labor (6: 490).

Yet among this decrying is what Berman calls "an impassioned, enthusiastic, often lyrical celebration of bourgeois works and ideas" (Berman 92). According to the *Manifesto*, the bourgeoisie have made "national one-sidedness and narrow-mindedness become more and more impossible" (*MECW* 6: 488). They have, apparently even more laudably, "rescued a considerable part of the population from the idiocy of rural life" (6: 488). More than this, however, it is the fact of bourgeois development, of the vastness of the possibilities which bourgeois power entails, which is compelling. Capitalism, just as it grievously thwarts human productive capacities, has nonetheless "been the first to show what man's activity can bring about" (6: 487). In this sense, the unprecedented vastness of capitalist productive power takes on a wondrous aspect: "[W]hat earlier century," it is asked, "had even a presentiment that such forces slept in the lap of social labour?" (6: 489). The processes of capitalism ultimately bring about the conditions for communism. The destruction of idyllic social relations compels "man [. . .] to face with sober senses, his real conditions of life, and his relations with his kind" (6: 487). The productive forces of capitalism can potentially be turned to an economy that does not depend on exploited labor, but in which "accumulated labour is but a means to widen, to enrich, to promote the existence of the labourer" (6: 499). The *Manifesto*, therefore, presents modern industry as at once terrifying and repulsive as well as exciting and compelling, just as is capitalism.

Terry Eagleton in *The Ideology of the Aesthetic* hints towards this ambivalence, but divides it into two distinct sublimes in Marx's thought, one of which is a "bad" sublime (Eagleton 212). Eagleton's implicitly "good" sublime is associated with communist society and its lack of need for formal strictures, which limit human potential—that is, communist society is one free from artificial strictures, one in which human powers and capacities are given full and untrammeled expression. Communist society is thus "no more than a continually self-expanding multiplicity bordered only by itself" and hence "the effect is then one of a certain sublimity" (217). The "bad" sublime, by contrast, is connected with the capitalist economy and the way in which exchange value levels out differences into a formless mass. It "resides in the restless, overweening movement of capitalism itself, its relentless dissolution of forms and commingling of identities, its confounding of all specific qualities into one indeterminate, purely quantitative process" (212). The key instance of this 'bad' sublime is money:

> Money for Marx is a kind of monstrous sublimity, an infinitely spawning signifier which has severed all relation with the real, a fantastical idealism which blots out specific value as surely as those conventional figures of sublimity—the raging ocean, the mountain crags—engulf all particular identities in their unbounded expanse. (212–13)

Eagleton thus links Marx's view of capitalism with Kant: "Like Kant's mathematical sublime, this endless accumulation of pure quantity subverts all stable representation, and money is its major signifier" (212).[5]

Eagleton's "bad" sublime is readily discernible in the "Bourgeois and Proletarians" section. Marx and Engels do present precisely "the restless, overweening movement of capitalism itself, its relentless dissolution of forms and commingling of identities" in the passages that characterize capitalism as a flood washing away all previous social relations (Eagleton 212). Indeed, Eagleton's talk of "relentless dissolution" seems clearly to be inspired by the *Manifesto*'s "[a]ll that is solid melts into air" (*MECW* 6: 487). Furthermore, this constant threat of dissolution is enacted in the rhetorical tension mentioned above between accumulation of examples and categorizing statement. The *Manifesto* also supports the point that this sublimity finds its paramount expression in money: capitalism has "left remaining no other nexus between man and man than naked self-interest, than callous 'cash payment'" (6: 487). Yet, Eagleton's dichotomy of a good and "bad" sublime does not quite capture the ambivalence of the *Manifesto*'s treatment of capitalism. It implies that the two aspects of the sublime are radically different, whereas the "bad" sublime of capitalism already, in its compelling terror, insinuates the positive potential of communism. To put it in terms of the Kantian sublime, the exploitative nature of capitalism might make it naturally threatening, but there is a positive excess to this feeling that suggests another possibility. This possibility is related to the text's rhetorical praxis. To fully appreciate it, however, I consider in some depth the text to which its rhetoric owes most: Thomas Carlyle's *Chartism*.

The Specter of *Chartism*

Carlyle was an important figure in the immediate context of the *Manifesto*, one with whom Marx and Engels can be said to share considerable common ground. He was a prominent and fierce critic of industrial British society and made his criticisms from the point of view of one steeped in German culture, enthusiastic particularly for the literature and thought of German romanticism. During his stay in Manchester in the early 1840s, Engels became well acquainted with Carlyle's work, and it is in Engels's writings of that period that the influence of Carlyle is most palpable (Hunt 202). Engels's *The Condition of the Working Class in England in 1844* makes frequent and generally approving reference to the work of Carlyle. Indeed, the very title of the work speaks of Carlylean influence, given that the first chapter of Carlyle's *Chartism* is entitled "Condition-of-England Question" (Carlyle 3: 255). Also in the book, Engels quotes Carlyle at great length on the subject of Irish immigration (*MECW* 4: 390). He echoes Carlyle's condemnation of the cynical acquisitiveness promoted by capitalist society. Engels thus characterizes the attitude of the bourgeois:

He cannot comprehend that he holds any other relation to the operatives than that of purchase and sale; he sees in them not human beings, but hands, as he constantly calls them to their faces; he insists, as Carlyle says, that "Cash Payment is the only nexus between man and man." Even the relation between himself and his wife is, in ninety-nine cases out of a hundred, mere "Cash Payment." (4: 563)

This passage refers to Carlyle's statements in *Chartism* and in *Past and Present* on "epochs when Cash Payment has become the sole nexus of man to man" (Carlyle 3: 293). Along similar lines, Engels quotes at length Carlyle's description in *Chartism* of the miserable existence endured by cotton spinners, adding that "Carlyle is perfectly right as to the facts and wrong only in censuring the wild rage of the workers against the higher classes" (*MECW* 4: 414). Engels's explicit engagement with Carlyle is carried further in another piece. In 1844 Engels produced a review of Carlyle's *Past and Present* for the *Deutsche-Französische Jahrbücher*. The review responds both to *Chartism* and to *Past and Present*, focusing on the latter text only because it is treated as an expanded version of *Chartism* (*MECW* 3: 447). Engels introduces the work with high praise:

Of all the fat books and thin pamphlets which have appeared in England in the past year for the entertainment or edification of "educated society" the above work is the only one which is worth reading. [. . .] Search as you will, Carlyle's book is the only one which strikes a human chord, presents human relations and shows traces of a human point of view. (3: 444)

For Engels, Carlyle's engagement with social developments, his posing of "the condition-of-England question" is his great achievement, even if the answers offered are insufficient. Thus Carlyle's point of view is characterized as "admittedly infinitely far in advance of that of the mass of educated people in England but still abstract and theoretical" (3: 466). The review closes by expressing the hope that Carlyle will "develop his German-theoretical viewpoint to its final conclusion" (3: 467). Both in this review and in *The Condition of the Working Class in England*, then, Engels shows, if not necessarily unalloyed praise, certainly a respect for Carlyle, in particular for his manner of articulating the social problems of the modern epoch.

Whilst the review focusses mainly on *Past and Present*, Engels's brief discussion of *Chartism* contains a remark that is particularly relevant to the *Manifesto*. In discussing Carlyle's move, marked by the pamphlet's publication, from popularizing German literature and philosophy toward addressing social conditions in England, Engels relates that:

> At that time the Whigs were in office and proclaimed with much trumpeting that the "spectre" of Chartism, which had arisen round 1835, was now destroyed. [. . .] The Whigs thought they had suppressed this Chartism, and Thomas Carlyle took this as his cue to expound the real causes of Chartism and the impossibility of eradicating it before these causes were eradicated. (3: 447)

This passage is strikingly reminiscent of the famous opening of the *Manifesto*: "A spectre is haunting Europe—the spectre of Communism" (6: 481). Just as what was vanquished was only the specter of Chartism, giving Carlyle occasion to bring forth its real existence, so the *Manifesto* aims to "meet this nursery tale of the spectre of Communism with a Manifesto of the party itself" (6: 481).[6] Other characteristic Carlylean phrases are to be found in the *Manifesto*. Engels's *Condition of the Working Class in England* quoted Carlyle's statement regarding the cash nexus, and this is used again in the *Manifesto*, which states that "[the bourgeoisie] has left remaining no other nexus between man and man than naked self-interest, than callous 'cash payment'" (6: 487). The initial use of this phrase in Carlyle concerns patriarchal relations between the aristocracy and lower classes:

> But it was their happiness that, in struggling for their happiness, they *had* to govern the Lower Classes, even in this sense of governing. For, in one word, *Cash Payment* had not then grown to be the universal sole nexus of man to man; it was something other than money that the high expected from the low, and could not live without getting from the low. (Carlyle 3: 292)

The latter text thus imports the phrase and largely the sentiment which accompanied it, that cash payment has replaced relations of loyalty or duty between social ranks.

The Carlylean phrases that appear in the *Manifesto* are accompanied by a deeper, structural relation of influence between the two texts. There is also in this passage another rhetorical feature of the *Manifesto* that Carlyle seems to have anticipated. The phrase "in one word" in Carlyle's passage above is telling. The phrase, used to sum up myriad things in a single statement, is a prominent element of the "Bourgeois and Proletarians" section, imparting a sense of a great many phenomena regarded together and conveying its impression of scope. This is no coincidence; *Chartism* itself uses a similar gesture in drawing together a broad sweep of history into a single discursive statement. Sure enough, the strategy of presenting the development of capitalism as a spectacular historical itinerary is anticipated in *Chartism*. This is clearest in the "New Eras" chapter of Carlyle's pamphlet. "New Eras," as the title suggests, expounds a series of historical epochs. It begins by asserting the particularity of the present moment: "For in very truth it is a 'new era'; a new practice has become indispensable in it" (Carlyle 3: 299). Carlyle immediately moves, as do Marx and Engels, to delineating eras, the advent of which is appreciable only in retrospect. Epochs, he says, "come quietly, making no proclamation of themselves, and are only visible long after" (3: 299). He moves on to assert that from these can be discerned the motive force behind historical upheavals. He states that in "the history of the English constitution" that "[r]ebellion is the means, but it is not the motive cause. The motive cause, and true secret of the matter, were always this: The necessity there was for rebelling?" (3: 303–4). This is strikingly reminiscent of the broad account of world history presented in the "Bourgeois and Proletarians" passage. In this section it is only now, in the disenchanted world of capitalist modernity, that it can be appreciated how "the history of all hitherto existing society is the history of class struggles" (*MECW* 6: 482) and how revolutions have been driven by a secret motive cause—namely, the development of successive modes and relations of production. This approach lends itself to treating the subject matter as a vast spectacle. The view that "New Eras" presents, like that of "Bourgeois and Proletarians," is extensive both temporally and geographically. Carlyle evokes the global reach of the rising middle class. Thus, as the *Manifesto* states "[t]he discovery of America, the rounding of the Cape, opened up fresh ground for the rising bourgeoisie" (6: 485), so Carlyle contributes:

> But now, on the industrial side, while this great Constitutional controversy, and revolt of the Middle Class had yet but begun, what a shoot was that that England, carelessly, in quest of other objects, struck out in the Ocean, into the waste land which it named *New England*! (Carlyle 3: 306)

Both texts' narratives present to the reader the intercontinental spread of the modern middle class as part of the grand spectacle of modern capitalism. There is evidence that this Carlylean approach fulfilled a pressing need for Marx and Engels during their composition of the

Manifesto. The previous drafts of the document, *Draft of a Communist Confession of Faith* and *Principles of Communism*, were both constructed as catechisms, consisting entirely of questions and answers. In a letter to Marx in January 1848, however, Engels expresses dissatisfaction with this structure. He opines that they would be better to "abandon the catechetical form and call the thing Communist *Manifesto*. Since a certain amount of history has to be narrated in it, the form hitherto adopted is quite unsuitable" (*MECW* 38: 149). Thus, given the many similarities, both rhetorical and structural, between the two texts, it seems probable that, having decided to refashion the *Manifesto* as a historical narrative, *Chartism* was for Marx and Engels ready to hand as a model.

Marx, Engels, and Carlyle

It is worth noting in passing that an appreciation of Carlyle's influence suggests something of a new angle on the collaborative authorship of the text. There is no consensus as to which author contributed in exactly which way to the final version of the *Manifesto*.[7] While it is unlikely that this question can be definitively settled, there is nevertheless a prevalent view in some quarters that ought, in light of these connections, to be queried. This is the opinion that what there is of literary interest in the *Manifesto* is attributable solely to Marx. Engels's more prosaic *Principles of Communism* is generally contrasted with the published version of the *Manifesto* and the difference in style, the addition of the many lyrical passages mentioned above, are attributed to Marx's particular genius.[8] With the influence of Carlyle in mind, this interpretation seems more questionable. Marx did read and make some notes on Carlyle, and he would have been familiar with some of Engels's writings on him (*MECW* 6: 416). Indeed, Marx edited the *Jahrbücher* in which Engels's review of *Past and Present* appeared. Yet it is nonetheless Engels who was deeply impressed by Carlyle's writings and whose texts show profound familiarity with Carlyle's ideas and style. There must, therefore, be a question mark attached to any assumption that the lyrical excellence of the *Manifesto* is attributable only to Marx, since many prominent features of its most eloquent passages seem to take their inspiration from Carlyle's English writings.

Neither is this characteristic simply an artefact of the text's English translation. By far the most widely used English translation of the *Manifesto* is that completed with Engels's oversight in 1888 by Samuel Moore (Stedman Jones, "Introduction" 191). Moore was an Englishman and old friend of Engels, with their acquaintance dating from the latter's time in Manchester (Hunt 203). As such, Moore, like Engels, was during that period in a milieu in which Carlyle was prominent. It might appear that the pair's subsequent translation of the text after Marx's death could have given the English document a more Engelsian, and by extension Carlylean, appearance than the 1848 original. Moore's translation of the *Manifesto* can be compared with Terrell Carver's alternative English version. Carver returns to the German of 1848 for his translation, bypassing Moore's and Engels's translation as well as Engels's subsequently added footnotes. Sure enough, Carver's version obscures some of the similarities with *Chartism* found in Moore's *Manifesto*. The passage referring to "Cash Payment" can be taken as an example. Carver translates the passage, "Die Bourgeoisie . . . [hat] kein anderes Band zwischen Mensch und Mensch übriggelassen als das nackte Interesse, als die gefühllose 'bare Zahlung'" (*MEW* 4: 464) as "The bourgeoisie . . . has left intact no other bond between one man and another than naked self-interest, unfeeling 'hard cash'" (Carver, "Re-Translating" 16), with no mention of a "nexus" or Carlyle's phrase "Cash Payment."

Yet it is not, or not simply, the case that there exists a more Marxian German version of the *Manifesto* and an English version more influenced by Engels and, through him, Carlyle. Many of the echoes of *Chartism* in the *Manifesto* are not, after all, simply a matter of lexical choice. The structure of the "Bourgeois and Proletarians" section, the conception of history as ages driven by an unappreciated principle and the metaphor of replacing a specter with its reality, all largely survive retranslation. Indeed, it is rather more likely that the "cash payment" passage is in a sense already in translation in the 1848 German. Certainly, Engels uses the same terms for "nexus" and "Cash Payment" as appear in the *Manifesto*, "Verbindung" and "bare Zahlung," when quoting Carlyle in his German version of *The Condition of the Working Class in England* (*MEW* 2: 487). Carver does not attempt to claim exclusive authority for his own translation, arguing instead that "there may very well be gains in seeing a more immediately political, less magisterially doctrinal *Manifesto* in English" (Carver, "Re-Translating" 55). Indeed, it seems that surprisingly one of these benefits is that it throws into sharper relief that Moore's English version has more to recommend than might be realized—that the canonical translation, with its lexical echoes of Carlyle, shows clearly this particular English strand in the text's genesis, something that is not so apparent in the German original or in the English version more faithful to it. The fact that Carlyle was himself painfully aware of his own ideas' Teutonic origins demonstrates the remarkably tangled interface between German and English culture in which this legacy of the sublime emerges.

The Naked Sublime

Regardless precisely how it came to be, *Chartism*'s influence also shows the *Manifesto*'s adaptation of the eighteenth-century sublime to encompass industrial modernity. Like the *Manifesto*, Carlyle presents history as a spectacle, invoking the paraphernalia of the sublime. His description of the present historical moment touches on the imagery of obscurity and flooding: the role of the English in world history can be discerned "[h]uge-looming through the dim tumult of the always incommensurable Present Time" (Carlyle 3: 303). Moreover, as in the *Manifesto*, industrialism is figured as dangerously powerful sorcery. Carlyle invokes *The Tempest*'s Prospero, a figure who "can send his Fire-Demons panting across all oceans; shooting with the speed of meteors, on cunning highways, from end to end of kingdoms" (3: 308). Most significantly, Carlyle makes explicit reference to the natural sublime:

> Manchester, with its cotton-fuzz, its smoke and dust, its tumult and contentious squalor, is hideous to thee? Think not so: a precious substance, beautiful as magic dreams, and yet no dream but a reality lies hidden in that noisome wrappage;—a wrappage struggling indeed (look at Chartisms and suchlike) to cast itself off, and leave the beauty free and visible there! Hast thou heard, with sound ears, the awakening of a Manchester, on Monday morning, at half-past five by the clock; the rushing off of its thousand mills, like the boom of an Atlantic tide, ten thousand times ten thousand spools and spindles all set humming there—it is perhaps, if thou knew it well, sublime as a Niagara, or more so. Cotton-spinning is the clothing of the naked in its result; the triumph of man over matter in its means. (3: 308)

As Carlyle slips easily between figures of power and plenitude, it is difficult to avoid connecting this passage with the "melting vision" of the *Manifesto*. The "boom of an Atlantic tide" immediately fragments into effectively innumerable "spools and spindles" and pours away towards "a Niagara." The concrete images of the tide, the spindles, and the waterfall are submerged in what is, after all, the description of a sound. Carlyle also reaches, as the *Manifesto* does, for the superlative: just as the wonders of modernity surpass the favored subjects of Romantic sublimity, Manchester's activity may well surpass Niagara Falls as the exemplum of natural grandeur *par excellence*. There is more in *Chartism* to compare with Marx's and Engels's evocation of capitalism, therefore, than turns of phrase or an approach to situating the present historical moment. That most remarkable quality of the *Manifesto*, its celebrated evocation of industrial modernity, is prefigured here in Carlyle's industrial sublime.

Carlyle's imagery here is influenced by his treatment of social crisis. Herbert Sussman discusses this passage in *Chartism* as an example of a technological sublime newly developed from the eighteenth-century convention. For Sussman, the accoutrements of industry, inevitably in themselves simply ugly, became sublime only through the symbolic relevance that authors such as Carlyle bestowed upon them. In this description, he argues, Carlyle's "[e]mphasis is on the response of the viewer to the scene's symbolism rather than its appearance" (Sussman 30). It is debatable whether Carlyle's description here entirely favors the symbolic; the sound of the "spools and spindles all set humming there" seems to find sublimity in the mills themselves, even if in their sonic rather than visual aspect (Carlyle 3: 308). The symbolic resonances are nevertheless important. The symbolism of clothing is bound up with Carlyle's ideas on social crisis. To see this it is necessary to consider the statements that bookend his invocation of Manchester. Immediately before the description comes the statement, "a precious substance, beautiful as magic dreams, and yet no dream but a reality lies hidden in that noisome wrappage;—a wrappage struggling indeed (look at Chartisms and suchlike) to cast itself off, and leave the beauty free and visible there!" (3: 308). Also, following the description, "Cotton-spinning is the clothing of the naked in its result; the triumph of man over matter in its means" (3: 308). In the first sentence is invoked the metaphor of unwrapping or disrobing. The second immediately directs the reader's attention away from the spectacle of the Manchester mills to the fact that they are spinning cotton to be used in the manufacture of clothing. Now, this is significant because the symbolism of clothing is one of Carlyle's favorite subjects. It is used in *Past and Present* synecdochically for maldistribution:

> What is the use of your spun shirts? They hang there by the million unsaleable; and here, by the million, are diligent bare backs that can get no hold of them. Shirts are useful for covering human backs; useless otherwise, an unbearable mockery otherwise. (Carlyle 9: 18)

The symbolism of clothes, however, receives its fullest explication in Carlyle's 1831 *Sartor Resartus*. This novel is largely an extended meditation on the metaphoric significance and resonance of clothes. It concerns a German philosopher, Diogenes Teufelsdröckh, who has written a volume entitled *"Die Kleider: ihr Werden und Wirken (Clothes, their Origin and Influence)"* (SR 6). The novel is composed of quotations from this fictional tome as well as commentary by an unnamed English narrator. The main thrust of the "clothes-philosophy" involves clothes standing for socially shared systems of symbols. Thus, says Teufelsdröckh, "Society, which the more I think of it astonishes me the more, is founded upon Cloth" (SR 48). The symbolic structures which are represented by clothes allow society to function, as in the criminal justice system:

> "You see two individuals," [Teufelsdröckh] writes, "one dressed in fine Red, the other in coarse threadbare Blue: Red says to Blue, 'Be hanged and anatomised;' Blue hears with a shudder and (O wonder of wonders!) marches sorrowfully to the gallows, is there noosed up, vibrates his hour, and the surgeons dissect him, and fit his bones into a skeleton for medical purposes. (47)

The defamiliarization of the process here reduces the whole institution of judicial authority, the ability to punish convicts without continually applying direct physical force, to its manifestation in symbolically charged outfits.

It is in this domain of clothes metaphors that Carlyle articulates his theory of social crisis. He contends that, in the current historical moment, the fabric of society is pulling apart. Teufelsdröckh believes the symbolic structures that formerly existed have begun to wear dangerously out, since "symbols, like all terrestrial garments, wax old" (SR 170). The deterioration of symbols has at the present moment reached an advanced and ominous stage. The "tatters and rags of superannuated worn-out Symbols (in this Ragfair of a World)" are "dropping off every where, to hoodwink, to halter, to tether you; nay, if you shake them not aside, threatening to accumulate and perhaps produce suffocation!" (171). The fact that inherited or traditional symbolic systems are losing their potency is dangerous indeed. Without these systems, society ceases to be and what is left is a mere brutish herding, one which threatens to topple into a Hobbesian state of nature:

> Teufelsdröckh is one of those who consider Society, properly so called, to be as good as extinct; and that only the Gregarious feelings,

and old inherited habitudes, at this juncture, hold us from Dispersion and universal national, civil, domestic and personal war! (176)

Had not the above-mentioned courtroom its particular red and blue clothes, the convict would have done only what he was physically forced to do. With this in mind, the concern in *Chartism* over "epochs when Cash Payment has become the sole nexus of man to man" (Carlyle 3: 293) becomes clear. The "Organic Filaments" of symbolic systems which connect humans to one another and allow them to coexist and function socially are falling away. This imagery also informs the *Manifesto*. The destruction that capitalist modernity has wrought on shared social norms and conventions is here also described using the imagery of clothes. In this case, the repeated metaphor is that of the torn veil. Thus the bourgeoisie has replaced "veiled" exploitation with "naked, shameless" exploitation (*MECW* 6: 487). It has also "torn away from the family its sentimental veil" (6: 487). The metaphors of nakedness once again stand for disenchantment and the loss of shared symbols in favor of straightforward self-interest. The *Manifesto* thus participates in the symbolic discourse, in which Carlyle was steeped, whereby the loss of clothes connotes a falling away of previous history, an approaching moment of apocalyptic crisis.

The Sublime and the Apocalyptic

Might the apocalyptic be a more appropriate category than the sublime, then? Both texts are certainly apocalyptic in the sense of being revelatory. In both cases the dissolution of the current epoch allows some overarching truth to be appreciated. For Carlyle, the tearing of the "noisome wrappage" of industrial Manchester will leave a "precious substance [. . .] free and visible there" (Carlyle 3: 308). Similarly, in the *Manifesto* the destruction of traditional and sentimental relations has the effect of clearing away ideological illusion. The underlying logic of historical development is exposed by capitalism's destruction of these and its turning loose of unalloyed material interest. Thus, capitalism cannot help but reveal man's "real conditions of life, and his relations with his kind" (*MECW* 6: 487). Furthermore, in each text not only is some large truth about history revealed, but this revelation presages a redemptive stage. The "Bourgeois and Proletarians" section, after all, ends by stating simply that the victory of the proletariat is inevitable (6: 496). This combination of revelation and redemption is linked to the use of clothes imagery. In discussing the use of this imagery, Berman contrasts Marx with figures such as Rousseau and Burke. The latter thinkers, he says, do not appreciate the dialectical ambivalence of nakedness. It is interpreted by them as "an unmitigated disaster, a fall into nothingness from which nothing and no-one can rise," or as "opening new vistas of beauty and happiness for all" (Berman 109). For Marx, capitalism is disastrous, but it still opens up the redemptive vista of communism. In this the *Manifesto* is once again preceded by Carlyle. He similarly intimates the redemptive potential of the current crisis. In his vision of Manchester, the succession of fragmenting images culminating in Niagara Falls's overpowering noise and magnitude evokes the threat of dissolution. Yet within this Carlyle suggests a paradox. This fragmenting image, treated symbolically as "a wrap-page struggling indeed . . . to cast itself off" is followed immediately by a focus on the literal work of cotton-spinning (Carlyle 3: 308). Carlyle plays upon the fact that the cotton mill, mainstay of the industrialism, which has caused so many rends in society's traditional cloth, is itself producing roll after roll of cloth. Cotton-spinning is "the clothing of the naked in its result" (3: 308). Thus Carlyle, like Marx and Engels, finds redemptive potential in the productive powers of industrialism.

Given this, it is widely observed that both Carlyle and the authors of the *Manifesto* resemble millenarian prophets, thematizing crisis and redemption as part of a predetermined narrative which some external agency is certain to bring about. Carlyle's voice is nearly universally described as prophetic. His prose is characterized by heavy use of archaisms, which recall the King James Bible. For example, the pronouns in the Manchester passage, as well as the construction "think not so" are more typical of the seventeenth than the nineteenth century (3: 308). Along with this, Carlyle at times explicitly invokes the deity. Part of the crisis of authority which marks the current historical moment, suggests Carlyle, is due to the fact that social hierarchy has lost its divine sanction: "It is not a light matter when the just man can recognize in the powers set over him no longer anything that is divine" (Carlyle 3: 315). Albert LaValley discusses the tension in Carlyle of his attempt to be a modern prophet. His imagery is that of the industrial revolution, but his prophetic mode shows "a nostalgia for the ordered religious life of the Middle Ages, a wish to retreat to the seventeenth-century world of Cromwell, to the old dialect" (LaValley 203). Carlyle's idiom can thus be viewed as an attempt to update the older theological structure with modern content, to produce, as LaValley claims, "a unitary vision that would be both religious and industrial" (203).

Similarly, the *Manifesto* has been interpreted as a millenarian document. Of course, Marx and Engels do not invoke the divine, and indeed they dismiss religion as being among "bourgeois prejudices" (*MECW* 6: 494–95). Nevertheless, the coincidence of the historical narrative presented in the *Manifesto* and the millenarian structure of crisis and redemption is suggestive. This becomes all the more so when the influence of Carlyle on the *Manifesto*'s rhetoric is taken into account. Ernest Tuveson notes the coincidence of Carlyle with Marx and Engels in his essay on the millenarian aspect of the *Manifesto*. He says that "to Carlyle the evils of industrialism and laissez-faire were the darkest of omens;" whereas "to Marx-Engels, in the true spirit of millenarianism, these same horrors seemed harbingers of the real, the universal judgement" and "[t]he fact that they are the very worst of evils humanity has ever known is evidence that, as in Revelation, the reversal is being prepared" (Tuveson 333). The interpretation of Carlyle here offered by Tuveson is rendered questionable by the positive potential Carlyle sees in the cotton mill, but it is the case that for Marx and Engels the widest-ranging world-historical crisis, the state of affairs which immiserates and dehumanizes the greatest number of people, is the condition for the most important liberatory development in human history. Tuveson therefore claims that "[i]t was the contribution of Marx and Engels to revive the old millenarian pattern in the forms of modern social and economic thought" and goes so far as to say that "there is reason to think of [Marx and Engels] as the last great prophets of the Judaic apocalyptic tradition" (327; 332). The *Manifesto*'s imagery is therefore linked to that of Old Testament prophets: Tuveson states that, since Isiah, "[t]he image of a great earthquake in nature [has been] the symbol of a great and levelling revolution in society, the sacrosanct distinctions of class being abolished" (328). In the face of this wealth of evidence, then, it is perhaps the case that the sublime might ultimately be an inappropriate category to describe *Chartism* and the *Manifesto*; perhaps what looks to be the sublime in these texts is a side-effect of the influence of the much older apocalyptic tradition.

There is no denying this aspect of these texts. However, this does not mean that the sublime is an inappropriate category under which to understand them, or that there is no more to say. This conclusion would seriously understate the complexity of the interacting themes and contexts of these texts. For one thing, it is not clear that the categories of the sublime and the apocalyptic necessarily exclude one another. James Kirwan and Morton Paley both propose an "apocalyptic sublime," which emerges in the nineteenth century. The paintings of John Martin are the most obvious examples of this development.[9] Certainly, given the pervasive influence the sublime had in the eighteenth century, it would be surprising if characteristics of the sublime aesthetic had not interacted with apocalyptic literature. The theme of ambivalent affect lends itself to the dual aspect of apocalyptic scenarios; the destruction of the world and the judgement of mankind are of course suited to provoke terror.

More than this, however, there is one sense in which the sublime is a more useful category and that focusing on it allows a deeper understanding of how these texts work. The rubric of the millenarian or apocalyptic does not capture a central aspect of the texts. This is apparent, for example, in Tuveson's reading of the *Manifesto*, where the account of history is interpreted as a preordained one: "Marx-Engels see history as process and judgement—the judgement of the 'determinism' of nature" (Tuveson 333). This is a misunderstanding of the *Manifesto* and misses some of its deeper connection with Carlyle's work. In fact, both texts engage in a distinctively modern staging of human freedom with reference to nature. This is not the Kantian view of individual freedom as moral autonomy. It is instead one which puts heavy emphasis on activity, particularly labor, and therefore the collective or social embeddedness of this freedom. Nevertheless, it retains a view of distinctively human freedom which is articulated through the structure of the sublime filtered through the post-Kantians Schiller and Hegel.

"The Triumph of Man over Matter"

Marx, Engels, and Carlyle do not formulate the ability of the subject to resist determination by the heteronomous forces of nature as precisely as Kant does. Instead they assume it and place their emphasis elsewhere. They are concerned with the positive ability of humans to shape nature according to their will. Jonathan Mendilow connects Marx and Carlyle on this point. He emphasizes the difference of this outlook from "earlier thinkers" such as Kant, who "tended to view the distinguishing characteristic of mankind as the possession of reason" (Mendilow 230). Instead Carlyle and Marx "argued that evolving man in an evolving world, in the evolution of which he not only participates but to which he contributes, must be judged in terms of his activity" (230). As a consequence, Marx and Carlyle associated freedom with an ideal of labor. Carlyle articulates his version of this outlook in *Sartor Resartus*. Diogenes Teufelsdröckh is a wholehearted advocate of the *vita activa*. On the one hand, he contrasts labor favorably with acquisition: "Not what I Have . . . but what I Do is my Kingdom" (*SR* 93). On the other, he presents thought, the traditional territory of those who consider humans rational animals, as just another kind of productive labor. He speaks of "the grand thaumaturgic art of Thought" and its miracles:

> [B]ut cannot the dullest hear the Steam-engines clanking around him? Has he not seen the Scottish brassmith's IDEA (and this but a mechanical one) travelling on fire-wings around the Cape; and across two Oceans; and stronger than any other Enchanter's Familiar, on all hands unweariedly fetching and carrying: at home, not only weaving cloth; but rapidly enough overturning the whole old system of Society. (92)

Thus, here we have creative thought figured as continuous with industrial production. The steam engine is not in some way caused by James Watt's having an idea; rather it simply is that idea. That is, having the idea and actually making the steam engine are not distinguished, and as that labor is just another form of creative thought, so thought is just another form of labor. This is central to Carlyle's philosophical attitude to work. Work has a distinctively human, and therefore supremely valuable, importance. In its comprehensive definition, which includes thought, labor becomes an expression of moral freedom. *Chartism* even contains a hint at an articulation of a labor theory of value: "the poor man also has property, namely, his 'labour'" (Carlyle 3: 292). The theme of labor's value is expanded upon in *Past and Present*, where Carlyle claims "there is a perennial nobleness, and even sacredness, in Work" and that "[w]ere he never so benighted, forgetful of his high calling, there is always hope in a man that actually and earnestly works: in Idleness alone is there perpetual despair" (9: 165). Here labor, even if it is a saleable property, is presented as being not only a commodity. It has, indeed, an overriding value such that the absence of work is synonymous with despair.

So for Carlyle, the value of work is an ethical one and this is significant because he inherits from post-Kantian German thought an ethics of autonomy. He was one of the few acolytes of German culture in England at the time, and was an important popularizer of its literature (Ashton 67). Although he probably had limited familiarity with Kant's writings themselves, he had written books on Goethe and Schiller (92). Schiller's philosophy and aesthetics, of course, included an emphasis on freedom, such that the sublime "establishes our moral self-sufficiency in an irrefutable manner" (Schiller 74). This was an aspect of Schiller's thought which Carlyle certainly embraced. As Tom Lloyd points out, his analysis of Schiller's work in his *Life of Friedrich Schiller* tended towards Carlyle's own interest in "the struggle of the will to gain victory over the oppressive fetters of material necessity" (Lloyd 93). As such, Carlyle's characterization of labor rests ultimately on an opposition between human freedom and the causality of material nature, with the two domains in explicit conflict. In the discussion in *Past and Present*, work is morally perfecting and this is intimately bound up with its status as free activity:

> Doubt, Desire, Sorrow, Remorse, Indignation, Despair itself, all these like helldogs lie beleaguering the soul of the poor dayworker, as of every man: but he bends himself with free valour against his task, and all these are stilled, all these shrink murmuring far off into their caves. The man is now a man. (Carlyle 9: 166)

These misfortunes beset the laborer like the serpents which assail Laocoön in Schiller's "On the Pathetic," and, like Laocoön, the laborer finds within himself courage and "free valour" to resist them. This exercise of autonomy is thus explicitly conducted against both the material world and against vices of character. What is more, these "helldogs," particularly "desire," evoke the appetitive inclinations against which the Kantian moral hero must struggle (9: 166). The conceptualization of labor as an assertion of human autonomy as against the domain of necessity is widespread in Carlyle's work. In *Sartor Resartus*, Teufelsdröckh describes the blacksmith, who "preaches (exoterically enough) one little textlet from the Gospel of Freedom, the Gospel of Man's Force, commanding, and one day to be all-commanding" (*SR* 56). In *Chartism*, Carlyle entertains the prospect of an entirely deterministic or materialist universe. This prospect is tellingly figured as a nightmarish machine:

> If men had lost belief in a God, their only resource against a blind No-God, of necessity and mechanism, that held them like a hideous World-Steamengine, like a hideous Phalaris' Bull, imprisoned in its own iron belly, would be, with or without hope,—*revolt*. They could, as Novalis says, by a "simultaneous universal act of suicide," *depart* out of the World-Steamengine. (Carlyle 3: 278)

While the countenancing of suicide is ethically un-Kantian, the choosing of destruction over inescapable heteronomy certainly chimes with the logic of the post-Kantian sublime, particularly as it is filtered through Schiller. Also, Carlyle does not usually take such a pessimistic view of humanity's prospects in the battle with nature. In *Past and Present*, the "Captain of Industry," Plugson of Undershot, conducts a military expedition from the domain of human freedom to the domain of necessity. "Bareness of back, and disobedient Cotton-fibre, which will not, unless forced to it, consent to cover bare backs" is "a most genuine enemy; over whom all creatures will wish him victory" (Carlyle 9: 163). He "enlisted his thousand men; said to them, 'Come, brothers, let us have a dash at Cotton!' They follow with cheerful shout; they gain such a victory over Cotton as the Earth has to admire and clap hands at" (9: 163). Here cotton stands for recalcitrant matter, the conquest and subjection of which is a victory for human freedom, and particularly for the "Captain of Industry." This idea of triumph over nature is clearly at stake in the description of Manchester. Manchester becomes, as Sussman puts it, "the embodiment of the sacrament of productive labor" (Sussman 30). Cotton spinning is "the clothing of the naked in its result; the triumph of man over matter in its means" (Carlyle 3: 308). It is important to note here the reversal of the expected order. The means usually precede the result, but here the process, the asserting of human purpose over cotton, is granted primacy and is thus implicitly more important, an end in itself.

Marxian Freedom

At first glance it might seem that, despite the demonstrable similarities and influence between Carlyle and Marx and Engels, this lauding of freedom must be where they part ways. In the *Manifesto*, it is material processes of production, not men and women, who appear as the real actors. Such an outlook would seem to leave little scope for a domain of human freedom. The description of the current historical moment in the "Bourgeois and Proletarians" section, for example, makes these entities the protagonists:

> For many a decade past, the history of industry and commerce is but the history of the revolt of modern productive forces against modern conditions of production, against the property relations that are the conditions for the existence of the bourgeoisie and of its rule. (*MECW* 6: 489)

Any revolt of concrete individuals, then, seems merely to be an epiphenomenon of the revolt of these impersonal productive forces. This is at play in the figuration of modern industry as akin to a flood or a supernatural being. The comparison of bourgeois society to "the sorcerer, who is no longer able to control the forces of the nether world whom he has called up by his spells," dramatizes precisely a lack of human control, particularly given that, according to the *Manifesto*, bourgeois society was unable to control itself in casting those spells in the first place (6: 489). After all, the bourgeoisie "cannot exist without constantly revolutionizing the instruments of production, and thereby the relations of production" (6: 487). Productive forces, therefore, have always been the driving force despite any volition of the bourgeoisie. Ultimately, then, the economic gigantomachy plays itself out such that "[the bourgeoisie's] fall and the victory of the proletariat are equally inevitable" (6: 496). This is the interpretation of those who, like Tuveson above, see the *Manifesto* as advancing a "historical determinism" (Tuveson 335). It is this quality that leads Tuveson to compare the *Manifesto*'s account of history to an eschatological timetable:

> Marx-Engels take great pains to set forth the cause-and-effect system, the process of "historical dialectic," eliminating any kind of supernatural intervention. But consideration will show that all this theorizing merely pushes back the ultimate source back beyond empirical knowledge. What set in motion this sequence of events? Why does there seem to be a built-in time scheme? (333)

Tuveson therefore suggests that for Marx and Engels the "historical dialectic" acts as much like a deity as makes no difference (334). Given this interpretation, Tuveson regards the fanaticism of communist agitators as a "rather curious fact" (339). He explains it with the caveat that "[a]lthough the series of events is prophesied, their *timing* may be retarded by the failure of mankind" (339). Under this interpretation, then, the scope of human freedom in the *Manifesto* is vanishingly limited, reduced at best to tinkering with the precise dates of events whose character is preordained.

This interpretation would seem also to find corroboration in some of the other writings of the *Manifesto*'s authors. Where Carlyle is broadly sympathetic to Kant and Kantian ethical ideas, Marx and Engels are withering. They comment on Kant in a manuscript on Max Stirner in what was to become *The German Ideology*:

> The characteristic form which French liberalism, based on real class interests, assumed in Germany we find again in Kant. Neither he,

nor the German middle class, whose whitewashing spokesman he was, noticed that these theoretical ideas of the bourgeoisie had as their basis material interests and a *will* that was conditioned and determined by the material relations of production. Kant, therefore, separated this theoretical expression from the interests which it expressed; he made the materially motivated determinations of the will of the French bourgeois into *pure* self-determinations of "*free will*," of the will in and for itself, of the human will, and so converted it into purely ideological conceptual determinations and moral postulates. (*MECW* 5:195)

Here again we find an emphasis on the determination of the material relations of production. Kant's positing of a free, self-determining will, it is suggested, is explained by the fact that he was unobservant of these secret determining factors. It would be tempting, then, to conclude that Marx and Engels reject the idea of autonomy or self-determination as so much naivety. However, this is not ultimately what is here being argued. It is not Kant's belief in self-determination *per se* that is attacked here, but rather the purity which he is supposed to accord it. The distinction made is between an actually existing "*will* that was conditioned and determined by the material relations of production" and "*pure* self-determinations of '*free will*'" (5:195). To say that a will is "conditioned and determined" by material factors is not to say that it is wholly determined thereby. Indeed, it may well still be in important ways *under*determined, just not *un*determined by them.[10] Indeed, by retaining the language of the will in relation to the French bourgeoisie and by emphasizing Kant's erroneously "pure" conception of free will, the argument clearly refrains from criticizing the concept itself.

Nor is the purported purity of Kantian freedom the main target in this discussion. Rather, Marx and Engels criticize Kant in terms which highlight their commonality with Carlyle:

While the French bourgeoisie, by means of the most colossal revolution that history has ever known, was achieving domination and conquering the Continent of Europe, while the already politically emancipated English bourgeoisie was revolutionising industry and subjugating India politically, and all the rest of the world commercially, the impotent German burghers did not get any further than "good will." Kant was satisfied with "good will" alone, even if it remained entirely without result, and he transferred the *realisation* of this good will, the harmony between it and the needs and impulses of individuals, to *the world beyond*. Kant's good will fully corresponds to the impotence, depression and wretchedness of the German burghers. (*MECW* 5:193)

Here Kant is excoriated not for holding to an idea of will, but for being satisfied with it. The good will of Kant's *Groundwork* is contrasted with the effects in the world that the wills of the French and English bourgeoisie were having. This is done, too, in terms that strikingly recall passages of the "Bourgeois and Proletarians" section of the *Manifesto*. The geographical scope of the bourgeoisie's activities, as well as their magnitude and dominating power, is highlighted. Here the difference in emphasis in Kant's view compared to that of the authors of the *Manifesto* is clear. Kantian freedom as resistance to the determination of nature is rejected in favor of an emphasis on activity, on engagement with, and shaping of, the world according to the will.

As with Carlyle, then, this freedom is valued inasmuch as it is manifested in activity and is understood within a social or economic context. This bears out Mendilow's linking of the two thinkers. Marx, too, accords a special place to labor. As Stedman Jones points out, Marx "developed a post-Kantian vision of the role of labor in history and its capacity for self-emancipation: a vision based on reason, spontaneity and freedom" (Stedman Jones, *Karl Marx* 202). In the *Economic and Philosophic Manuscripts of 1844*, Marx lays out the relationship between labor and this post-Kantian spontaneous subjectivity. For Marx, freedom is united with activity in the natural disposition of humans. He writes that the "whole character of a species—its species-character—is contained in the character of its life activity; and free, conscious activity is man's species-character" (*MECW* 3:276). Marx is here not interested in freedom and consciousness as pure or isolable things, but in the context of human activity. They are nevertheless essential aspects of that activity. Elsewhere in the *Manuscripts*, Marx explicitly identifies this activity with labor (3:333). He attributes to Hegel the recognition of labor's importance:

> The outstanding achievement of Hegel's *Phänomenologie* [. . .] is thus first that Hegel conceives the self-creation of man as a process, conceives objectification as loss of the object, as alienation and as transcendence of this alienation; that he thus grasps the essence of *labour* and comprehends objective man—true, because real man—as the outcome of man's *own labour*. (*MECW* 3:332–33)

This passage expresses Marx's particular synthesis of labor with radical freedom. Labor does not just alter the natural world, it is a process by which humans create themselves. Since freedom is an aspect of that activity that constitutes human species-character, then human self-creation can also be characterized by freedom. In other words, humans are free and self-determining, but only become so through labor. The material conditions of production are important because they determine how labor occurs, hence Marx's and Engels's objection to Kant's neglecting them, but the fact that labor itself alters these conditions means that humans are nevertheless always underdetermined with respect to the natural world.

"Lordship and Bondage" and the *Manifesto*'s Sublime

Since Marx credits the achievement of conceiving human self-determination through labor to Hegel's *Phenomenology of Spirit*, it is no surprise that this text provides the direct source of the *Manifesto*'s staging of the sublime. The relevant section is that known as "Lordship and Bondage." Its influence is felt in the *Manifesto* in subtle ways. In their descriptions of modern history under the "economical and political sway of the bourgeois class," Marx and Engels place the proletariat in the position of Hegel's bondsman (6: 489).[11] The relevant chapter of Hegel's text has the full title "Independence and Dependence of Self-Consciousness: Lordship and Bondage" (Hegel, *Phenomenology* 111). One of its major concerns is the role of fearful affect in the development of consciousness towards an apprehension of its independence. The passage describes a consciousness, which engages in a life-or-death struggle with another and, in the event that it becomes the bondsman, experiences subjection to, and mortal fear of, the lord. This fear is described as a particularly all-encompassing one:

> For this consciousness has been fearful, not of this or that particular thing, or just at odd moments, but its whole being has been seized with dread; for it has felt the fear of death, the absolute lord. In that experience it has been quite unmanned, has trembled in every fibre of its being, and everything solid and stable has been shaken to its foundations. But this pure, universal movement, the absolute melting-away of everything stable, is the simple, essential nature of self-consciousness, absolute negativity, *pure being-for-self*, which consequently is *implicit* in this consciousness. (Hegel, *Phenomenology* 117)

Tom Furniss in his study *Edmund Burke's Aesthetic Ideology* reads "Lordship and Bondage" with reference to the sublime. He sees in Hegel's characterization of the bondsman's experience an echo of "Burke's account of the physiological processes of the body or mind undergoing the sublime crisis" (Furniss 56). Hegel's emphasis on all-encompassing dread in the dialectic is doubtless reminiscent of Burke. However, "Lordship and Bondage" is in fact much more readily comparable to Kant's "Analytic of the Sublime." Both Hegel's and Kant's accounts present narratives by which the subject proves its own independence by countenancing the prospect of the "absolute lord," death. In the "Analytic," of course, an object can be dynamically sublime only if it is "fearful," and it is fearful only if "we judge it in such a way that we merely think of the case in which we might wish to resist it, and think that in that case all resistance would be altogether futile" (CJ 144). The examples that Kant gives of fearful objects, "volcanoes with their all-destroying violence, hurricanes with the devastation they leave behind, the boundless ocean set into a rage," make it clear that they have the capacity to destroy the person (144). The thinking of a case in which resistance to such objects would be vain would therefore be to countenance death. Yet, in the experience of the sublime, the subject discovers that it has the ability to resist such forces nevertheless, they "allow us to discover within ourselves a capacity for resistance of quite another kind, which gives us courage to measure ourselves against the apparent all-powerfulness of nature" (144–45). This, too, is the case in "Lordship and Bondage." At the outset of this section of the *Phenomenology*, two consciousnesses fight one another to the death because each wishes to show "that it is not attached to life" (Hegel, *Phenomenology* 113). Hegel's statement that "it is only through staking one's life that freedom is won" accords with the implicit logic of Kant's "Analytic" (114). Kant's subject, as we saw, must find itself confronted with a situation in which it would have to stake its life against overwhelming power. It is only then that the subject can appreciate its freedom from nature. Beiser offers a gloss of Hegel's life-or-death struggle, which makes clear its Kantian foundation. He says that it is "only in risking its own life that [the self] demonstrates its rational status, that it has a power over the realm of mere biological life and its animal desires" (Beiser, *Hegel* 187). Both "Lordship and Bondage" and the "Analytic of the Sublime" share an underlying intuition that willingness to countenance death implies rational independence. Both describe a situation in which such a staking of life is brought to the fore by a confrontation with a fearful object and both assert that in this way the subject's autonomy can be discovered.

The *Manifesto* inherits the staging of the sublime in "Lordship and Bondage," particularly Hegel's description of the bondsman's fear. Evocations of fearful power are, as we have seen, everywhere in "Bourgeois and Proletarians," and one particular passage, which is central to the *Manifesto*'s celebrated "melting vision," is clearly heavily influenced. For Hegel's bondsman, "everything solid and stable has been shaken to its foundations" in an "absolute melting-away of everything stable" (Hegel, *Phenomenology* 113). The *Manifesto* states that under bourgeois rule:

> All fixed fast-frozen relations with their train of ancient and venerable prejudices and opinions, are swept away, all new-formed ones become antiquated before they can ossify. All that is solid melts into air, all that is holy is profaned. (*MECW* 6: 487)

Hegel's description, of course, is of a subjective affective state—the bondsman's fear—whereas Marx and Engels are here discussing the social conditions of capitalism. Nevertheless, in its universality the *Manifesto*'s passage presents the overturning of these external social conditions in a way hardly distinguishable from the bondsman's experience. In both cases, the dissolution is not related to any particular object, but rather is a total falling-away of objects in general. Thus, Hegel's description of the bondsman's fear becomes difficult to distinguish from the *Manifesto*'s account of modern history. What Hegel discusses as a feeling for the bondsman, Marx and Engels present as the fact of capitalist society. This is important because in Hegel's dialectic, the all-encompassing fear is key to the bondsman's development. As he says, the fear "is the simple, essential nature of self-consciousness [. . .] which consequently is *implicit* in this consciousness." (Hegel, *Phenomenology* 117). When combined with work, this implicit self-consciousness results in an explicit recognition on the part of the bondsman of his own independence (118). Similarly, the possibility of proletarian revolution is implicit in the power of the bourgeoisie; it compels the subject to face "his real conditions of life, and his relations with his kind" (*MECW* 6: 487). Thus, in rendering the bondsman's fear as a characteristic of the capitalist spectacle, the *Manifesto* repurposes the bondsman's "independence of self-consciousness" toward suggesting the possibility of "independent, self-conscious" action on the part of the proletariat.

There is, however, one particular element that places the aesthetic of the *Manifesto* closer to Kant's "Analytic" than to Hegel's dialectic. This is that the power of the bourgeoisie is figured in the *Manifesto* as a natural force or supernatural irruption; it is an icy flood or sorcery gone awry. Both of these things are distinguished by their being specifically nonhuman kinds of power. This recalls, more than Hegel's bondsman's fear of his master, the spectacle that incites Kant's sublime. Kant identified the dynamically sublime with "[n]ature considered in an aesthetic judgement as a power that has no dominion over us," and his examples are all drawn from mute nature (*CJ* 143). Now, this may seem like an odd and inappropriate piece of reification to appear in the *Manifesto*. The treatment of contingent social conditions and relations as unalterable forces of nature was something that Marx and Engels set their faces against. After all, much of the "Proletarians and Communists" section of the *Manifesto* is spent arguing that institutions such as property and current family relations are historically contingent rather than naturally determined. The bourgeoisie have, after all, "been the first to show what man's activity can bring about," and have achieved unprecedented "subjection of Nature's forces to man" (*MECW* 6: 487; 489). The choice of metaphor here is thus surprising, that the changes produced by the conditions of capitalist industrialism should find their images in suggestions of these very natural forces rather than being expressions of human power. This presentation has also, as we saw in the case of Tuveson, led to the misinterpretation that the *Manifesto* suggests productive forces really are necessarily beyond human control.

The opposite is in fact the case. These natural metaphors are apt because, for the modern proletarian, the forces of industry do seem to be inhuman natural ones, even if they are not. This is consistent with Marx's and Engels's Hegelian source. After all, in "Lordship and Bondage," each consciousness is alienated from the other, and each regards the other as no more than an object for it. The imagery of the natural sublime in the *Manifesto* encodes the idea that it is society's productive power that is alienated. In the central text of Marx's theory of alienation, the *Economic and Philosophic Manuscripts*, the discussion also uses imagery that recalls "Lordship and Bondage." In this case, it is the machine or the product that takes the place of Hegel's other consciousness. Marx observes that "[s]ince the worker has sunk to the level of the machine, he can be confronted by the machine as a competitor" (*MECW* 3: 238). More than this, the inanimate product, which the machine produces, thereafter assumes the position of the lord. It "becomes a power on its own confronting him," and ultimately subjects him (3: 272). Under capitalism, therefore, "realization of labour appears as a *loss of realization* for the workers; objectification as *loss of the object and bondage to it*; appropriation as *estrangement, as alienation*" (3: 272). It is this alienation and subjection to the machine and to its product that is behind the *Manifesto*'s statement that the worker "becomes an appendage of the machine" (6: 491). It is therefore through this alienation that the human world of production becomes the wild tempest of the industrial sublime. In appropriating the rhetoric of the natural sublime, the *Manifesto* works to expose and thereby undermine this sense of alienation from the world.

The Captain of Industry

Both *Chartism* and the *Manifesto*, then, represent a particular strand of mid-nineteenth-century sublimity. This strand emerges from post-Kantian German thought and derives many themes from it. Not least, it builds a conception of human freedom, which takes Kant's autonomous subject and adds an emphasis on labor as an expression of self-determination. Because of this, it is a sublime with an emphasis not on the solitary individual confronting mute nature, but rather one embedded in the context of the modern industrial society and economy. This industrial world thus becomes the sublime object, the cotton mill becomes Niagara, and the whirl of modernization the sublime terror. The subject, too, is inseparable from its position within the social world of production. Yet exactly how the subject is immersed in the social world is by no means the same in both texts. Indeed, the depiction of the sublime subject captures the most salient difference between the texts; it is not just a matter of how the sublime is used, but rather has profound implications for how these pamphlets work as polemical texts. The *Manifesto* is unique in creating a collective subject of the sublime in the form of the proletariat, where *Chartism*'s model of freedom is limited by its aristocratic view of political agency.

As we saw, Carlyle held workmanship to be of central ethical importance and situates his discussion of human freedom in terms of economic activity. However, in *Chartism* this is in tension with his interest in social renewal—that is, for Carlyle the capacity for freedom through work does not necessarily translate into social or political agency. Indeed, one of *Chartism*'s main concerns is to deny agency to the Chartists. The pamphlet opens by asserting the requirement for intervention in social affairs. The disposition of the working class constitutes "a matter in regard to which if something be not done, something will *do* itself one day, and in a fashion that will please nobody" (Carlyle 3: 255). Agency is here already removed from the working class. What is referred to is social conflict, a potential outbreak of unrest, but this is presented as an agentless event, something doing itself. Carlyle continues by stating that "[t]he time has verily come for acting in it" (3: 255). It is not clear, however, who is to act. It is certainly not to be the Chartists themselves. In the pamphlet, Carlyle does not grant them the ability even to articulate the problems affecting the condition of England, much less the ability to act and solve them. Carlyle recognizes the presence of Chartist demands. He says the "'National petition' carts itself in wagons along the streets" (3:255). Yet here again the petition is figured as only an agentless circumstance, by no means the gesture or action of any rational beings. The specific contents of the petition are not heeded. What Carlyle instead recommends is "a genuine understanding by the upper classes of society what it is that the under classes intrinsically mean" (3: 258). The upper classes need "a clear interpretation of the thought which at heart torments these wild inarticulate souls, struggling there, with inarticulate uproar, like dumb creatures in pain, unable to speak what is in them!" (3: 258). The working classes, and by extension the Chartists, are with relentless reiteration cast as inarticulate and ineffectual, in dire need of help from those able to act on their behalf. Thus, as John Plotz notes, "Carlyle, from the very beginning of *Chartism*, introduces a fundamental uncertainty about agency that makes Chartist claims to be performing legible speech-acts seem absurd" (Plotz 95–96). Carlyle's characterization of Chartism, indeed, is summed up in the pamphlet's epigraph: "It never smokes but there is a fire" (Carlyle 3: 253). The Chartists are reduced to sign or symptom, and are as ineffectual as smoke.

Carlyle's conception of political agency is ultimately an aristocratic one. Consistent with his dismissal of the Chartists' demands for suffrage as inarticulate, he has no time for parliamentary representation. The right to participate in representative government is merely "one's right [. . . to send one's 'twenty-thousandth part of a master of tongue-fence to National Palaver'" (Carlyle 3: 313). Carlyle has little time for democracy, which "is found but as a regulated method of rebellion and abrogation" that "abrogates the old arrangement of things; and leaves, as we say, *zero* and vacuity for the institution of a new arrangement" (3: 289). Democracy only negates, whereas positive progress is found in a government ordained by natural hierarchy. This is the view of Teufelsdröckh in *Sartor Resartus*: "[C]an I choose my own King? I can choose my own King Popinjay [. . .] but he who is to be my ruler, whose will is to be higher than my will, was chosen for me in Heaven" (*SR* 188). Thus the Chartists' demands for representation can be interpreted as inarticulate ones for enlightened government, "[b]ellowings, *in*articulate cries as of a dumb creature in rage and pain; to the ear of wisdom they are inarticulate prayers: 'Guide me, govern me! I am mad and miserable and cannot guide myself!'" (Carlyle 3: 288). Carlyle's solution, therefore, is for social agency to be taken up by a new aristocracy. This is still one embedded in industrial society, however. It is thus only in the figure of the "Captain of Industry" that Carlyle's outlook finds expression. *Past and Present*'s "Plugson of Undershot" is described as a "born member of the Ultimate genuine Aristocracy of this Universe" (Carlyle 9: 163). He behaves like a chivalric leader of men, having "enlisted his thousand men" for his "dash at Cotton" (Carlyle 9: 163). This, then, is the Carlylean political agent. He is indeed a participant in modern industry and one who employs labor, but it is not this which is his defining feature. Rather it is that he is above all a member of a natural aristocracy.

The assumptions about freedom that animate Carlyle's use of the sublime in *Chartism*, then, are not continuous with the model of political agency that this polemical text assumes. Carlyle's message is inevitably addressed only to a small group. Moreover, because this group is a natural aristocracy who are latent in the current period of laissez-faire misrule, they cannot be readily identified. What is more, given that they have a monopoly on social agency, Carlyle can only doubtfully exhort:

> How an Aristocracy, in these present times and circumstances, could, if never so well disposed, set about governing the Under Class? What they should do; endeavour or attempt to do? That is even the question of questions:—the question which *they* have to solve; which it is our utmost function at present to tell them, lies there for the solving and must be solved. (Carlyle 3: 295)

Yet the vast majority of readers are presumably not part of the new governing aristocracy, and are by definition therefore incompetent to answer this question of questions. Also, these new aristocrats, if they do read the pamphlet, must still solve for themselves the condition-of-England question. This doubtfulness about reaching an audience is a perennial issue in Carlyle's work and one that becomes only intensified when the text in question is, like *Chartism*, a polemical one. This is an issue discussed by Martin Puchner in his study of manifestoes, *Poetry of the Revolution*. Puchner contrasts *The Communist Manifesto* with Machiavelli's *The Prince*. The latter text suffers from the same problem as does *Chartism* in that its effectiveness is belied by its aristocratic assumptions. Puchner points out that "there is an incongruity between the figure, or 'subject' of political agency this text creates—namely, the prince—and the text's own agency," and because the text is committed to all agency residing with the prince, "the manifesto can only intervene indirectly by hoping that this imaginary prince will adopt its suggestions" (Puchner 29–30). Carlyle's quotation above, in which he proposes only to frame the salient questions which his new aristocracy must address, surely suffers from this same incongruity.

The Communist Subject

In the *Manifesto*, by contrast, there is a continuity between its presentation of human autonomy and its model of political agency. This is accomplished by conceiving of the proletariat as if it were a collective subject. As we saw, Marx and Engels regarded labor as an essential aspect of freedom in the world. Unlike Carlyle, the authors of the *Manifesto* carry this through into a conception of political agency, in that they conceive the agent of revolution to be a class defined by its relationship to labor—that is, the proletariat understood as the class of those who own only their own capacity for labor. The proletariat are, in other words, a class in the position of Hegel's bondsman. This Hegelian conception is echoed in the definitive statement in "Bourgeois and Proletarians" of the revolution. As was mentioned above, the relevant section of the Phenomenology was concerned with the bondsman's development towards "independence of self-consciousness." At the end of "Bourgeois and Proletarians," the *Manifesto* states that "[t]he proletarian movement is the self-conscious independent movement of the immense majority, in the interest of the immense majority" (6: 495). What the bondsman himself acquires, then, is predicated of a collective. More precisely, this self-consciousness is attributed to the communists, who are positioned as the plural speaker of the *Manifesto*. They identify themselves simply as members of the proletariat who are the "most advanced and resolute section of the working-class parties," and "have the advantage of clearly understanding the line of march, the conditions and the ultimate general results of the proletarian movement" (*MECW* 6: 497). If there is a collective subject of the proletariat, the communists are presented here like its Kantian rational faculty, understanding the nature of history and perceiving the potential for action not determined by the capitalist world. It is therefore telling that Georgy Lukács, a writer sensitive to the Hegelian in

Marx, invokes the sublime in describing the communists, saying they are "assigned the sublime role of *bearer of class consciousness of the proletariat and conscience of its historical vocation*" (Lukács 41).

Of course, at the time of the *Manifesto*'s writing, self-conscious communists were even rarer than Carlylean "Captains of Industry." Puchner argues that the text is profoundly shaped by that fact, arguing that the text shows a "mutual reinforcement of theory and practice" (Puchner 30). This is because it "is written from the point of view of the proletariat, which is also the true agent of its revolution" (30). There is, however, a problem with this "happy unity of theory and practice," which is that "[e]ven though the rise of capitalism has created a proletariat in the most advanced countries, this proletariat is not yet fully conscious of being the proletariat in the sense of the *Manifesto*" (30). As he puts it, the *Manifesto* "[u]nable to rest comfortably on the existence of the proletariat as a class for itself, [. . .] must create such a self-conscious class in a projective manner" (30–31). Puchner thus argues that the text does this by "show[ing] the proletariat who and what it is by creating a figure, the figure of the proletariat," thus "anticipating and enacting the proletariat in the manner that is, for the time being, theatrical." (Puchner 31). When considered this way, the role that the sublime plays in the *Manifesto* becomes clearer. The text needed a way to rhetorically create a figure that embodies the potential for freedom. As I argue, the sublime after Kant became just such a way of staging human freedom. The sublime was ready to hand as a way to conjure theatrically an independent, self-conscious subject of revolution. Influenced by both Carlyle and Hegel, then, the modern world was presented as a sublime spectacle, terrifying and alienated but also compelling in that it intimated the potential of the human subject to achieve independence from it. In this way, one terminal point of the sublime's post-Kantian career was to become an integral part of the revolutionary praxis in this unparalleled depiction of modernity.

CHAPTER 3

Orders of Magnitude

The Time Machine, Deep Time, and Wells's Mathematical Sublime

All that is solid melts into air before the protagonist of H.G. Wells's 1895 novella *The Time Machine*. The *Manifesto*'s powerful image for the modern world becomes a realized spectacle under the eyes of Wells's Time Traveller. As the character turns the lever on his machine, he sees the world undergo just this process of transforming from solid to fluid:

> The landscape was misty and vague. I was still on the hillside on which this house now stands, and the shoulder rose above me grey and dim. I saw trees growing and changing like puffs of vapour, now brown, now green; they grew, spread, shivered, and passed away. I saw huge buildings rise up faint and fair, and pass like dreams. The whole surface of the earth seemed changed—melting and flowing under my eyes. (*TM* 19)

The syntax itself begins to flow in waves. In the sentence "I saw huge buildings rise up faint and fair, and pass like dreams," the comma marks a caesura between the two phrases, suggesting the rise and fall of the transient houses (19). The comma in the second sentence of the above quotation, the semicolon in the third, and the dash in the final sentence repeat the structure. The passage describes a world speeded up until it seems to become a flowing liquid, and this finds formal expression in furious description counterpointed by this regular, washing motion of the syntax. Both Wells and Marx and Engels use the same arresting image: the entirety of the landscape, "all that is solid," changing so rapidly that it seems to melt and to become a vapor. Yet the spectator in Wells's text could not be more different from the communist subject imagined by the *Manifesto*; a middle-class inventor, using his ingenuity and the amazing discoveries of nineteenth-century science to conquer the fourth dimension. This is the paradigm of the kind of subject that Wells's employment of the sublime constructs, a technocratic and scientifically minded one who helps humanity conquer the natural world with ever-increasing thoroughness. Yet, just as the Time Traveller is immediately thrown out of equilibrium by his own machine, so Wells's sublime ultimately only destabilizes the prospect of such human conquest of nature.

Subliming Solids

Like the relevant passage in the *Manifesto*, Wells's time travel sequence appeals to the ambivalent affect associated with the sublime. The ineffability of its quality is, to be sure, insisted upon: "I'm afraid I cannot convey the particular sensations of time travelling" (*TM* 19). Yet what description is offered makes it clear that the experience partakes of the sublime's characteristic ambivalence. It is marked by fear and physical threat: "There is a feeling exactly like one has upon a switchback–of a helpless headlong motion! I felt the same horrible anticipation, too, of an imminent smash" (19). This feeling is "excessively unpleasant," but it is also complex (19). The fear comes to gain an admixture of excitement or attraction without completely losing its terrifying character. Thus, as the Time Traveller's journey progresses, we are told that

> [t]he unpleasant sensations of the start were less poignant now. They merged at last into a kind of hysterical exhilaration. I remarked indeed a clumsy swaying of the machine, for which I was unable to account. But my mind was too confused to attend to it, so with a kind of madness growing upon me, I flung myself into futurity. At first I scarce thought of stopping, scarce thought of anything but these new sensations. But presently a fresh series of impressions grew up in my mind—a certain curiosity and therewith a certain dread—until at last they took complete possession of me. (20)

With the "fresh series of impressions," there comes another mixed feeling. There are thus two distinct feelings described in this passage: the first is helplessness, which is mixed with exhilaration; the second is curiosity mixed with dread. Both appeal to the structure of ambivalence in that each has a negative element tinged with danger and a positive element mixed with it. Emphasis is placed on the fact that the threatening and attractive components of the feelings are inseparable.

The helplessness, once it becomes somewhat diminished, "merg[es]" with exhilaration, and the curiosity and dread likewise occur together. The Time Traveller's statement that he "scarce thought of anything but these new sensations" implies a supremely powerful and fascinating experience (20). All this adds up to an extremely detailed meditation on qualities of ambivalent feeling.

It is early on in the novel that the protagonist is introduced as the subject of this sublime experience. The complexity of the state of mind is thrown into relief afterwards by contrast with the uncomplicated stimulus-responses of the Eloi which the Time Traveller finds at the end of his journey. The affective life of the Time Traveller's Eloi companion, Weena, shows very little nuance. The protagonist recalls her being "fearless enough in the daylight," but she "dreaded the dark, dreaded shadows, dreaded black things" with "a singularly passionate emotion" (*TM* 43). The Eloi seem incapable of the ambivalence that the Time Traveller experiences in the seat of his machine. They have instead a simple binary reaction, which includes only untroubled composure or an extreme fear of the dark.

It is therefore worth pausing over the commonalities between Wells's time travel passage and the *Manifesto*'s "melting vision." Both share very similar imagery and both appeal to a feeling of being fearful yet compelled, with Marx and Engels communicating this in their descriptions of capitalist productive forces and Wells, like Hegel, describing impressionistically the feeling of everything melting away. In the original German of the *Manifesto*, what is rendered into English as "melts into air" is linguistically somewhat more drastic, being contained in the single verb "verdampft" (*MEW* 4: 465). This comes from "Dampf," meaning "steam," and thus implies a sudden evaporation from a solid state into gas (Puchner 53). Likewise, the trees in the time travel passage are made of solid wood that nonetheless behave "like puffs of vapour" (*TM* 19). In chemistry, the process of heating a solid until it becomes immediately gaseous is denoted by the verb "to sublime." This is likely the oldest sense of the word in English, being derived from alchemical usage as early as around 1400 (*OED*). This context, of course, is one very far removed from the eighteenth-century aesthetics through which the term gained its other sense. Nevertheless, its applicability here may not be entirely a matter of coincidence. There is etymological common ground between the two applications in the Latin 'limen,' in that the aesthetic sense involves rhetoric that is raised up towards the highest limit and the chemical process involves a substance being brought to the limit of its solid state. As will become clear, the chemical sense of an object approaching the limit of its palpability evokes the psychological processes of Wells's sublime particularly well.[1] As we saw, the rhetorical strategy of the *Manifesto* involved giving the impression of a great many things being held unsteadily in a single view in a spectacle that strains at the boundaries of its comprehensibility. This is at the heart of Wells's sublime. The process of subliming is also one in which states of matter are altered through heating—that is, through a thermodynamic process. This hints toward the scientific context that gives Wells's sublime its particular character.

Natural Science and the Natural Sublime

The texts of Marx and Engels and of Carlyle participate in what can be thought of as an industrial sublime. This means that, in them, the powerful products of human artifice take the place of mute nature as the object that occasions the sublime feeling. Now, there are examples of Wells's writing that show a similar kind of interest in technology. In discussing *The Time Machine*, Brian Aldiss differentiates the "modern sublime" from other iterations in part because the modern iteration does not restrict itself to natural objects but can be found in objects of human making. It thus "embraces anything imposing in scale, whether human-made or natural" (Aldiss 189). The comparison made in *Chartism* between industrial Manchester and the sublimity of Niagara Falls is a clear instance of this approach. As Aldiss notes, Wells was keenly interested in the hydro-electric power station that was built near Niagara Falls (192). This shift in attention, it seems, almost literally plays out Carlyle's metaphor before Well's eyes, as Niagara itself becomes industrialized. Furthermore, the language Wells uses to evoke the power station is reminiscent of Carlyle's; he calls its turbines "will made visible, thought translated into easy and commanding things" (Wells, *Future in America* 74). Carlyle's description in *Sartor Resartus* of a steam engine as an idea made physical seems to stand behind Wells's rhetoric here. It could be, then, that the Time Traveller's sublime experience is to be read as a kind of variation on the earlier theme.

Yet in *The Time Machine*, it is not artificial objects which primarily provide the occasion for the sublime. The time machine itself does not constitute an impressive spectacle in the way Carlyle's Manchester does. Instead, it facilitates the presentation of the spectacle. The machine functions, as Caroline Hovanec puts it, as a "visual technology," part of Wells's procedure of "transform[ing] scientific visual instruments into aesthetic ones" (Hovanec 471). In the time travel passages, it is the landscape itself that is the focus for the description. There are other passages in the novel that evoke the sublime, and these objects are generally natural ones. Tellingly, when Aldiss discusses the sublime in *The Time Machine* it is Wells's landscapes that predominate (Aldiss 189–90). The novel returns several times to the numerousness and vastness of heavenly bodies. In one scene, the Time Traveller meditates under the strange sky of the Eloi's and Morlocks' world:

> Looking at these stars suddenly dwarfed my own troubles and all the gravities of terrestrial life. I thought of their unfathomable distance, and the slow inevitable drift of their movements out of the unknown past and into the unknown future. (*TM* 61)

Here Wells employs the rhetoric of cognitive failure; distances are "unfathomable" and both the past and future are "unknown." The Time Traveller feels a sense of his own smallness and limitation.[2] Further in the future, the size of heavenly bodies is again treated in this way. In this scene, the sun appears to have grown staggeringly: "At last, more than thirty million years hence, the huge red-hot dome of the sun had come to obscure nearly a tenth part of the darkling heavens" (84). This "further vision" displays a starkly sublime landscape. The barren solitude of the future world is emphasized. Every aspect of the vista is enumerated with each part in its own way inimical to human life.

> I cannot convey the sense of abominable desolation that hung over the world. The red eastern sky, the northward blackness, the salt Dead Sea, the stony beach crawling with these foul, slow-stirring monsters, the uniform poisonous-looking green of the lichenous plants, the thin air that hurts one's lungs; all contributed to an appalling effect. (83)

The breadth of the view given here serves to underline the solitude of the lone Time Traveller. This theme of solitude is related to another kind of privation, silence:

> From the edge of the sea came a ripple and a whisper. Beyond these lifeless sounds the world was silent. Silent? It would be hard to convey the stillness of it. All the sounds of man, the bleating of sheep, the cries of birds, the hum of insects, that makes the background of our lives—all that was over. (85)

The silence here is fittingly so still that it cannot even be effectually spoken of. An insistence on the ineffability of the impression is a common thread which links these scenes to the Time Traveller's ecstatic experience as he hurtles through time.

The Cosmic Process

It is natural objects, then, that are most strongly associated with the sublime in *The Time Machine*. This marks the novel out from the industrially situated sublime of Carlyle, Marx, and Engels. Yet the novel's aesthetic is clearly not a simple return to any kind of pre-industrial natural sublime. Instead, *The Time Machine* depicts nature as conceived through nineteenth-century scientific discourses, in particular evolutionary biology, geology, and thermodynamics. The latter two were intimately linked with the developments that brought about the industrial world described in the previous chapter. Geology emerged as a science around the time of the early industrial revolution, and this process was given much impetus by the increased demand for coal mining. Likewise, the study of thermodynamics was given impetus by the advent of steam engines, which constituted a uniquely convenient opportunity to study the relationship of heat to dynamic effect (Cardwell 189). The industrial revolution certainly influenced many of the sciences that *The Time Machine* draws upon, even though it is on those sciences' reflections on the natural world that provide the novel's primary subject matter.

There are two main ways in which these scientific shifts are important here. The first of these relates to the positioning of the human within nature. This became a subject of fresh anxiety in the later nineteenth century. Developments in biology in particular questioned, or drew renewed attention to problems with traditional distinctions between the human and the natural. Yet, importantly, this questioning nevertheless happened in an intellectual climate in which post-Kantian ways of thinking about humanity's ethical position were still prevalent. Two essays by Thomas Henry Huxley are particularly illustrative. These are "Evolution and Ethics" and "On the Hypothesis that Animals are Automata and Its History." Huxley's writing is particularly useful because of its influential engagement with the contemporary intellectual cross-currents, particularly commenting on matters of evolutionary biology but also addressing broader philosophical themes. Moreover, beginning with his lectures at the Normal School of Science, Huxley had an enormous influence on the worldview of the young Wells.

The effects of Darwinism on anxiety about the status of the human in the natural world are well known, and it is these anxieties that provide Huxley's starting point in "Evolution and Ethics." He begins by pointing out how a great many human characteristics can be traced back to the struggle for existence:

> For his successful progress, throughout the savage state, man has been largely indebted to those qualities which he shares with the ape and the tiger; his exceptional physical organization; his cunning, his sociability, his curiosity, and his imitativeness; his ruthless and ferocious destructiveness when his anger is roused by opposition. (Huxley, "Evolution" 51–52)

The list given here emphasizes the breadth of the continuity between human characteristics and those of the ape and tiger; it is not just the aggression or savagery that such metaphors may immediately imply, but other universal aspects of human life such as curiosity and sociability. The persistence of these continuities with the animal kingdom is also emphasized: "[C]ivilized man would gladly kick down the ladder by which he has climbed. He would be only too pleased to see 'the ape and tiger die.' But they decline to suit his convenience" (Huxley, "Evolution" 52). The continuity between human and animal qualities is deep as well as broad. The use of the phrase "the ape and tiger" is also somewhat unsettling here, as it slips between synecdochic use (representatives of fellow organisms), and metaphorical use (naming these atavistic qualities), dramatizing a deeply uncertain relationship between the human and the animal. Alongside this, the retreat to rational volition is called into question. This is addressed in "On the Hypothesis that Animals are Automata and Its History." This essay discusses advances in physiology, particularly reflex action, which in the late nineteenth century were creating an increasing challenge to ideas of free will (R. Smith 18–19). In the essay, Huxley again uses an analogy between human and animal. This time the animal is a frog, which has had most of its brain amputated, such that it is "devoid of all spontaneity" (Huxley, "Hypothesis" 223). The frog nonetheless exhibits very many behaviors that are typical of an ordinary frog (224–25). The frog's actions are then compared to that of humans who have sustained brain injuries (226). Huxley comes to the conclusion that consciousness does not appear to determine action. Famously, he says that it is "as completely without any power of modifying that working as the steam-whistle which accompanies the work of a locomotive engine is without influence on its machinery" (240). He draws conclusions from this for the sense of volition: "[T]he feeling we call volition is not the cause of a voluntary act, but the symbol of that state of the brain which is the immediate cause of the act" (244). Because of this, Huxley arrives at a compatibilist definition of free will, one that conceives of freedom in negative terms as the absence of external obstacles:

> We are conscious automata, endowed with free will in the only intelligible sense of that much abused term—inasmuch as in many respects we are able to do as we like—but none the less parts of the great series of causes and effects which, in unbroken continuity, composes that which is, and has been, and shall be—the sum of existence. (244)

Ultimately, then, there seems to be no great divide between the sphere of human action and that of nature; the former is entirely assimilated to the processes of nature.

Yet Huxley is still working within a post-Kantian intellectual climate and has recourse to Kantian ways of thinking about ethical questions. Huxley was familiar with Kant and read him in the original German (Lyons 26).[3] In the essays, he is clearly familiar with the concepts, language, and thinkers of the Kantian moment. In "On the Hypothesis," for example, he states that "the shibboleth of the materialists that 'thought is a secretion of the brain' is the Fichtean doctrine that 'the universe is the creation of the Ego'" (Huxley, "Hypothesis" 211). Also in this essay, he uses terminology reminiscent of Kant. He describes the croak of a frog and the cry of an infant as "*à priori*" (231–32). Likewise, a presumption of familiarity with Kantian ethics is in the background of "Evolution and Ethics." In the discussion of Stoicism in the essay, it is ultimately compared to Kant's system. Huxley says of the Stoic conception of the soul that "the one supreme, hegemonic, faculty, which constitutes the essential 'nature' of man, is most nearly represented by that which, in the language of a later philosophy, has been called the pure reason" (Huxley, "Evolution" 74). He sums it up explicitly, saying that the Stoic system "reverences the categorical imperative as strongly as that of any later moralists" (75). These mentions suggest important things about the place of Kantianism in Huxley's outlook. Ideas such as pure reason and the categorical imperative are made reference to, but it is not felt necessary to explain their source and context. Kant's system, it seems, provides a familiar background theory by which the relatively unfamiliar philosophy of ancient Stoicism can be illuminated. Huxley does not only assume familiarity with Kant. Rather, the background of Kantianism informs the way in which humanity and nature are treated in "Evolution and Ethics." The essay is based around an opposition between the natural and the ethical. On the one hand, Huxley talks of "the cosmic process," which is associated with the Darwinian struggle for existence. This is opposed to an "ethical process; the end of which is not the survival of those who may happen to be the fittest, in respect of the whole of the conditions which obtain, but of those who are ethically the best" (88). The relationship between these processes is an antagonistic one. As with Kant, the cosmic process is devoid of intrinsic moral worth: "[T]he cosmos works through the lower nature of man, not for righteousness, but against it" (76). Because of this, the human must act in opposition to nature. Huxley says that "the ethical progress of society depends, not on imitating the cosmic process, still less in running away from it, but in combating it" in order that humans can "subdue nature to his higher ends" (83). All this recalls the heroic view of ethical struggle between the domains of nature and morality familiar from the *Groundwork of the Metaphysics of Morals*. This view, of course, is embodied in that vision of the sublime in which the subject does battle with nature both within and without. To put it in Huxley's terms in "Evolution and Ethics," then, the struggle to subdue the ape and tiger within and the cosmic process without is one redolent of the Kantian view.

These essays show how the post-Darwinian approach to nature can still retain enough of the Kantian picture to make a staging of the sublime viable. There is also in Huxley's writing an echo of the approach to the sublime of the earlier writers Marx, Engels, and Carlyle—that is, these writings maintain the emphasis on considering humans collectively or socially, rather than individually, as pitted against nature. Huxley expresses optimism that the ethical process can meet the challenge of the cosmic process because "the organized and highly developed sciences and arts of the present day have endowed man with a command over the course of non-human nature greater than that once attributed to the magicians" (84). This sentiment echoes the *Manifesto*'s celebration of the "subjection of Nature's forces to man" and Carlyle's "triumph of man over matter" (*MECW* 6: 487; 489; Carlyle 3: 308). Yet for all this, there are subtly different assumptions at work. Marx, Engels, and Carlyle emphasize humanity collectively in the main because of their emphasis upon labor, and the social organization that work in an industrial society implies. For Huxley, the emphasis on the macrocosm seems to be motivated differently. When looked at too closely, as in "On the Hypothesis that Animals are Automata and Its History," the rational will which drives the ethical process is elusive. The distinctness of human purpose from the cosmic process can be more easily perceived on a large scale. For this reason, "Evolution and Ethics" concludes much more optimistically than the former essay, by quoting Tennyson with a summons to "play the man 'strong in will/ to strive, to seek to find, and not to yield'" (Huxley, "Evolution" 86). The different implication for the domain of freedom when different scales are considered is, as we will see, at the heart of Wells's use of the sublime.

Geology and Imagination

The second way in which nineteenth-century scientific discourses are relevant to the *The Time Machine* also concerns an idea of scale. In the middle and late century, both geology and thermodynamics became involved in the issue that furnishes the main subject matter of the novel—that is, the temporal extent of the world. Geology, since at least Charles Lyell's 1830 *Principles of Geology*, had argued for the reality of "deep time," that the earth's history reached back in time vastly further than previous chronologies suggested. Lyell, indeed, viewed the extent of the past as indefinite and thus potentially infinite. This view was tempered by the work of William Thompson, Lord Kelvin. In 1862, Kelvin estimated the lifespan of the sun to be somewhere from ten to one hundred million years (Burchfield 31). By implication, the earth's habitable lifespan at least must be similar. Thus, time, whilst still extremely long, was held by this thermodynamically-informed account to be limited. Thus, geology and thermodynamics became entwined in a contention over the past, and by extension also the future, extent of the earth's lifespan. *The Time Machine*, of course, is strongly informed by both of these discourses. In the epilogue, for instance, the Time Traveller is speculated to be "wandering on some plesiosaurus-haunted Oolitic coral reef or beside the lonely saline lakes of the Triassic age" (*TM* 91). Elsewhere, there occurs a digression on the theories of George Darwin as they relate to the sun's lifespan (45). The Time Traveller speculates that the warm climate he feels might be explained by the sun's being fueled anew by planets that have fallen into its furnace. These speculations strongly resemble a consideration of Kelvin's as he was making his own calculations, by which he supposed that the sun was partially fueled by the impacts of meteors (Burchfield 29). *The Time Machine* thus draws its subject matter from both of the scientific strands relevant to the duration of the world at the late nineteenth century. This is relevant in that both branches of natural science, though they differed on the figures, attributed sublime dimensions to the world's duration and this in turn influences the particular natural sublime of *The Time Machine*.

In the "further vision," the Time Traveller's Richmond location has become situated on the coast. This circumstance does much more than facilitate the inclusion of crab-like monsters. The time machine's ending up on the margins of the land as it simultaneously arrives near the furthest limit of life on earth carries a symbolic resonance, and this goes deeper than might initially appear. In contrast to the melting landscape around the Time Traveller, the sea is presented as a figure of eternity. We are told that "[o]nly a slight oily swell rose and fell like a gentle breathing, and showed that the eternal sea was still moving and living" (*TM* 82). The opposition, then, is between a landscape, which is presented as mutable, and a sea, which is changeless and eternal. This particular opposition has its roots in the geology of the late eighteenth and early nineteenth century. The field was devoted to studying the extensive history of changes that the earth's rocks had undergone. This was not the case for the sea, which must have remained much as it presently appears while these geological processes were taking place. Indeed, in the late eighteenth century the main controversy within geology, one carried out "with a degree of bitterness, almost unprecedented in questions of physical science," was that between Neptunists and Vulcanists (Lyell 60). This debate focussed on the question of whether the action of the sea or of volcanoes constituted the main agent of observed geological change. Amid this debate, the changing nature of the land was not in doubt, and the sea was considered either as inert or as the factor that molds a malleable landscape. In both cases there is a clear reversal of the usual assumptions about the seas' and the land's relationship. Lyell is probably the most important exemplar of this particular attitude. As Michael Tomko points out, Lyell praises Byron for his use of the sea as a symbol of permanence (Tomko 118). Lyell suggests, indeed, that geologists should "overcome those first and natural impressions which induced the poets of old to select the rock as the emblem of firmness—the sea as the image of inconstancy" and instead should draw on Byron's "more philosophical spirit" that saw in the sea "The image of Eternity," contrasting "the fleeting existence of the successive empires which have flourished and fallen, on the borders of the ocean, with its own unchanged stability" (Lyell 459). What is striking about this is the equivalence that Lyell makes between geological and poetic or imaginative thought. Indeed, the issue of the imagination's power is one of central importance in the *Principles of Geology*. This text is credited with bringing deep time to the forefront of nineteenth-century consciousness. It did this by arguing for a position known as uniformitarianism, which claimed that the present state of the earth's rocks can, and in proper scientific methodology should, be explained with reference to processes that are currently observable. The implication of this view is that these slow processes must have been acting over huge periods of time to produce those drastic changes that are observed in the earth's surface. Yet, as Martin Rudwick argues, this theoretical position of Lyell's could not be advanced in isolation. He says that "the nature of his task of persuasion" was determined by the fact that "although his scientific colleagues (unlike the Mosaic pseudo-scientists) readily accepted a vast timescale on an intellectual level [. . .] it was their scientific imagination that needed transforming" (Rudwick in Lyell xviii). Thus Lyell's persuasive project operates simultaneously at the level of theory and of imagination. Were Lyell merely to make a theoretical argument, he would not have the desired effect on his audience. These scientific colleagues, not having fully come to terms with the long history of the earth that they tentatively allowed, could be susceptible to (for Lyell, unscientific) catastrophist theories which did not require such long timespans. Lyell had therefore to engage both formally and discursively with this problem of imagination. Thus when Rudwick speaks of the "detailed argument" of the *Principles*, it is not only the content of that argument, but also its form, which is necessary to his purpose. A Reading of Lyell's *Principles* that takes this into account is given by J.M.I. Klaver, who holds elements of literary form to be of high importance in the text. In particular, he says that narrative is "clearly an essential part of *Principles*" (Klaver 46). Klaver sees this as, among other things, part of Lyell's aforementioned imaginative argument. It is a "strategic necessity, both as a control of his place in the history of geology and as an instrument in limiting the bewilderment of the mind before the immensity of the subject matter" (46). Narrative, then, is a way to stave off an intuitive rejection of Lyell's examples by having their scope seem more easily comprehensible to his readership.

Yet the hedging effects of narrative can take Lyell only so far. He responds to this in one extraordinary passage by frankly admitting the incomprehensibility of the timescales suggested. This occurs when discussing his precursor, James Hutton. Hutton had before Lyell suggested a view of geology that considered its processes as occurring over a potentially infinite period of time.

> "In the economy of the world," said the Scotch geologist, "I can find no traces of a beginning, no prospect of an end"; and the declaration was the more startling when coupled with the doctrine, that all past changes on the globe had been brought about by the slow agency of

existing causes. The imagination was first fatigued and overpowered by endeavouring to conceive the immensity of time required for the annihilation of whole continents by so insensible a process. [. . .] Such views of the immensity of past time, like those unfolded by the Newtonian philosophy in regard to space, were too vast to awaken ideas of sublimity unmixed with a painful sense of our incapacity to conceive a plan of such infinite extent. Worlds are seen beyond worlds immeasurably distant from each other, and beyond them all innumerable other systems are faintly traced on the confines of the visible universe. (Lyell 63)

The invocation of the sublime here is full-throated, and it displays Lyell's investment in the imagination in both its content and its form. Lyell's formal engagement is demonstrated in the last sentence of the passage, which slips entirely away from discursive argument and instead presents a poetic image of the vast expanse of space standing as a metaphor for vistas of time. The shrinking of the individual subject is encoded by the use of the passive voice: worlds "are seen," but by subjects rendered irrelevant by the extent of the objects described. At the level of content, too, Lyell's argument makes use of the aesthetics of the sublime. There is no sublime feeling here that is "unmixed" with pain, but this mixing with pain of course only intensifies the ambivalent affect. The rhetoric of cognitive failure proliferates. Time and space are "infinite," "immeasurable," and "innumerable," and account for changes that are "insensible." The insistence on negatives hammers home the sense of imaginative lack. Combined with this is a particular conception of the imagination current in the discourse of the sublime. The description of the imagination as something capable of fatigue speaks of a faculty psychology reminiscent of Kant's philosophy. Lyell here also displays an appreciation of the history of sublime aesthetics, particularly its rise to prominence in the late seventeenth and early eighteenth centuries as a part of Newton's cultural impact.[4] Lyell thus situates Hutton's, and by extension his own, discoveries in the context of a figure of as high a stature as Newton by appealing to the continuing tradition of the sublime. Beyond this, the appeal to the sublime is crucial to Lyell's imaginative argument. His admission of the difficulty of imagining deep time posits a psychological explanation for the rejection of Hutton's ideas, something convenient for the thesis that he is advancing. Moreover, the invocation of the sublime allows the baffling nature of deep time to be admitted, but also to be valorized. In his later writings, Lyell continued to return to the imaginative impossibility at the heart of his ideas. In 1863's *The Antiquity of Man*, he returns to the old theme from the *Principles*: "How absurd and fruitless every recourse to calculation on the subject of antiquity! The stretch of human conception necessarily fails us" (Lyell in Klaver 30). Lyell's insistence on cognitive failure in his theories of deep time may have had some interesting consequences; Kelvin avoided directly criticizing Lyell even though, as we saw above, he was an advocate of a limited solar lifespan. Joe Burchfield argues that this may have been influenced by Kelvin's interpretation of Lyell's emphasis on cognitive failure:

> Lyell always spoke rather vaguely of "indefinite" or "limitless" expanses of time, never in concrete numerical terms. For Kelvin a million years was clearly vast enough to be inconceivable or "indefinite" on a human scale. In fact, he casually mentioned in 1854 that two million years should be ample for the speculations of geologists. (Burchfield 33)

These two representatives of their fields thus find a modicum of common ground in a shared belief in the inadequacy of the human mind to comprehend the world's age. This agreement among figures from across disciplines shows what Vybarr Creggan-Reid argues is a characteristically Victorian approach to time, one which he calls the "historical sublime." Creggan-Reid defines the historical sublime as "a way of describing the new paradigms of time and history that emerge in the nineteenth century as a result of geological endeavour and debate," one which centers around a "descriptive and epistemological criteria of lack or absence" (Creggan-Reid 8–9). As such, the commonality that Lyell and Kelvin find here speaks of a common investment in the historical sublime, since it is precisely an epistemological lack that forms the point of agreement between them.

A note nearly identical to Lyell's is struck by Wells in some of his own educational texts. One example is his 1929 *A Short History of the World*, which situates its historical overview with introductory chapters, entitled "The World in Space" and "The World in Time." The second of these chapters includes an indication of up-to-date thinking on the age of the earth:

> It now seems probable that the earth has had an independent existence as a spinning planet flying round and round the sun for more than 2,000,000,000 years. It may have been much longer than that. This is a length of time that absolutely overpowers the imagination. (Wells, *Short History* 3)

The vastness of the duration is emphasized by the decision to represent the quantity not lexically but as a figure including a long string of zeroes. In addressing the relation of deep time to the imagination, even the phraseology Wells uses could be taken from Lyell's discussion. The imagination is once again overpowered, and in this case, the cognitive failure is not recovered from. The above quotation closes the first paragraph of the chapter "The World in Time," and Wells's following paragraph moves on to discussing various astronomical theories of planetary formation. The subject of the conceivability of the earth's lifetime is thus left with this unqualified negation.

Structures of Scale

In another educational text, *The Science of Life*, which Wells authored along with his son G.P. Wells and Thomas Henry's grandson Julian Huxley, a similar remark is made. Discussing the deposition of geological layers, Wells says that "[t]he time must evidently have been prodigious; and when we look at the actual figures in years [. . .] they are indeed staggering" (Wells et al. 198). The emphasis on figures is carried on from the reference in *A Short History*. But here, unlike in the former text, the defeat of the imagination in front of deep time is not left as an insoluble fact. Wells instead sets out a system under which it can be circumvented:

> To think in such magnitudes is not so difficult as many people imagine. The use of different scales is simply a matter of practice. We very soon get used to maps, though they are constructed on scales down to a hundred-millionth of natural size; we are used to switching over from thinking in terms of seconds and minutes to some other problem involving years and centuries; and to grasp geological time all that is needed is to stick tight to some magnitude which shall be the unit on the new and magnified scale—a million years is probably the most convenient—to grasp its meaning once and for all by an effort of imagination, and then to think of all passage of geological time in terms of this unit. (199)

For Wells, then, the problem of thinking deep time is simply a case of orders of magnitude. If the right scale is chosen by which to contemplate the findings of geology, then bafflement can be avoided. It seems unlikely that this difference in position compared to *A Short History* is wholly down to the collaborative authorship of the book. In *A Short History*, Wells suggests a similar method as a means of understanding the distances between the planets of the solar system (Wells, *Short History* 2). Wells had a longstanding imaginative interest in scales of magnitude. His novel of the relatively near future, *The Sleeper Awakes*, features a society in which the decimal system has been replaced with new and unfamiliar units. The protagonist is told,

> [o]f course things, even these little things, have altered. You lived in the days of the decimal system, the Arab system—tens, and little hundreds and thousands. We have eleven numerals now. We have single figures for both ten and eleven, two figures for a dozen, and a dozen dozen makes a gross, a great hundred, you know, a dozen gross a dozand, and a dozand dozand a myriad. Very simple? (Wells, *Sleeper* 34)

Wells, then, was consistently interested in the nature and possibilities of scales. In *The Sleeper Awakes* he plays with their arbitrariness and in *The Science of Life* he advocates their usefulness to scientific thought.

Taking these together, it is evident that Wells understood some of the implicit psychology behind the practice of thinking in magnitudes. As such, it is worth looking closely at the structure of this psychology as it appears both in Wells's educational texts and in *The Time Machine*. Wells's method of dealing imaginatively with deep time is particularly comparable with Kant's explanation in the "Analytic of the Sublime" of how magnitude is estimated logically. This link can help illuminate the particular structure of the sublime in *The Time Machine*. Whilst it is not clear precisely how closely Wells had read Kant, he nevertheless shows familiarity with and respect for his thought. This is perhaps attributable to Huxley's educational influence. Wells held Kant in high esteem: in a letter to the editor of the *Fortnightly Review*, Wells complains that Herbert Spencer "quite preposterously refuses to read Kant" (Wells, *Correspondence* 79). This letter was written in 1905, but there are references by Wells to Kantian philosophy as early as *The Time Machine*. In the version of the novel that appeared in the *New Review*, one of the characters begins an objection to this text's staunchly determinist Time Traveller:

> "Kant," began the Psychologist.
> "Confound Kant!" said the Time Traveller. (Wells, *Definitive Time Machine* 176)

This is, of course, a very passing reference, but it at least indicates Wells's familiarity with Kantian philosophy. Wells's interest in Kant, moreover, encompassed territory associated with the latter's sublime. In *God, the Invisible King*, Wells makes several references to the famous lines from the conclusion to the *Critique of Practical Reason* that "[t]wo things fill the mind with ever new and increasing admiration and reverence, the more often and more steadily one reflects on them: *the starry heavens above me and the moral law within me*" (PP 269). This pronouncement, in linking the vastness of the natural world to the appreciation of moral vocation, anticipates the mathematical sublime that is expounded in the third *Critique*. Wells cites approvingly this statement of Kant's, both in expounding his concept of immanent religion and in discussing how a belief in moral prescription can be reconciled with a scientific materialism (Wells, *Invisible King* xiv; 101–2). Wells thus had at least some familiarity with Kantian ideas, particularly with those ideas clustered around the mathematical sublime. This is particularly important when seen in the context of Wells's clear interest in the structures by which magnitude can be imagined. His presentations of magnitudes that strain at the limits of comprehensibility are strikingly Kantian.

Kant conceives estimation of magnitude as involving two parallel psychological processes. These he calls "apprehension" and "comprehension" (*CJ* 135). Apprehension in its barest form consists in mentally placing things in a series. To estimate the height of a tree in terms of an average person's height, for example, it is necessary to imagine the latter height being duplicated and stacked one on top of another.[5] This repetitive stacking is the action of apprehension. As such, it has no particular limit to speak of; as Kant says, "[I]t can go on to infinity" (135). Yet to truly estimate magnitude, apprehension by itself is insufficient. This is because it takes no heed of the units with which it works. The other operation, comprehension, is thus required. Comprehension focusses on what is to be put together: it gives the quanta as such. In the above example, then, the height of an average person must be comprehended if the action of the apprehension is to have any meaning. It is clear, then, that these two operations as Kant has defined them must work in parallel with one another. Without apprehension, comprehension cannot move beyond the understanding of a single quantity and so estimation of magnitude cannot begin. However, without comprehension, the apprehension has no sense of what is to be put in sequence. Also, the duplicating action of apprehension, given that it can go on indefinitely, will eventually become useless. This is because at some point the beginning of the series will be forgotten. As Kant says:

> For when apprehension has gone so far that the partial representations of the intuition of the senses that were apprehended at first already begin to fade in the imagination, as the latter proceeds on to the apprehension of further ones, then it loses on one side as much as it gains on the other. (135)

Thus, to estimate any magnitude, both of these operations must play their part. Not only this, however, but the comprehended unit must be of an appropriate size, because if it is too small the apprehension will have too much work to do and become adrift as described above. Thus, once apprehension goes so far, another, larger, quantum must be given in comprehension, and then the process can start again. This is what happens in counting. As Kant describes:

> For in the understanding's estimation of magnitudes (in arithmetic) one gets equally far whether one pushes the composition of the units up to the number 10 (in the decadic system) or only to 4 (as in the tetradic system). (137)

Now, in logical estimation of magnitude, this comprehended quantum can be of any size: "a foot or a rod, or whether it chooses a German mile or even a diameter of the Earth" (137). Thus, any magnitude whatsoever, given the appropriate combination of apprehension and comprehension, can logically be estimated.

In *The Science of Life*, Wells suggests that deep time be estimated according to this essential structure. The principle of estimating magnitude is evidently in Wells's view the same whether it is spatial or temporal extent in question. Thus he points out the fact that "[w]e very soon get used to maps" as evidence that his method is broadly applicable (Wells et al. 199). For Wells, as for Kant, all rests on the size of the comprehended quantum. The appropriateness of the basic unit is the only thing necessary for successful estimation of geological timescales: "[A]ll that is needed is to stick tight to some magnitude which shall be the unit on the new and magnified scale" (199). Not to comprehend an appropriate unit is to risk lapsing into cognitive failure; thus we must "stick tight" to it lest we become unmoored. The new unit chosen can be of any arbitrarily large size, the only consideration being its relevance to the amounts of time which must be estimated. Thus Wells breezily states that "a million years is probably the most convenient" (199). In describing it this way he singles out the process of comprehension, the intuition of a unique quantum, as a distinguishable mental effort. Moreover, he states that it is only when this is done that the other processes of ordinary estimation can begin. He recommends his readers should endeavor to "grasp [the new unit's] meaning once and for all by an effort of imagination, and then to think of all passage of geological time in terms of this unit" (199). Thus, once we have made the "effort of imagination" implied in comprehension, we can resume the duplicative process of apprehension to "think of all passage of geological time" (199).

Kant, however, distinguishes the kind of estimation that Wells here advocates from a truly aesthetic one. The distinction involves two separate kinds of comprehension, which Kant terms "*comprehensio logica*" and "*comprehensio aesthetica*." *Comprehensio logica* works with abstractions given by the understanding. As Kant says, "[T]he understanding, however, guides this by numerical concepts, for which the former must provide the schema" (*CJ* 137). It is therefore this kind of comprehension that is involved in decimal counting. *Comprehensio aesthetica*, by contrast, works with quanta given "in an intuition of the imagination" (137). With this distinction in mind, the aforementioned arbitrarily large units (such as the diameter of the earth) are for Kant more like the numerical abstractions that apply to *comprehensio logica* than the sensible intuitions of *comprehensio aesthetica*. They are quantities "whose apprehension but not composition is possible in an intuition of the imagination (not through *comprehensio aesthetica*, though certainly through *comprehensio logica* in a numerical concept)" (137–38). Thus, though apprehension can always carry on, there comes a point at which the imagination fails and *comprehensio aesthetica* collapses; this does not happen with the solely arithmetical process of logical estimation, since the numerical concepts of the understanding have no such maximum. Kant is describing *comprehensio aesthetica* when he says "comprehension becomes ever more difficult the further apprehension advances, and soon reaches its maximum, namely the aesthetically greatest basic measure for the estimation of magnitude" (135). More succinctly, he says that "there is in the comprehension a greatest point beyond which it cannot go" (135). In this collapse of comprehension is found the mathematical sublime. Kant explains this by analogy with an observer's entry into Saint Peter's Basilica:

> For here there is a feeling of the inadequacy of his imagination for presenting the ideas of a whole, in which the imagination reaches its maximum and, in the effort to extend it, sinks back into itself, but is thereby transported into an emotionally moving satisfaction. (136)

The collapse of *comprehensio aesthetica* is ultimately the factor that precipitates the sublime experience. This is because when the imagination fails to comprehend the magnitude presented, the idea of wholeness is supplied by the reason in the form of a concept of the infinite (138). Thus the "feeling of inadequacy" is thereby juxtaposed with "emotionally moving satisfaction" to produce the ambivalent "negative pleasure" of the Kantian sublime (138; 129).

"The Year Eight Hundred and Two Thousand Odd"

Wells in *The Science of Life* does not make the distinctions that Kant here makes. His method of coming to terms with deep time makes no strong division between understanding and imagination: the reader is urged to grasp by "an effort of imagination" a unit large enough that only a concept of number—that of a million years—can encompass it. Nonetheless, at a broader level a distinction of this kind can be posited in Wells's writings. It makes sense that the explanation in *The Science of Life* is of a method that resembles Kant's logical rather than aesthetic estimation. The text is, after all, an educational one, and the relevant passage comes immediately before a discussion of the fossil record and the evolutionary history of life. Wells's educational burden in this text is very different from Lyell's polemical one in *Principles of Geology*. Lyell's initial readership was composed primarily of geologists already familiar with much of the evidence but undecided about the validity of uniformitarian principles. Their imaginations needed to be engaged in favor of their embracing the consequences of what Lyell saw as sound science. Wells, however, is writing an introductory text for a non-specialist audience. The sublime, therefore, must at this point be bracketed out in favor of the ability to relay information discursively.

This is not the case in *The Time Machine*. In this novel, the structures of scale bear much more towards the collapse with which Kant associated the mathematical sublime. The focus falls far more intently on the dizzying and frightening profusion of apprehended units, rather than any shift to a larger scale. The year in which most of the plot takes place is given as "Eight Hundred and Two thousand Seven Hundred and One A.D." (*TM* 28). The Gregorian calendar is used. This is done despite the fact that the length of time thereby represented utterly dwarfs the length of recorded history. A system conceived in a different context is carried on with no change of scale until it has become perversely cumbersome. By contrast, when geologists speak of times in even relatively recent geological history, dates are generally given in round numbers before the present, since the two millennia or so between the present day and the advent of the common era are negligible. The Time Traveller initially has trouble with the date, calling it "Eight Hundred and Two Thousand odd" (25). However, after this, the date is given with the exactitude mentioned above. On one level, the exactness of the given date mockingly recalls James Ussher's precision in his estimate of the date of the creation. Wells mentions Ussher's date in *The Science of Life*, saying "Archbishop Ussher, less than three hundred years ago, dated the creation of the world in 4004 B.C. (and gave the day and hour, too!)" (Wells et al. 198). The juxtaposition of cosmic event with Ussher's anthropocentric precision clearly struck Wells, as it has done many others, as ripe for ridicule. More importantly, however, the exactitude of the figure that Wells gives for the year emphasizes its cumbersome size and thus the incomprehensibility of the timespan it represents. It drives home that in these hundreds of thousands of years we are dealing with a timescale outside anything that the human imagination, habituated to the day or the lifetime, can comprehend.[6]

This is even further exaggerated in the Time Traveller's final trip into the future. In the sequence that precedes the "further vision" there comes a description of the dials on the time machine. These, it turns out, are based on perhaps the most intuitively imaginable quantum of time in everyday human experience, the day. The narrator states that "[o]ne dial records days, another thousands of days, another millions of days, and another thousands of millions" (*TM* 81). This is an apt example of the bewildering effect of apprehension unaccompanied by appropriate comprehension. There is, of course, a concept of number by which the days are arithmetically counted, but the lack of any other quantum intuitive to the imagination means that Kant's *comprehensio aesthetica* fails. By the time thousands of millions of days are counted, any imaginative sense of the amount of time referred to becomes lost. A similar effect might prevail if someone were to describe, say, the time spent working on a book in terms of seconds rather than hours, months, or years. The narrative dramatizes this confusion of units:

> Now, instead of reversing the levers I had pulled them on so as to go forward with them, and when I came to look at these indicators I found that the thousands hand was sweeping round as fast as the seconds hand of a watch—into futurity. (81)

The identification of thousands of days with the passage of seconds demonstrates the telescoping effect here. The difference between the day and the second are on this journey negligible. If anything, the day seems paradoxically even shorter than the second. This passage, moreover, plays rhetorical expectation off against semantics to aid the sense of vertigo. The phrase "into futurity" occurs after a dash and at the close of the paragraph. Such a phrase is therefore in the usual position of a narrative coda or a reflection, appended to and marked off from the main discourse. In one way, of course, it is such a phrase: it clarifies the direction of the previously narrated movement, where the time machine is going. However, its semantic content and its sounding almost like a standalone imperative, is uncompromisingly open-ended. Indeed, the choice of the word "futurity" in the coda is itself telling. Creggan-Reid notes that the word enjoyed a vogue in the late nineteenth century, suggesting that this is because it captures well a sense of being temporally adrift. Compared to "the future," futurity "describes a vision of the future stripped of its 'the'-ness, stripped of its grammatical trace of fixity," evoking a "'deep' future," which is a mirror image of the geological past (Creggan-Reid 209). This passage which describes the falling away of comprehensible quanta ends by wrong-footing the reader on a syntactic level, while employing a term that itself evokes the impalpable extent of the future.

The imagery of collapsing scales extends beyond the time machine's dials. As the Time Traveller journeys farther, he observes a change in the earth's natural cycles:

> The palpitating greyness grew darker; then—though I was still travelling with prodigious velocity—the blinking succession of day and night, which was usually indicative of a slower pace, returned, and grew more and more marked. This puzzled me very much at first. The alterations of night and day grew slower and slower, and so did the passage of the sun across the sky, until they seemed to stretch through centuries. (*TM* 81)

Far into the future, then, the length of a day on earth changes until it is much longer than a century. The days on the Time Traveller's dials have therefore lost any referent in nature. In this way, while the apprehension of moving ever onward into the future continues, comprehension has failed in both ways. After all, comprehension, as remarked above, not only allows newer, large units to be given once apprehension goes too far, but also gives the unit in the first place. The Time Traveller's fundamental unit of the day, then, besides being too small to measure these durations, has lost any intuitive meaning it had in the first place. The Time Traveller is finally utterly adrift.

There is yet another way in which the observed world itself connects with the collapsing of comprehensible structures. The needle that measures days on the time machine's control panel is described as having been during this final acceleration "a mere mist upon its scale" (*TM* 82). The imagery discussed above of melting and subliming is thus applied directly to this succession of units. The "melting vision" of the landscape changing state under the Time Traveller's eyes can be seen as more than simply a representation of the malleability of the natural world across time. The melting is identified with the breaking down of comprehensible scales on the time machine's controls. In turn, it represents particular mental processes related to the imagination of quantities. Apprehension runs indefinitely on and eventually melts away when it does not find a new quantum that can be comprehended. The melting of the world in front of the Time Traveller therefore represents this cognitive failure.

So the language of sublime affect in the description of the Time Traveller's journey is joined to a rehearsal of the structure of the Kantian sublime. This experience is provoked by the revelation of a natural extent in a temporal dimension that can logically be understood but cannot be imagined in terms of anything in human life. Thus the Time Traveller—conscious the whole time and no mere sleeper—witnesses deep time itself, something that is categorically unimaginable. In turn, what he experiences can only be depicted in terms of that very imaginative impossibility and the terrifying cognitive dissolution it induces.[7]

"One Cannot Choose But Wonder"

These time travel scenes, then, dramatize the mind's operations when confronted with the discoveries of nineteenth-century science. This is an important issue for Wells. The psychological structure of the mathematical sublime serves as a paradigm for the new kind of scientifically literate thought that Wells advocated. Sussman claims that Wells was "the only nineteenth-century writer who understood science well enough to create psychologically believable scientists," and this new way of thinking was something Wells hit upon early in his career (Sussman 164). It found articulation in one of his very first published articles, 1891's "The Rediscovery of the Unique." The idea, moreover, was something he maintained interest in and returned to repeatedly, in 1917's *First and Last Things* and in 1932's *The Work, Wealth and Happiness of Mankind* (Parrinder 101). This reiterated idea of Wells's is called by Patrick Parrinder "neo-nominalism" (101).[8] Neo-nominalism is basically an ontological position, but Wells's emphasis falls largely on its epistemological ramifications. Its fundamental claim is that no two things are exactly alike. As he put it in "The Rediscovery of the Unique": "*All being is unique*, or, nothing is strictly like anything else" (Wells, *Early Writings* 23). No matter how similar entities appear, closer study will always reveal differences between them. This applies even to the most fundamental constituents of the material world. He says of atoms that "it is possible to think of them as unique things each with its idiosyncrasies, and yet regard the so-called verification of the atomic theory with tranquillity" (28). This extraordinary claim has profound epistemological consequences. For Wells, it means that we must come to terms with the fact that common-sense understandings of the world in which things are supposed to be identifiable with one another ultimately rest on "an unconscious or deliberate disregard of an infinity of small differences" (23). This expresses itself in a semiotic skepticism with both linguistic and numerical parts, so that "The Rediscovery of the Unique," he says, could just as suitably titled "The Fallacy of the Common Noun" (22). Wells explains: "[T]he *common noun* is really the verbal link of a more or less arbitrarily determined group of uniques" (24). Numbers also falsify the multiplicity of reality: "[N]*umber* is a purely subjective and illusory reduplication of uniques" (25). The epistemological implications here described for Wells necessitated a radical change in modes of thought: "It should, it will, decimate every thoughtful man's views as pestilence thins a city" (22). He suggests the broad range of subjects in which his argument will have consequences, from cab regulations to philosophy and science (22).

Yet before these conclusions are reached, the realization of the neo-nominalist position, the "rediscovery of the unique" itself, must be achieved. Psychologically, this realization will inevitably resemble the structure of the mathematical sublime described above. To see the world as the neo-nominalist does is to realize that apprehension is, in reality, impossible. If "all being is unique," then to duplicate anything identically is to stray from accuracy. This means that the mind that imagines such a world cannot simultaneously perform any estimation of magnitude like that which Kant describes. Relatedly, this position makes the initial comprehension of a quantum prohibitively difficult, when it is understood that any real object must after all be composed of very many incommensurable and unique parts down to its very atoms. To truly understand neo-nominalism, then, the mind must become aware of this "infinity of small differences" (Wells, *Early Writings* 23)— that is, as in Kant's sublime, this breakdown of apprehension must lead to the arrival at an idea of infinity supplied by reason. For Wells, of course, number can still be used, but it must be used in the knowledge that in another, more accurate, way of regarding the world it would have to be discarded. We saw in Kant that concepts of number can be used for logical estimations of magnitude, but not for aesthetic ones. Likewise, for Wells, numbers will inevitably be used in everyday thinking, but in the mind as it considers the neo-nominalist view of reality they cannot be applied.

This outlook is pervasive in *The Time Machine*, underlying both imagery and narrative. The melting and subliming imagery of the time travel sequences can be further appreciated here, particularly as it relates to the common ground between the aesthetic and scientific senses of "sublime." The impossibility of comprehending an object as a unity when it is understood to be composed of innumerable unique atoms finds expression in solid objects becoming suddenly liquid or gas. These passages also display the linguistic skepticism that is mandated by the neo-nominalist view. It is signaled that many of the events that the Time Traveller attempts to narrate ultimately defeat linguistic expression. The possibility that narrative cannot capture reality is a preoccupation of the novel. The Time Traveller "cannot convey the peculiar sensations of time travelling" (*TM* 19). Likewise, the stillness of the silent world in the "further vision" "would be hard to convey" (85). These qualities are, importantly, indescribable because they are so singular, so unique that their particularity defeats the generalizations on which language relies. The inadequacy of the Time Traveller's language finds a thematic echo in the clumsiness of the Eloi's speech. His communication with the Eloi is severely limited and he states that "[e]ither I missed some subtle point, or their language was excessively simple—almost exclusively composed of concrete substantives and verbs" (38). As if chastened by this caricature of language, the Time Traveller displays in his narrative an extraordinary willingness to disavow his own glosses. He offers a succession of interpretations on how the present-day world became that of the Eloi and Morlocks. The first is dismissed laconically: "Very simple was my explanation, and plausible enough—as most wrong theories are!" (33). The second is left with a severe disclaimer:

> So I say I saw it in my last view of the world of Eight Hundred and Two Thousand Seven Hundred and One. It may be as wrong an explanation as mortal wit could invent. It is how the thing shaped itself to me, and so I give it to you. (79)

This manner of proceeding through provisional hypotheses is of course part of a usual scientific practice and does not necessarily indicate the more extreme linguistic skepticism for which Wells's neo-nominalism calls. Yet the Time Traveller goes further than this, disclaiming his whole narrative, caveats and all. He tells his listeners after he has finished to "[t]ake it as a lie—or a prophecy. Say I dreamed it in the workshop" (87). The Time Traveller's story is difficult to believe because it is so extraordinary; it is an event which is too unusual to describe and must inevitably be told with a sense of linguistic communication's inadequacy in the face of the unique. This is followed by a moment that neatly expresses the tension:

> The Time Traveller turned to us. "Where are the matches?" he said. He lit one and spoke over his pipe, puffing. "To tell you the truth ... I hardly believe it myself ... And yet ..."
>
> His eye fell with a mute inquiry upon the withered white flowers upon the little table. (88)

The Time Traveller begins to doubt his own narrative and, having no more words, trails off. He directs his attention immediately to the two white flowers that he brought from his journey. These flowers are emblems of the unique; the Medical Man subsequently tells the Time Traveller that he cannot place their natural order (88). They defy taxonomic categorization just as the Time Traveller's experiences defy linguistic description.

This juxtaposition, and the consequent qualification of the Time Traveller's narrative, could not be achieved were it not given at one remove, embedded in that of the primary narrator. It is perhaps ultimately this frame narrator who best exemplifies Wells's ideal habits of thought. He displays the same keen linguistic skepticism as the Time Traveller. In embarking on his rendering of the story he is conscious of its ineffable particularity: "In writing it down I feel with only too much keenness the inadequacy of pen and ink— and, above all, my own inadequacy— to express its quality" (*TM* 16–17). This attitude can be contrasted with that of the newspaper editor who also hears the Time Traveller's story. When the Time Traveller arrives back in Richmond, the journalist does not allow his incomprehension of the situation to prevent him from summing it up in an easy phrase: "Then, 'Remarkable Behaviour of an Eminent Scientist,' I heard the Editor say, thinking (after his wont) in headlines" (14). The headline, with its compression and necessary reliance on general terms, is an exaggerated case of how language does not capture the multiplicity and uniqueness of the world; in this case, while it is accurate in its way, the Editor's headline falls spectacularly short of capturing the situation. Moreover, this reliance on headlines is said to be a psychological characteristic of the Editor's. Again we are reminded that the rediscovery of the unique must have profound consequences for modes of thinking; if we are to be skeptical of common nouns and numerals we must certainly no longer think in headlines. This new kind of thinking can be seen nowhere more strongly than in the frame narrator's epilogue to the novel. It begins by speculating on what has become of the Time Traveller. The first sentence, however, is a categorical one: "One cannot choose but wonder" (91). This is contextualized only in the next sentence with "will he ever return?" (91). The great vistas of possibility that the Time Traveller's story has opened up, signaled by this initially unqualified summons to wonder, hang over the epilogue and echo the profoundly unsettling implications of the natural extent and multiplicity that constitute Wells's sublime objects. It is fitting that the epilogue should close with an image taken from "The Rediscovery of the Unique" (91n3). That essay finishes by imagining humanity as a man who stands in darkness and strikes the match of science, "to see his hands lit and just a glimpse of himself and the patch he stands on visible, and around him, in place of all that human comfort and beauty he anticipated— darkness still" (Wells, *Early Writings* 30–31). When the narrator of the epilogue states that "to me the future is still black and blank—is a vast ignorance, lit at a few casual places by the memory of his story," he signals that, in listening to the terrible and baffling narrative of the Time Traveller, he has himself come some way towards the rediscovery of the unique (*TM* 91).

"Capable, Rational Men"

There is another way in which the narrator of the epilogue is representative of Wells's ideal, scientifically literate subject. This is that, in contrast to the Time Traveller, he finds a way to be steadfastly socially optimistic. Considering the question of where the Time Traveller may have ultimately arrived, he foresees a possible utopian future. This will be a state of affairs in which "the riddles of our own time [are] answered and its wearisome problems solved" (*TM* 91). This is in contrast to the Time Traveller's own outlook:

> I, for my own part, cannot think that these latter days of weak experiment, fragmentary theory and mutual discord are indeed man's culminating time! I say, for my own part. He, I know—for the

> question was discussed among us long before the time machine was made—thought but cheerlessly of the Advancement of Mankind, and saw in the growing pile of civilization only a foolish heaping that must inevitably fall back and upon and destroy its makers in the end. (91)

The narrator countenances the startlingly grim prediction of the Time Traveller. Yet he rejects it, even after he has heard the Time Traveller relate a narrative that seems to corroborate the pessimistic view. He draws a line under his statement of the Time Traveller's opinion with a note of hard-nosed practicality: "If that is so, it remains for us to live as though it were not so" (91).

This statement of the necessity of practical action is a succinct summation of the attitude that Wells prescribes for the rulers of the future. Immediately after his first clutch of scientific romances, beginning with *The Time Machine* and ending with *The First Men in the Moon*, Wells turned to producing nonfiction works on the subject of social and technological progress. The first of these was the pamphlet *The Discovery of the Future* and its associated bestseller, *Anticipations*. In both of these texts, Wells makes the case that humanity must approach scientific development in a self-conscious and directed way. This necessitates that society be reorganized in order best to deploy the possibilities of modern science. In this society, Wells believes, political authority should be exercised by a specialist managerial or technocratic class. He envisages, as he says, "a Republic that must ultimately become a World State of capable, rational men, developing amidst the fading contours and colors of our existing nations and institutions" (*A* 157). This class is variously called by Wells the "New Republicans," the "Samurai" and the "open conspirators." A significant part of *Anticipations* is given over to advocating investment in education so that such a class can emerge and take on the mantle of leadership. It is in this way that, for Wells, the "riddles" and "wearisome problems" of the nineteenth century will be answered and solved. The new modes of thought heralded by Wells's neo-nominalism are central to this project since neo-nominalism represents the correct response to the multifariousness of the world uncovered by modern science. It is a form of thinking appropriate to the science that the New Republicans will master and wield. The optimism that the narrator evinces in the epilogue, rests, therefore, a great deal on the abilities of practical and scientifically literate subjects to remake the world. In *The Science of Life*, the possibilities for humanity are even expanded onto the canvas of deep time.

An optimistic conclusion is reached in contemplating the resources of evolution guided by the power of human reason:

> If that self-same stream of life that flows through our human generations and that we call man was once fish, and if those fishy ancestors could be transformed into our present selves in three-hundred million years, without the aid of conscious purpose in any of the prehuman forbears, who shall prophesy what our race may not achieve and into what it may not transform itself before another such period in the history of life on earth has passed? (Wells et al. 258)

The expanse of the future here allows rational freedom to be played out on a grand scale. This mention of the possible fate of a future society as it stretches off into geological time inevitably recalls *The Time Machine*. The view expressed in Wells's later educational work once again links back to that of his earlier novel. The earlier novel can be illuminated thereby, but it nonetheless shows itself to be much more complex in its structures and implications.

The Cosmic Process Reasserted

There are hints that the ideal of the scientific subject influenced the writing of *The Time Machine*. In his early speculations on the origins of the future world, the Time Traveller supposes a golden age of human potency, a "perfect conquest of Nature" (*TM* 32). Huxley's ethical process seems to have proceeded far from the ape and tiger as this hypothesised future society works its will on the natural world: "One triumph of a united humanity over Nature had followed another. Things that are now mere dreams had become projects deliberately put in hand and carried forward" (31). The society that the Time Traveller envisages is striking in its resemblance to that of the "New Republicans" advocated in *Anticipations*:

> The whole world will be intelligent, educated, and cooperating; things will move faster and faster towards the subjugation of Nature. In the end, wisely and carefully we shall readjust the balance of animal and vegetable life to suit our human needs. (31)

So, despite his opinions as revealed in the epilogue, the Time Traveller is not entirely immune to belief in a more advanced future civilization. Moreover, he displays some of the qualities of Wells's New Republicans.

He uses his scientific knowledge, ingenuity, and intelligence to navigate and ultimately escape the world that confronts him. John Hammond notices the proliferation of images involving being pulled backwards and downwards, and of struggling to escape bonds. The number of these is so marked that he calls disentanglement a "powerful theme" in the novel (Hammond 77). He puts this in a biographical context, saying "[t]he Traveller's escape from the clinging Morlocks and emergence to the surface is paralleled by Wells's escape from drapery and from his cramping environment" (Hammond 77). Inasmuch as this motif can be understood to express a longing for personal freedom and autonomy, it can also be read to point in the direction of a validation of the Time Traveller's agency. He has after all, as Aldiss mentions, conquered time itself, applying his scientific knowledge to gain a hitherto barely imagined kind of freedom (Aldiss 193).

There are therefore aspects of *The Time Machine* that chime with Wells's stated opinions concerning a new kind of scientific thinking and a corresponding new class of scientific subjects. Yet a reading of *The Time Machine* that ultimately vindicates optimism about the ethical process is hard to sustain. The factors that point to this are part of a text that is marked by profound tension on the matter. This tension is part of the late-Victorian climate, which marks Huxley's writings and, as we see below, is reflected in, and perhaps even generated by, the particular nature of Wells's scientific sublime. First of all, this can be thrown into greater relief by a consideration of *The Time Machine*'s textual history. Several versions of a story concerning the invention of time travel saw print before the novel's ultimate publication. The first of these was 1888's *The Chronic Argonauts*. In this text, the explanation of the notional physics behind time travel touches on that motif of breaking free. The realization of the fourth dimension is presented as a moment of liberation from nature's strictures:

> "When we take up this new light of a fourth dimension, and re-examine our physical science in its illumination," continued Nebogipfel, after a pause, "we find ourselves no longer limited by hopeless restriction to a certain beat of time—to our own generation." (Wells, *Definitive Time Machine* 150)

This is figured as part of a march of progress characterized by successive realizations of power over nature:

> First, the keel of Jason cut its way between the Sympeglades, and then in the fullness of time, Columbus dropped anchor in a bay of

Atlantis. Then man burst his bidimensional limits, and invaded the third dimension, soaring with Montgolfier into the clouds, and sinking with the diving bell into the purple treasure-caves of the waters. And now another step, and the hidden past and unknown future are before us. We stand upon a mountain summit with the plains of the ages spread below. (150)

This narrative of progress is unambiguously linked to the activities of pioneering and adventurous individuals. It features a parade of heroes, from mythical voyager Jason to the Montgolfiers, who win victories over the limits of nature and so capture the heights. This can be compared with the corresponding section in a later version, published in January 1895 in the *New Review*. Here the explanation of time travel has a far different, much more deterministic, flavor. The dynamic man on the mountaintop is replaced by an "omniscient observer" akin to Laplace's famous demon. This omniscient being "would see, as it were, a rigid universe filling space and time—a Universe in which things were always the same. He would see one sole unchanging series of cause and effect to-day and to-morrow and always" (Wells, *Definitive Time Machine* 177). The deterministic implications of this view are driven home: "From the absolute point of view the universe is a perfectly rigid unalterable apparatus" (177). In this version, then, the principles that allow humans to travel in time also state that they can do nothing to alter events. There is no exhilarating sense of breaking free and mastering nature to be had, but instead a repeated emphasis on rigidity and the ultimate powerlessness of any individual in relation to a series of events that exists as a chain from one end of time to the other.[9] The novel's final version does not dwell so intently on the deterministic implications of its time travel theory, but it certainly does not celebrate the heroic human breaking free from the bonds of time as does *The Chronic Argonauts*. The rigidity of the temporal dimension is still subtly insisted upon in *The Time Machine*: the Time Traveller this time uses the example of a person's life to demonstrate his theory of the temporal dimension. In contrast to the partial description of their three-dimensional bodily existence, a person should fully be considered "a Four-Dimensioned being, which is a fixed and unalterable thing" (*TM* 5). Rather than being an agent who can freely change things in the world and in their own self, then, the person when viewed as extended across time is necessarily rigid and inert.

Indeed, the emphasis on the triumph of the cosmic process increases across versions of the novel. Subsequent iterations of *The Chronic Argonauts* have the intervention of the time-travelling protagonists causing a future society to burst into revolution (Wells, *Definitive Time Machine* 153). This makes a clear contrast with the final version of *The Time Machine*. In the later text, the narrative is instead given over wholly to the Time Traveller's efforts to survive and recover his time machine. His main fear during his journey is that the beings he encounters would be "something inhuman, unsympathetic, and overwhelmingly powerful," with him correspondingly appearing "a foul creature to be incontinently slain" (*TM* 22). He worries, in short, that the future would be governed by the wills of powerful human descendants. What he finds, however, is an apparently rigidly stable ecosystem. The Morlocks may be dangerous, but their threat is more like that of a wild animal than the coercive apparatus of a state. The intervening time between then and the present day has served to draw out the illusory nature of any ethical process because it has allowed unregarded factors such as natural laws or social dynamics to prevail over conscious purpose. In contrast to the optimistic evocations of *The Science of Life*, the initially hypothesized "triumph of a united humanity over Nature" gives rise to a world indistinguishable from one of untamed nature (31). The great spans of deep time in front of humanity are in this novel not a blank canvas upon which to shape the future, but an expanse across which the cosmic process eventually but irresistibly reasserts itself.

The thesis of mankind's conquest of nature is not, of course, the Time Traveller's final one; the discovery of the Morlocks forces him to revise it. Yet his concluding interpretation hardly vindicates human agency either. In the Time Traveller's new interpretation of the future world, the expanse of time has drawn out unexpected aspects of the class system: "It seemed clear as daylight to me that the gradual widening of the present merely temporary and social difference between the Capitalist and the Labourer, was the key to the whole position" (*TM* 48). In this revised view, it is the less deliberate tendencies of the present-day social arrangement that have proven decisive. Considering the Morlocks' subterranean lifestyle, he says:

> [E]ven now there are existing circumstances to point that way. There is a tendency to utilize underground space for the less ornamental purposes of civilization; there is the Metropolitan Railway in London, for instance, there are new electric railways, there are subways, there are underground workrooms and restaurants, and they increase and multiply. Evidently, I thought, this tendency had increased till industry had gradually lost its birthright in the sky. (48)

In this description, the shift from passive to active constructions is notable. The longest sentence starts in the passive voice with "[t]here is a tendency." The tendency is presented as a fact with no agent behind it. More examples of this drive toward subterranean construction are introduced in similar passive constructions. However, in the final phrase, these examples suddenly become agents: "[T]hey increase and multiply." Not only, then, does the tendency to underground dwelling increase and multiply its instances, but it begins to acquire a causal power of its own. In discussing the Eloi's ancestors, the case is the same: "[T]he exclusive tendency of richer people [. . .] is already leading to the closing, in their interest, of considerable portions of the surface of the land" (48). The grammatical agent here is again the tendency, and it is this tendency that is seen to make itself felt long after any conscious agency on the part of these richer people has dwindled.

The two interpretations to which the Time Traveller comes, then, have in common the theme of the futility of human activity in the face of deep time. Both involve unintended factors proving decisive above the conscious purpose of the actors: the quest for a victory over nature turning into a degenerate return to it, or social stratification becoming speciation. These more fundamental factors prove ultimately determining, rendering mastery over the natural world only provisional and apparent. There is, moreover, no sense that the tale is only cautionary, that humanity could avoid this fate by becoming still more effective and rational agents. The Time Traveller himself has no stomach for this kind of attitude:

> I even tried a Carlyle-like scorn of this wretched aristocracy in decay. But this attitude of mind was impossible. However great their intellectual degradation, the Eloi had kept too much of their human form not to claim my sympathy, and to make me perforce a sharer in their degradation and their Fear. (*TM* 62)

There is no reason to believe that, had the social utopia been achieved, the result would have been limitless progress instead of a process of degeneration like that which the Time Traveller first supposed to have happened. On this point his identification with Weena in the above passage is significant. The sympathy between the two is perhaps more than a trick played by physical appearance. He refuses to scorn the Eloi and identifies with their plight. The connection that the human form makes between the Time Traveller and Weena only prompts the recognition that modern humans are just as helpless as the Eloi before these unseen determining factors.

Here the difference between the conceptions found in *The Time Machine* and in the texts discussed in the previous chapter can be most clearly distinguished. *The Time Machine*, indeed, quite clearly rejects both the *Manifesto*'s and *Chartism*'s constructions of the relationship between the human and nature. Shortly after first arriving in the world of the Eloi, the pastoral landscape and the gregarious living habits of the Eloi lead the Time Traveller to conclude that he is witnessing communism (*TM* 29). This initial supposition is revealed, of course, to have been seriously mistaken. The shape of the Eloi's world is likely to be the result of the ossification of productive relations like those prevailing under capitalism. The agency that the *Manifesto* aims to impart is shown after all to have been illusory. The proletariat has never been able to stage any "self-conscious, independent movement" such as Marx and Engels foresaw and has lapsed into a permanently subterranean existence (*MECW* 6: 495). Productive relations were indeed determining and there was no way to break free of them. A revolution of sorts might be said to have happened, with the Morlocks finding themselves higher on the food chain than the Eloi, but this is only the result of natural appetites asserting themselves and utterly different from the human autonomy that the communists envisage (*TM* 62). Likewise, the Time Traveller above explicitly rejects Carlyle's conception of the aristocratic agent. Even though Wells's scientifically educated technocrat may seem like a Carlylean "Captain of Industry," there are important intellectual differences between Wells and Carlyle. In *Chartism*, Carlyle contemplates the threat of determinism in the passage regarding the "World-Steamengine" (Carlyle 3: 278). This, however, is passed over relatively quickly. For Carlyle, if such a belief were to be taken too seriously, a universal suicide would be the only acceptable course of action and Carlyle does not dwell at length on the possibility that determinism may be an accurate description of the world (3: 278). This is not the case for the Time Traveller. In the above passage, he sees Weena as a sharer in his human condition. It is her fate ultimately to be at the mercy of natural processes, as is it his. He cannot scorn her, as would Carlyle, for the failure of her people's civilizational development. Wells takes much more seriously the possibility that this development is simply impossible.

The conflict between freedom and determinism is generally, and justly, regarded as a productive tension animating *The Time Machine*.[10] The conflict between the optimistic, practical outlook of the frame narrator and the contents of Time Traveller's narrative is captured and presented without being resolved, enacting in the novel the dynamics at work in any speculation about the future. Robert Philmus and David Hughes see this capturing of contradictory positions as an example of Wells's interest in "complementarity," the position that ideas that seem intractably to contradict one another are merely the result of artificially "projecting them upon the same plane" (Wells, *Early Writings* 6). These interpretations of *The Time Machine*'s dynamics do indeed capture a large part of what makes it such a compelling text. However, there is a crucial further point that should be made about the ambivalence of freedom and determinism in this novel. This is that the tensions animating the aesthetics of *The Time Machine* cannot themselves necessarily be neatly levelled out with the discursive theories Wells elsewhere expounds and which leave their traces in the text. The juxtapositions that the novel uses, in fact ultimately undermine Wells's construction of autonomy. Within the bounds of the novel at least, the sublime inescapably redounds upon Wells's neo-nominalist subject and undercuts its agency.

The Revenge of Entropy

This is because in his discursive writings on the subject, Wells always insists on a strict distinction between the areas in which free will and determinism can be said to exist. In *First and Last Things*, he speaks of this distinction as one between "planes of thought," which must not be confounded: "I have it very much in mind that various terms in our reasoning lie, as it were, at different levels and in different planes, and that we accomplish a large amount of error and confusion by reasoning terms together that do not lie or nearly lie in the same plane" (*FLT* 27). He uses, as a signal instance of this, "the old theological deadlock between predestination and free will" (29). We must, in other words, never attempt to think of the world in which determinism prevails and that in which free will prevails together, lest we fall helplessly into muddle. The idea finds articulation again towards the end of *Anticipations*. Here Wells is describing the worldview appropriate to his "capable, rational men":

> The men of the New Republic will hold and understand quite clearly the doctrine that in the real world of man's experience, there is Free Will. [. . .] The conflict between Predestination and Free Will, which is so puzzling to untrained minds, will not exist for them. They will

know that in the real world of sensory experience, will is free, just as new-sprung grass is green, wood hard, ice cold, and toothache painful. In the abstract world of reasoned science there is no green, no colour at all, but certain lengths of vibration, no hardness, but a certain reaction of molecules; no cold and no pain, but certain molecular consequences in the nerves that reach the misinterpreting mind. In the abstract world of reasoning science, moreover, there is a rigid and inevitable sequence of cause and effect; every act of man could be foretold to the uttermost detail, if only we knew him and all his circumstances fully; in the abstract world of reasoned science all things exist now potentially down to the last moment of infinite time. But the human will does not exist in the abstract world of reasoned science, in the world of atoms and vibrations, that rigidly predestinate scheme of things in space and time. (A 160)

Wells here separates reality into two epistemological domains, which do not overlap on one another and can thus be said to have different properties. In the world of everyday phenomenal experience freedom does exist; in the abstract world of scientifically posited but sensually unobservable entities it does not. This distinction allows Wells to preserve the political agency of his New Republican technocrats undamaged. At times, indeed, Wells uses his compatibilist distinction as a means not only to divide free will and determinism, but to defend human freedom against the threat of determinism, therefore explicitly to relegate the determinist worldview to a subordinate position: "If you ask me, I think I should say I incline to believe in predestination and do quite completely believe in free will. The important working belief is free will" (FLT 57). With this, Wells institutes a pragmatic hierarchy between his planes of thought. The domain of determinism is more distant and can be safely regarded noncommittally, whereas that of free will is immediate and must be assented to. The distinction between these spheres thus at times takes on the aspect of a defensive line protecting the agency of the subject from the threat of determinism.

It is important to discern exactly how this distinction is made. How is the world of determinism different from that of free will? In the above passage from *Anticipations*, Wells gestures toward the distinction between a qualitative, phenomenal world and an abstract one. Yet the distinction is not only definable in these terms; it is also articulated as a difference in orders of magnitude in spatial or temporal dimensions. In the above quotation, the phenomenal realm is also the macroscopic, and the abstract is the molecular. The world of determinism is also "the world of atoms and vibrations," of things that are abstract precisely because the entities are too small to see. He prefaces this with "[i]n the abstract world of reasoned science there is no green, no colour at all, but certain lengths of vibration, no hardness, but a certain reaction of molecules; no cold and no pain, but certain molecular consequences in the nerves that reach the misinterpreting mind" (*A* 160). Here Wells repeatedly contrasts phenomenal qualities with material entities distinguished by their smallness; "hardness" with a "reaction of molecules," "pain" with "molecular consequences in the nerves" (160). The use of these contrasts suggests that Wells takes, on the one hand, the difference between phenomenal and abstract, and on the other that between microscopic and macroscopic, to be in effect one and the same difference. Moreover, the very same distinction between libertarian and deterministic worlds is played out in *The Discovery of the Future* across timescales. The passage in this essay, like that in *Anticipations*, comes as Wells is considering the idea of his world state. What comes beyond this political reorganization is unforeseeable, although it may be speculated upon in general terms:

> That world state of more vivid, beautiful and eventful people is, so to speak, on the brow of the hill, and we cannot see over, although some of us can imagine great uplands beyond and something, something that glitters elusively, taking first one form and then another, through the haze. (*DF* 52)

The image of the "brow of the hill" here represents a line between domains analogous to that used in *Anticipations*. As in *Anticipations*, the more directly known domain, that closest to the human scale, is the realm of human purpose. On this side of the hill there resides the world state under the New Republicans. Though a note of cautious optimism is struck in this passage, the further realm past the hill is associated with determinism. As Wells talks more about the unforeseeable future, the limitations of freedom emerge and come to dominate the discussion. He continues by granting that "it is impossible to show why certain things should not utterly destroy and end the entire human race and story, why night should not presently come down and make all our dreams and efforts vain" (*DF* 54). These possibly inescapable disasters culminate in a statement of inevitability in the form of entropy. He says:

> And finally, there is the reasonable certainty that this sun of ours must radiate itself toward extinction; that, at least, must happen; it will grow cooler and cooler, and its planets will rotate ever more

> sluggishly until some day this earth of ours, tideless and slow moving, will be dead and frozen, and all that has lived upon it will be frozen out and done with. There surely man must end. That of all such nightmares is the most insistently convincing. (*DF* 55–56)

What is significant here is that this solar extinction is a conclusion extrapolated from Kelvin's second law of thermodynamics—that is, it comes from that domain of scientific abstraction, which Wells is at such pains in *Anticipations* to distinguish from the domain of human liberty. The far future, therefore, like that of the world of molecules, is one in which materially determined processes hold sway and which must be separated from the domain of everyday human experience in order to preserve meaningful agency in the latter.

Yet the particular sublime of *The Time Machine* depends entirely upon destabilizing this separation. This sublime, as we saw above, occurs when it becomes impossible to comprehend a quantum appropriate to estimate a particular magnitude. The quantum that is imaginatively given, as in Kant's *comprehensio aesthetica*, must be something accessible to the imagination. It must, then, come from that domain of qualitative experience. The magnitude that constitutes the sublime object, on the other hand, must exceed this domain. Thus the Time Traveller witnesses geological periods of time passing before his eyes. Those sequences were marked by the rhetoric of cognitive failure and sublime affect. *Comprehensio aesthetica* fails because the expanses of time seen cannot be represented by any quantum found in everyday experience. The result is a passage marked by dissolving imagery and the rhetoric of cognitive failure and ambivalent affect. In the "further vision," the Time Traveller journeys to behold with his own eyes the throes of a dying sun. This sun can no longer heat the earth: "A bitter cold assailed me. Rare white flakes ever and again came eddying down" (*TM* 84). The sea, that image of eternity, has too become fringed with ice (84). This depiction is clearly echoed in Wells's statement above about how inescapably "this earth of ours, tideless and slow moving, will be dead and frozen" (*DF* 55). The heat death of the sun is the ultimate example of cosmic determinism. Yet, of course, it is experienced by the Time Traveller not as "certain molecular consequences" of thermodynamic principles, but as sensible cold itself. The second law of thermodynamics, the law that determines the extinction of the sun, has ceased to be a piece of only "reasoning science," and has become phenomenal, painted in vivid reds and white flakes. The Time Traveller's journey into the far future, then, sees the boundaries that Wells tried in his own future to construct as already in a state of collapse. The same can be said of the imagery of chemical subliming or evaporation in the time travel sequences. In these sequences, melting and evaporation appear as metaphors for the psychological consequences of the neo-nominalist worldview. Yet it also shows the world as if it were materially to come apart into these unique entities. This, too, then, involves a world of another scale, that of molecules, being made visible to human eyes. It is not, as Philmus and Hughes suggest, merely a case of juxtaposing two standpoints. This sublime occurs when the domain of natural determinism collides with that of autonomy. The abstract is brought into the phenomenal, the microscopic into the macroscopic, deep time into the waking moment.

Just as the Time Traveller ultimately pays a high price to see what no other human can, so the young Wells's aesthetic achievement came at a high price for his later project. *The Time Machine* formulates a compelling vision of the sublime, uniquely drawing on the sublime tradition and the discourses of nineteenth-century science. Its power ultimately comes from the recognition, which Wells shared with Huxley, that the discoveries he draws upon could amaze and disturb in equal measure. It is for just this reason that, when Wells attempts thereafter to articulate a vision of human freedom in the natural world, the staging of the sublime in his first novel lingers like the epilogue's melancholy and unsettling memory of the Time Traveller himself.

CHAPTER 4

Details and Detonators

The Secret Agent, Schopenhauer, Nietzsche, and the Ironizing of the Sublime

Mr. Vladimir, the embassy official of Joseph Conrad's *The Secret Agent*, would likely pronounce a withering judgement on the sublimes both of *The Time Machine* and of *The Communist Manifesto*. Inasmuch as Wells's sublime is invested in human progress through science, Vladimir would have little time for it. Far from scientific education being key to the development of future society, Vladimir sees the social value attached to science as little more than a superstition. He calls science a "wooden-faced panjandrum" and a "fetish" (*SA* 25). He openly mocks the middle class's high opinion of scientific progress: "They believe that in some mysterious way science is at the source of their material prosperity. They do" (27). With his coda "[t]hey do," he suggests that his listener might find the bourgeoisie's faith difficult to believe. Wells's technocratic New Republicans would under such a view be only another example of this fetishism. Yet Vladimir would have even less time for Marx's and Engels's sublime rhetoric in the *Manifesto*. Besides his being an arch-reactionary, he is very much of the opinion that poetry makes nothing happen. On being presented with the pamphlets that Verloc's secret society, the "Future of the Proletariat," publishes, he is unimpressed: "Isn't your society capable of anything else but printing this prophetic bosh in blunt type on this filthy paper—eh? Why don't you do something?" (21). Rhetoric, for Vladimir, is defined against efficacious action. He is considerably less impressed than is *Heart of Darkness*'s Charlie Marlow at the prospect of a powerful voice. On Verloc's demonstrating his own vocal abilities, Vladimir responds that "[v]oice won't do. We have no need for your voice. We don't want a voice. We want facts— startling facts—damn you!" (20). The envoi "damn you!" delivered "right into Verloc's face," underlines the point with its particularly blunt lack of eloquence (20). Vladimir wants "activity—activity," both on the part of Verloc and of the British establishment (18). He insists that "the proper business of an 'agent provocateur' is to provoke" (20). He believes, moreover, that causing this activity is a relatively simple matter, that Verloc need only create a sufficiently "startling fact," to achieve this end. Yet the outcome of Vladimir's provocation is far from straightforward. Ultimately both he and Verloc are helpless to prevent its consequences from redounding upon them, as well as on third parties of varying degrees of innocence.

The scene that puts into motion the events of *The Secret Agent*, then, captures many of the intellectual shifts that affect its treatment of the sublime. In his scorn for science and rhetoric, Vladimir represents a move away from the optimistic view that concerns itself with how humans can best exercise their freedom over the natural world. In the ultimate, messy failure of his scheme, which takes up the rest of the novel, it becomes clear that the issue at hand is instead a response to the inescapable bleakness of the world as viewed through pessimism. It is this latter issue to which Schopenhauer's sublime addresses itself. Schopenhauer develops the Kantian sublime within a metaphysical view that privileges opting out of nature rather than acting autonomously within it. *The Secret Agent*, in turn, interrogates this view, drawing out the consequences of Schopenhauer's theory until it leaves us with a thoroughly ironic sublime. Ultimately, Conrad comes close to Nietzsche's Dionysiac in finding within this irony itself a glimpse of a response to Schopenhauerian pessimism.

Propaganda by Deed

Standing behind Vladimir's declarations is the practice of "propaganda by deed." This refers to a tactic, much used by anarchists in the final years of the nineteenth century, in which targets associated with state structures were attacked with a view to inciting and encouraging revolution. The attacks, that is to say, were conducted for symbolic rather than "military" purposes and aimed to inspire political action on the part of the proletariat rather than to be intrinsically damaging. The tactic may be traced back to Mikhail Bakunin, Marx's great antagonist within nineteenth-century socialism. In 1870, Bakunin called upon his fellow anarchists to "spread our principles no longer by words but by deeds" (Bakunin in Cahm 76). The explicit renunciation here of words in favor of deeds runs against a Marxian praxis which emphasizes the continuity of discursive theory and physical action. It was in the context of the widespread adoption of the propaganda by deed tactic by anarchists in the late nineteenth century that the event that inspired *The Secret Agent* occurred. In February 1894, Frenchman Martial Bourdin was walking through Greenwich Park when he was killed by the detonation of a bomb, which he was carrying (SA xiii). Conrad, in the "Author's Note" to the 1920 edition of *The Secret Agent*, cites this event as the germ of his idea for the novel (249). In the note, he dwells upon the inexplicable and irrational appearance of the action: "[A] blood-stained inanity of so fatuous a kind that it was impossible to fathom its origin by any reasonable or even unreasonable process of thought. For perverse unreason has its own logical processes" (249). Despite this inanity, when Conrad comes to fictionalize the event, he places it firmly within the logic of propaganda by deed. Vladimir's "philosophy of bomb throwing" resembles a mirror image of the Anarchism of Bakunin and his heirs (26). Vladimir shares the assumption that only deeds can be potent enough to awaken political action; the difference lies only in that he desires the middle classes be awoken from their complacency and moved to repression.

Given this particular conception of propaganda, it might seem unlikely that the sublime can provide an area here in which propaganda and aesthetics converge as they do in the *Manifesto*. Carlo Pisacan, another figure identified as a possible source for the tactic (Cahm 76), demonstrates a trenchant refusal to go beyond materiality:

> The propaganda by the idea is a chimera, the education of the people is an absurdity. Ideas result from deeds, not the latter from the former, and the people will not be free when they are educated, but will be educated when they are free. (Pisacan in Cahm 76)

Aesthetics of any kind might be thought to be given short shrift when an outlook so hostile to "the idea" is held. Yet it is not necessarily true that anarchists have no time at all for the sublime, even if the rhetorical sublime is precluded by their suppositions. George Sorel's *Reflections on Violence* comes in the wake of the 1890s heyday of propaganda by deed, being published in French in 1906. Sorel addresses himself to the syndicalist movement and, like Pisacan before him, is concerned with justifying the value of physical violence as a form of socialist propaganda. Sorel makes extensive use of the concept of the sublime, using it to describe the feeling that disposes the individual to extraordinary effort. Strikingly, Sorel praises Kautsky, since "for [him] morality is always subordinate to the idea of sublimity" (Sorel 246).

The Schopenhauerian Object

The sublime thus impinges upon anarchist thinking about propaganda by deed and when Conrad comes to write about it he is most certainly interested in its aesthetic implications. The Greenwich plot in the novel is conceived in aesthetic terms—that is, important characteristics of the Greenwich bomb mirror the epistemological structure of the aesthetic object as theorized by one of Conrad's primary philosophical influences. It is worth pausing here to consider an earlier instance in which Conrad addresses issues of socialism and political action. In a letter of December 1897 to his relatively new but already close friend R.B. Cunninghame Graham, Conrad discusses Graham's political commitments and his own relation to them. Conrad protests that he shares the humanitarian values behind Graham's socialist politics but regards radical social change of the kind Graham proposes as simply unfeasible: "What makes you dangerous is your unwarrantable belief that your desire may be realized. That is the only point of difference between us. I do not believe. And if I desire the very same things no one cares." (*CLJC* 1: 425) In explaining this difference Conrad cites not a political analysis but what may be called a metaphysical pessimism. It is expounded in an arresting piece of imagery:

> There is—let us say—a machine. It evolved itself (I am severely scientific) out of a chaos of scraps of iron and behold!—it knits. I am horrified at the horrible work and stand appalled. I feel it ought to embroider—but it goes on knitting. You come and say: "this is all right; it's only a question of the right kind of oil. Let us use this—for instance—celestial oil and the machine shall embroider a design in purple and gold." Will it? Alas no. You cannot with any special lubrication make embroidery with a knitting machine. And the most withering thought is that the knitting machine has made itself; made itself without thought, without conscience, without foresight, without eyes, without heart. It is a tragic accident—and it has happened. You can't interfere with it. The last drop of bitterness is in the suspicion that you can't even smash it. In virtue of that truth one and immortal which lurks in the force which made it spring into existence it is what it is—and it is indestructible!
>
> It knits us in and it knits us out. It has knitted time space, pain, death, corruption, despair and all the illusions—and nothing matters. I'll admit however that to look at the remorseless process is sometimes amusing. (1: 425)

The pessimism here articulated can be thought of as resting on two elements: first, the idea that the universe tends towards suffering and, second, that it is outside our power to do anything about it. The second element is discussed later in the chapter. Here, however, it is sufficient to note that the machine does indeed busily produce suffering. Conrad's evaluative language certainly tends this way. The activity is "horrible," the machine a "tragic accident" and its indestructibility is "the last drop of bitterness" (1: 425). Conrad stresses the lack of sympathy on the part of this universe-machine for those who must experience its output: it is "without conscience" and "without heart" and its process is "remorseless" (1: 425). Finally, its products are enumerated as "time space, pain, death, corruption, despair and all the illusions" (1: 425). In the catalogue, the categories of time and space run seamlessly into "pain, death, corruption, despair" (1: 425). These latter, then, are given the status of inescapable parts of the universe's fabric.

Conrad's view thus bears comparison with the most prominent proponent of metaphysical pessimism of Conrad's time, and indeed of modern times, Arthur Schopenhauer. Concerning Schopenhauer there are no explicit avowals or disavowals of influence by Conrad (Panagopolous 17–18). There are some factors, however, which make such influence seem likely. Conrad's friend John Galsworthy, writing in 1927, testifies that "[o]f philosophy he had read a good deal, but on the whole spoke little. Schopenhauer used to give him satisfaction twenty years and more ago" (Galsworthy in Johnson 23). Suggestively, this places Conrad's reading of Schopenhauer around and before 1907, the date of *The Secret Agent*'s writing and publication. This would not be surprising. Schopenhauer's cultural influence in the decades either side of the turn of the twentieth century was huge. Owen Knowles asserts that Schopenhauer's influence on Conrad was indirect, but nevertheless says of Schopenhauer that "his voice echoed throughout Europe as ubiquitously as Kurtz's through the African jungle" (Knowles 77). There is good reason, then, to take the prospect of Conrad's being acquainted with Schopenhauer seriously.[1] Moreover, the knitting machine passage above is another piece of evidence that Conrad was well acquainted with Schopenhauerian ideas. The juxtaposition of time and space with pain and despair are reminiscent of Schopenhauer's conception of the will as thing-in-itself. This will, an objectless striving, is the fundamental reality (hinting that, as Conrad says, "nothing matters" [*CLJC* 1: 425]). The will, according to Schopenhauer, is objectified into categories such as time and space simultaneously as its individuation into subjects causes the personal suffering that is for him the inescapable content of life.

Importantly for the treatment of the sublime in *The Secret Agent*, it is possible to find Schopenhauer's influence in some of Conrad's most explicit statements on his conception of art as a whole, and therefore to consider the influence as extending broadly through his oeuvre. Paul Kirschner and Mark Wollaeger dwell on this aspect of Conrad's preface to *The Nigger of the Narcissus* (Kirschner 272–75; Wollaeger 33). In this preface, Conrad conceives art as the attempt to communicate a kind of truth that is distinguished from particulars. He calls it "a single-minded attempt to render the highest kind of justice to the visible universe, by bringing to light the truth, manifold and one, underlying its every aspect" (Conrad 5). He goes on to differentiate this truth from the sort of truth that the philosopher and scientist seek. The latter is a truth that helps satisfy the individual will, which aids us in the satisfaction of our quotidian interests and desires. The philosopher and scientist "make their appeal to those qualities of our being that fit us best for the hazardous enterprise of living," and "their words are heard with reverence for their concern is with weighty matters: [. . .] with the attainment of our ambitions; with the perfection of the means and the attainment of our precious aims" (5). It is against this that Conrad defines his conception of the truth realized by aesthetic objects. He follows the above passage with the single-sentence paragraph: "It is otherwise with the artist" (5).

Standing behind this conception of art is much that is prominent in Schopenhauerian aesthetics. Schopenhauer makes a distinction between aesthetic knowledge and practical scientific knowledge. Indeed, as in Conrad's preface, the two are opposed to one another in terms of their relation to individual desire. Aesthetic knowledge for Schopenhauer is attained when something frees the subject from its condition of constant desire and frustration:

> When, however, an external cause or inward disposition suddenly raises us out of the endless stream of willing, and snatches knowledge from the thraldom of the will, the attention is no longer directed to the motives of willing but comprehends things free from their relation to the will. (*WWR* 1: 196)

Thus the truth that can be known when apprehending things aesthetically is different from the truth that concerns, in Conrad's words, "the attainment of our precious ends." Now, this notion of aesthetic disinterestedness is of course a common post-Kantian theme. Nevertheless, the distinctiveness of the Schopenhauerian conception in Conrad becomes clearer when we consider the opposition made between particular phenomena and the universal nature of the truths that are the goal of art. Conrad views art as

> an attempt to find in [the universe's] forms, in its colours, in its light, in its shadows, in the aspects of matter and in the facts of life, what of each is fundamental, what is enduring and essential—their one illuminating and convincing quality—the very truth of their existence. (Conrad 5)

Schopenhauer also sets in opposition the universal aesthetic Idea and the multiplicity of particular phenomena. Consider the following account of aesthetic experience:

> Raised up by the power of the mind, we relinquish the ordinary way of considering things and cease to follow under the guidance of the forms of the principle of sufficient reason merely their relations to one another, whose final goal is always the relation to our own will. Thus we no longer consider the where, the when, the why, and the whither in things, but simply and solely the *what*. (*WWR* 1: 178)

Thus Schopenhauer conceives the Idea, which we come to know through aesthetic contemplation, to be a Platonic one, an essential truth that underlies existence. This truth is not known in the ordinary way. It is knowable because it is an object, but it is a particularly generalized object, which "has not assumed any other form peculiar to knowledge as such" (1: 175). This means that it is not bound by what Kant would call the categories of perception; neither space, time, nor causality apply to it. Thus, Schopenhauer states that "where" and "when" do not concern us, and nor do the "why" and the "whither" of its existence. Both the *"principium individuationis"* (Schopenhauer's term for that which makes particulars in the world distinguishable from one another) and the principle of sufficient reason are here absent.

"Sudden Holes in Space and Time"

The Greenwich bomb in *The Secret Agent* is intended by Vladimir to be just such an aesthetic object. This is clear from the involved explanation he gives Verloc of his rationale for its particular target. Most basically, the bomb is meant to impress upon its spectators a particular idea, in this case the idea of anarchism's destructiveness. Moreover, it must, judging by Vladimir's disquisition, do this in the most generalized possible way, the way furthest removed from ordinary means of regarding the world. At one point Vladimir suggests that "it would be really telling if one could throw a bomb into pure mathematics. But that is impossible" (SA 27). Failing this level of generality, then, the bomb becomes instead an attack on science. As we saw, Vladimir believes science has its status as "sacrosanct fetish of to-day" because it is felt to serve the phenomenal wills of the middle classes: "[t]hey believe that in some mysterious way science is at the source of their material prosperity" (27). Vladimir's explanation thus recalls the distinctions drawn by both Schopenhauer and Conrad between useful scientific truths on the one hand and aesthetic truths on the other. More than this, the bomb plot targets the very categories of space and time. These, of course, are represented by the Greenwich observatory: the building stands on the notional line that marks zero degrees longitude and from which the global time standard is measured. Vladimir specifically thinks of the attack in these abstract terms. He says that "the blowing up of the first meridian is bound to raise a howl of execration" (28). His characterization of the attack is here technically inaccurate: even if the observatory were to be completely annihilated, the meridian, as a cartographical fiction, would still be there. What Vladimir is thinking of when he says this, therefore, appears to be an attack on a symbolic level on space and time as such. This resonance of the Greenwich plot has, of course, long been observed. R.W. Stallman, in his early and influential essay on time in the novel, comments that "[i]t's no wonder that Mr. Verloc is unnerved by Mr. Vladimir's orders. *His mission is the destruction of space and time*" (Stallman 236). This is not quite right, because Vladimir would seem to have little use for the destruction of space and time per se. What he does want, on the other hand, is a symbolic act that is so expressive that it places itself in opposition to spatial and temporal categories of perception.

In so doing the spectacle can claim the universality that both Conrad and Schopenhauer attach to the aesthetic truth. Inasmuch as the bomb attacks space and time, it also attacks causality and Schopenhauer's *principium individuationis*. It is intended that the bombing should have particular power because it will be apparently causeless, or at least motiveless. Vladimir holds that it "must go beyond the intention of vengeance or terrorism. It must be purely destructive. It must be that, and only that, beyond the faintest suspicion of any other object" (SA 27). He further elaborates that the attack should be "an act of destructive ferocity so absurd as to be incomprehensible, inexplicable, almost unthinkable; in fact, mad" (27). This description echoes Conrad's "Author's Note" with its emphasis on the apparently causeless nature of the Greenwich bomb, that "blood-stained inanity," which was "of so fatuous a kind that it was impossible to fathom its origin by any reasonable or even unreasonable process of thought" (249). As the attack seems to stand outside of causation, it thereby also resists individuation. Contingent personal circumstances should not be seen behind the bomb. Thus Vladimir is careful to avoid "the suggestion of a non-political passion: the exasperation of a hungry man, an act of social revenge" (26). All these factors give the intended outrage a universal aspect. Vladimir notes that "[t]he whole civilized world has heard of Greenwich. The very boot-blacks in the basement of Charing Cross station know something of it" (29).

Thus, even though no one will enjoy the state of will-less serenity that Schopenhauer conceives to be the result of contemplating an aesthetic object, in its conception as a universal spectacle breaking through the categories of perception, the bomb is nonetheless a parodic version of the Schopenhauerian aesthetic object and represents a prime example of Schopenhauerian aesthetics at work in *The Secret Agent*. It can be read further as a sublime object. Important in this regard is Chief Inspector Heat's reaction to the Greenwich bombing. The bomb appears to Heat very much in the terms above outlined—that is, it stands in opposition to the epistemology that governs Heat's everyday activities and to his will-bound desires and goals. Shortly before the explosion, he has assured the Home Secretary that an attack such as the Greenwich plot could not happen without the foreknowledge of the police. This at the time seemed a particularly opportune thing to have said: "He had made that statement with infinite satisfaction to himself, because it was clear that the high official desired greatly to hear that very thing" (SA 67). The easy hyperbole of "infinite satisfaction" reflects Heat's complacency. This reassurance is consonant with Heat's usual means of understanding, his "wisdom" that is "of an official kind," which presumably involves relying on probability and trusting his informers (68). This is explicitly a kind of understanding that, like Conrad's conception of science, is fitted to aid everyday desires and interests:

> True wisdom, which is not certain of anything in this world of contradictions, would have prevented him from attaining his present position. It would have alarmed his superiors, and done away with his chances of promotion. His promotion had been very rapid. (66)

The incident which actually happens in Greenwich is not anticipated by, and indeed does not fit within, this schema of everyday understanding. It points, therefore, to a truth different from that of Heat's usual, utility-focussed, approach to the world:

> His wisdom was of an official kind, or else he might have reflected upon a matter not of theory but of experience that in the close-woven stuff of relations between conspirator and police there occur unexpected solutions of continuity, sudden holes in space and time. A given anarchist may be watched inch by inch and minute by minute, but a moment always comes when somehow all sight and touch of him are lost for a few hours, during which something (generally an explosion) more or less deplorable does happen. (68)

Those facts that stand outside Heat's official wisdom, are presented explicitly in contrast to the categories of perception. The "holes in space and time" are, somewhat paradoxically, "sudden" (68). They are certainly objects, but ones outside Heat's usual epistemology. The parenthetical "(generally an explosion)" enacts the consequent sense of irruption (68). The Greenwich incident, then, as it applies to Heat's circumstance, mirrors the structure of the Schopenhauerian aesthetic object. Not only is the bombing incomprehensible according to the will-serving everyday epistemology used by Heat, but it is actively threatening to his will. He has "had a disagreeably busy" day since the bombing (67). The very fact of its occurrence emerges as a threat to the professional interests served by his "official wisdom." His reaction when confronted with the telegram of the news "had not been impressive," and this vexes him because his "instinct of a successful man had taught him long ago that, as a general rule, a reputation is built on manner as much as on achievement" (68). Heat reflects with annoyance that the exchange with the Assistant Commissioner had been "[v]ery damaging" to him (68). The opposition to the individual will, as we shall later see, is the defining feature of Schopenhauer's sublime object. The bomb, therefore, not only blows a hole in space and time for Heat, but menaces the interests he pursues in these parameters, and so appeals to the theme of the threatening sublime object.

Andrew Smith reads detective figures as key in introducing the sublime into an urban milieu, and in this respect his commentary can shed light on how the sublime object confronting Heat might be read (A. Smith 103; 113). Specifically, Smith detects an echo of Kant in Edgar Allan Poe's detective stories (103). He argues that the detective, as an urban subject confronting the mysterious, can be read according to a Kantian psychology of the sublime. His first example is the narrator of Poe's story "The Man of the Crowd." This character is not explicitly a detective, but the tale is nonetheless one in which the criminal and the mysterious are identified, since the narrator's encounter with a physiognomicaly unreadable face in the crowd leads to an assumption that the titular man is, as the narrator says, the "essence of all crime" (113–14). Smith points out that the narrator is "animated" by this encounter just as the sublime moves the Kantian subject (116). Smith elaborates this claim with reference to Poe's detective tales, in which again crime becomes identified with an absorbing mystery. He argues that there are "a range of similarities between Poe's detective tales and Kant's version of the subject," the first being that "the mystery, the 'crime' to be solved, stimulates reason" in a similar way to how "the sublime stimulates an idea of reason and gestures towards the idea of a totalizing reason" (119). As a mystery, then, the crime works like a Kantian sublime object, baffling attempts to comprehend it. In this, it moves the mind from its usual state of inertia. As Smith says of Poe's Dupin, he "is typified by inertia, an inertia transcended in the advent of a mystery which animates him" (124). Dupin proceeds to solve the crime using his own rational faculty, something with which he is put in touch by the initial cognitive failure: "The mysterious refers the subject to a different order of rationality because the failure of reason gestures towards the supersensible" (124).

Using the structure mapped out by Smith, Heat's own encounter with the mysterious can be understood as being comparable, if with a decidedly Schopenhauerian tinge. Indeed, if Dupin is read as displaying influences from Kantian psychology, Heat appears very much like a Schopenhauerian answer to him.[2] Heat, too, is moved from inertia by the advent of a mystery. It shakes him out of a self-satisfied complacency. He had given reassurance to the Home Secretary because "[i]f ever he thought himself safe in making a statement, it was then," and so he made the statement "with infinite satisfaction to himself, because it was clear that the high official desired greatly to hear that very thing" (SA 67). Heat is shaken out of this ease by the advent of the Greenwich case. Here, however, the two begin to diverge. The mystery does not call Heat to the appreciation of supersensible reason. Indeed, reason is implied to be impotent in this particular case. Heat initially rejects the very possibility of establishing the identity of Stevie's remains: "The first term of the problem was unreadable" (71). Heat is, however, moved to a different realization in his encounter with the sublime. This is an insight into the futile and obscure nature of the world, and into the grievousness of human suffering. As was seen above, Heat's reassurance of his superior is contrasted with a different possible wisdom, one which "is not certain of anything in this world of contradictions" (66). What is gestured towards, then, is the fact of the world's obscurity and the consequent tenuousness of all human endeavor. This is consonant with the experience of the sublime subject according to Schopenhauer. This subject "forcibly tear[s] himself from his will and its relations" (*WWR* 1: 201). This affords the opportunity to develop a sublime character and thus "look less at [one's] own individual lot than at the lot of mankind as a whole" (1: 207). The subject of Schopenhauer's sublime in this way sees the world from above an individual standpoint and thus apprehends human suffering per se. Heat, in contemplating Stevie's remains, rejects reason, and instead comes to just this kind of knowledge:

> The shattering violence of destruction which had made of that body a heap of nameless fragments affected his feelings with a sense of ruthless cruelty, though his reason told him the effect must have been as swift as a flash of lightning. The man, whoever he was, had died instantaneously, and yet it seemed impossible to believe that a human body could have reached such a state of disintegration without passing through the pangs of inconceivable agony. No physiologist, still less of a metaphysician, Chief Inspector Heat rose by the force of sympathy, which is a form of fear, above the vulgar conception of time. Instantaneous! [. . .] The inexplicable mysteries of conscious existence beset Chief Inspector Heat till he evolved a horrible notion that ages of atrocious pain and mental torture could be contained between two successive winks of an eye. (70)

In this passage, Heat is undergoing the experience of the sublime subject according to Schopenhauer. His contemplation is aesthetic: he is not thinking as a theorist and he has transcended the category of time. The phrase "Chief Inspector Heat rose by the force of sympathy, which is a form of fear," implicates the sublime themes of elevation, force, and terror in a single cognitive movement, a movement which is then enacted by the interruption of free indirect discourse from within Heat in the exclamation "Instantaneous!" (70). Heat, then, has been moved through a recognizably sublime experience into contemplation, arriving at a higher truth concerning not reason, as in a Kantian sublime, but the nature of "conscious existence" and of the potential for suffering which it contains.

Schopenhauer and Kant's Sublime

This comparison brings into focus Schopenhauer's post-Kantian development of the sublime. The precise nature of this development is beset by something of an ambivalence concerning Schopenhauer's relationship to his predecessor's theory. Sandra Shapshay points out that Schopenhauer both praises and dismisses Kant's account of the sublime in different texts (Shapshay 479–80). There is nonetheless an identifiable thread of Schopenhauer's commentary on the sublime at play in *The Secret Agent*'s treatment of aesthetic objects. This is apparent when considering particularly Schopenhauer's difference with Kant concerning the sublime's relation to the beautiful. Schopenhauer maintains Kant's distinctions between the beautiful and the sublime, as well as that between the mathematical and dynamic sublime. However, he gives an importantly different account of the nature of the beautiful-sublime distinction. Kant holds the beautiful and the sublime to refer to different kinds of entities—that is, the beautiful describes the quality of objects in the world fit to stimulate the free play of our faculties, whereas the sublime may be properly attributed only to aspects of human thought (*CJ* 160). For Schopenhauer, however, the sublime and beautiful are distinct but continuous. He claims that it is only a "special modification" of the beautiful that distinguishes the two (*WWR* 1: 208). In addition, Kant's description of the sublime is attended by a careful delineation of the psychological processes that culminate in the negative presentation of an idea of reason (*CJ* 137–38). This is not the case for Schopenhauer. In this instance he is scathing of Kant's "Analytic," stating that "we differ from him entirely on the inner nature of that impression, and can concede no share in this either to moral reflection or to hypostases from scholastic philosophy" (*WWR* 1: 205). Schopenhauer replaces Kant's account with a simplified relation to the phenomenal will:

> The difference between the beautiful and the sublime depends on whether the state of pure, will-less knowing, presupposed and demanded by any aesthetic contemplation, appears of itself, without opposition, by the mere disappearance of the will from consciousness, since the object invites and attracts us to it; or whether this state is reached by free, conscious exaltation above the will, to which the contemplated object itself has an unfavourable, hostile relation, a relation that would do away with contemplation if we gave ourselves up to it. (1: 208–9)

The account that emerges in Schopenhauer's response to the Kantian sublime, then, is one that puts much greater emphasis on the relation of an object to the individual will as the defining feature of the sublime. Schopenhauer is Kantian in that he maintains the staging of an agonistic relationship between the object and the subject, requiring that the object be considered as a potential threat to the subject. In fact, Schopenhauer follows and is more explicit than Schiller in making this relationship both necessary and sufficient for the sublime, where in Kant it was one aspect of a multifaceted distinction between the sublime and beautiful. It is only this that distinguishes the sublime from the beautiful for Schopenhauer.

The continuity with the beautiful that Schopenhauer's view implies has important implications. This is an increased emphasis on the subject in identifying the sublime. Schopenhauer's writings on the sublime participate in a trend whereby the distinction between the sublime and beautiful increasingly breaks down. Schopenhauer sees the sublime and beautiful as less different from one another than does Kant. He states that it is only a special modification "on the subjective side," which distinguishes the two (*WWR* 1: 208). This is an instance of the broad trend of the sublime's "ultimately being absorbed into a cognitive interpretation of the beautiful" (Guyer, "German Sublime" 105). It is therefore crucial that the essential characteristic of the sublime for Schopenhauer is explicitly restricted to the subjective circumstance of the experience. This extends the direction of movement in the discourse of the sublime to which Kant was himself a major contributor. This development, as expounded by Samuel Monk's early study, charts a shift in theories of the sublime from seeing the affect as produced by the qualities of external objects to a focus on subjective elements. Thus, early British theorists of the sublime such as Addison and Shaftesbury, and to some extent Burke, found the sublime in the qualities of specific natural objects. With Kant, however, the sublime could only be properly attributed to "the manner of thinking, or rather to its foundation in human nature" (*CJ* 160). Nevertheless, though it is properly only our states of mind that may be sublime, Kant maintains that the sublime is felt upon contemplation of only certain kinds of objects. Now, Schopenhauer can be read as implicitly rejecting this supposition of Kant's. By placing greater emphasis on the Kantian theme of ambivalent affect, Schopenhauer advances the implications of this subjective shift even further than his predecessor. Whereas for Kant the distinction between the sublime and beautiful involves the beautiful being potentially found in nature where the sublime cannot be, for Schopenhauer the difference between the two is purely subjective. Dale Jacquette draws out the implications:

> It is, if Schopenhauer is right, all a matter of how we as representing subjects feel in the presence of such objects. Just as every object is actually beautiful for Schopenhauer, so every object is potentially sublime, depending on whether or not we experience any sort of threat to our phenomenal will to life in its presence. It is possible, then, that the simplest, most innocent appearing objects could be sublime as well as beautiful, if they happen circumstantially to arouse a sense of fear. (Jacquette 162)

There are, it must be said, ambiguities in this aspect of Schopenhauer's theory. Just as Schopenhauer's expressed attitudes to Kant's theory are contradictory, so there is some license to read Schopenhauer's account in a way that is closer to Kant's. Sandra Shapshay argues that for Schopenhauer the sublime object must still be of a kind that is threatening to mankind per se (Shapshay 493–94). Schopenhauer does suggest this, discussing sublime objects as having "a hostile relation to the human will in general" (*WWR* 1: 201). This, however, is incompatible with Schopenhauer's insistence that the difference between the beautiful and the sublime is entirely "on the subjective side" and does not depend at all on the status of the object (*WWR* 1: 208). Moreover, it seems to conflict with Schopenhauer's further statements on the matter in the second volume of *The World as Will and Representation*. Here, Schopenhauer discusses how the phenomenal will influences our perception of objects:

> [L]et us picture to ourselves how much every emotion or passion obscures and falsifies knowledge, in fact how every inclination or disinclination twists, colours, and distorts not merely the judgement, but even the original perception of things. Let us recall how, when we are delighted by a successful outcome, the whole world at once assumes a bright colour and a smiling aspect, and on the other hand looks dark and gloomy when care and sorrow weigh on us. Let us then see how even an inanimate thing, which is yet to become the instrument of some event we abhor, appears to have a hideous physiognomy; for example the scaffold, the fortress to which we are taken, the surgeon's case of instruments, the travelling coach of loved ones, and so on; indeed, numbers, letters, seals can grin at us horribly and affect us like fearful monsters. (*WWR* 2: 373)

This passage thus describes how the will's relation to an object can add that directly perceived fearful quality that is necessary for an object to occasion the sublime. What is significant here is that no distinction is made between objects that have generally fearful connotations and those that have more circumstantial ones. Thus, the scaffold is listed along with the travelling coach, even though the latter's negative aspect depends very much more on a contingent personal circumstance—namely, that of being parted from one's particular loved ones. The addition of "numbers, letters, seals" likewise implies such contingent circumstances, which are here unstated (2: 373).[3] Furthermore, Schopenhauer claims that knowledge and judgment are also affected by this coloring effect. In this case, it would seem to be difficult to make a judgment as to whether the object is hostile to the human will in general or to ourselves in particular. Thus, while there are perhaps conflicting interpretations possible in Schopenhauer's theory, the subjective reading is more strongly suggested by the texts, and it is this one which is clearly drawn out in *The Secret Agent*.

The Devil in the Details

The Secret Agent clearly comments on the structure of the Schopenhauerian sublime and is filled with objects that correspond with this expanded conception of the sublime object. Winnie's thoughts immediately after the murder of her husband are evocative of Schopenhauer's list:

> Mrs Verloc, who always refrained from looking deep into things, was compelled to look into the very bottom of this thing. She saw there no haunting face, no reproachful shade, no vision of remorse, no sort of ideal conception. She saw there an object. That object was the gallows. Mrs Verloc was afraid of the gallows. (SA 211)

Her fear manifests itself not directly in the thought of being caught and convicted, but instead in an object. The gallows appears charged with all the fear entailed by Winnie's position of having committed a capital offence. Furthermore, taking after Schopenhauer's "numbers, letters, seals," *The Secret Agent* abounds with seemingly harmless objects that, through contingent circumstances, become tinged with menace (WWR 2: 373). Indeed, this well describes the bomb plot as it is conceived by Vladimir. He emphasizes that the bomb is to seem "an act of destructive ferocity" (SA 27). However, this is not expressed in physical danger to life: "'These outrages need not be especially sanguinary,' Mr Vladimir went on, as if delivering a scientific lecture, 'but they must be sufficiently startling—effective'" (25). The Greenwich plot as planned by Verloc does not involve harming anyone and in the event its only victim is killed by accident. Yet its superlatively startling impact depends entirely on its circumstances, on the beliefs of the subjects who witness it, ultimately their faith in science as the foundation of their prosperity. During Vladimir's conversation with Verloc, the same structure is repeated in miniature in the discomposure Verloc feels upon noticing a fly:

> In the silence Mr Verloc heard against a window-pane the faint buzzing of a fly—his first fly of the year—heralding better than any number of swallows the approach of spring. The useless fussing of that tiny energetic organism affected unpleasantly this big man threatened in his indolence. (22)

That the fly and Verloc are translated into general signifiers, "organism" and "man" respectively, suggests that we are here dealing with the universality of the aesthetic object. The plight of the fly is certainly a symbol of the human condition going back to *King Lear*. However, the emphasis here is nonetheless squarely on the subjective unpleasant feeling that is wrought on Verloc. The harmlessness of the fly is emphasized along with its menace; the buzzing is "faint" and the fly is "tiny," especially in contrast with Verloc's ample size. Nevertheless, the small thing takes on disproportionate importance because it seems circumstantially to underscore the threat to his livelihood. Another example comes late in the novel, after Verloc's murder. Ossipon's realization that he has become mixed up in the murder comes through an encounter with a trivial detail:

> But the true sense of the scene he was beholding came to Ossipon through contemplation of the hat. It seemed an extraordinary thing, an ominous object, a sign. Black, and rim upward, it lay on the floor before the couch as if prepared to receive the contributions of pence from people who would come presently to behold Mr Verloc in the fullness of his domestic ease reposing on a sofa. (226)

The slight incongruity of the hat's being turned upward on the floor is enough to charge it with the whole gravity of the situation and the danger that Ossipon now realizes he is facing. Thus it is no longer an everyday, harmless thing to Ossipon but an "ominous object, a sign."

Indeed, a terror of small details is a preoccupation in *The Secret Agent*. In his conversations with the Assistant Commissioner, the Home Secretary Sir Ethelred insists that the details of the Greenwich case be kept from him at all costs. This is initially presented as the necessary expedient of a busy legislator: "'I would like to know if this was the beginning of another dynamite campaign,' he asked at once in a deep, very smooth voice. 'Don't go into details. I have no time for that.'" (*SA* 108). The insistence takes on a farcical aspect as the avoidance of details is returned to and dwelt upon at length: "Very well. Go on. Only no details, pray. Spare me the details." (109); "What is your general idea, stated shortly? No need to go into details." (110); "I am keeping clear of details, Sir Ethelred." (112); "I am trying to be as lucid as I can in presenting this obscure matter to you without details" (113). This self-defeating insistence on brevity hints at an import given to details as such that is blown out of proportion. Later in the novel they reach the status of a terror to Sir Ethelred:

> "Is there anything more you'd wish to tell me now?"
> "I think not, Sir Ethelred, unless I were to enter into details, which—"
> "No. No details, please."
> The great shadowy form seemed to shrink away as if in physical dread of details. (175)

Once again the bodily size of a character is used to demonstrate the disproportionate effect that a seemingly insignificant thing can have. Shortly after this, Verloc provides yet another instance of this leitmotif. His involvement in the Greenwich bomb and therefore in Stevie's death is revealed by Heat's discovery of a name tag sewn into the collar of Stevie's jacket. This detail, overlooked by Verloc in his preparation for the operation and overlooked also by the police in the park, makes the difference between escape for Verloc and his discovery and ultimate murder at the hands of his wife. After Winnie has discovered Stevie's fate, Verloc reflects that "[a] small, tiny fact had done it. It was like slipping on a bit of orange peel in the dark and breaking your leg" (187). Again there is the theme of the seemingly small and innocuous object that becomes devastatingly threatening. This theme is noticed by Stallman, who comments that

> [i]t is the insignificant *things* in The Secret Agent, the minute particulars of life, that manifest reality; and the characteristic of these pieces

of reality is their absurdity—the cracked bell, the cracked wedding ring, the lonely mechanical piano, Verloc's round hat rocking on its crown, Stevie's coat-label, the buzzing fly. All "mere trifles," but not one of these pieces of reality is too insignificant, too absurd to be disregarded. They each signify the unpredictable, the absurdly incongruous thing which disturbs routine existence by the sudden fact of its unexpected and uncalled for intrusion. The nature of reality in *The Secret Agent* is irrational, incongruous and incalculable. (Stallman 244)

The disturbance of routine existence, which Stallman emphasizes here, often constitutes just that threat to the characters' individual will that makes an aesthetic object sublime. Stallman gestures here towards a link with Schopenhauer in the idea that reality is fundamentally and terribly irrational. It is just such an appreciation of absurdity to which Heat comes on contemplating the Greenwich bomb's effects.

"Unsuspected and Deadly"

The line between thing and character in *The Secret Agent* is often an uncertain one, and as such, it is not only things which admit of this kind of treatment. A character, the Professor, also becomes this type of sublime object. Sure enough, the Professor is small and seemingly insignificant, yet intensely threatening. Indeed, his very first appearance in the narrative foregrounds this tension:

> His flat, large ears departed widely from the sides of his skull, which looked frail enough for Ossipon to crush between thumb and forefinger; the dome of the forehead seemed to rest on the rim of the spectacles; the flat cheeks, of a greasy, unhealthy complexion were merely smudged by the miserable poverty of a thin, dark whisker. The lamentable inferiority of the whole physique was made ludicrous by the supremely self-confident bearing of the individual. His speech was curt, and he had a particularly impressive manner of keeping silent. (SA 49–50)

The emphasis is first upon the Professor's slight body. His head could be easily crushed; the forehead resting on spectacles suggests that the Professor's body has not even enough integrity to hold itself together, and it is on the point of simply collapsing under its own weight. This lack of soundness is insisted upon though the "unhealthy" cheek and the "poverty" of the moustache. Yet just after this, the contradiction between his visage and the Professor's mien is pointed out. The effect of this tension is initially that he appears risible. The self-confidence he shows is merely ludicrous in conjunction with his feebleness. Yet the final sentence of the paragraph with its "particularly impressive" is left unqualified. The emphasis, then, shifts from the humor to be found in the Professor's incongruously impressive manner to its reality and possible implications. This shift enacts narratively a growing sense of misgiving about the feeble figure. We subsequently learn that such a misgiving is more than justified. The man's small, insignificant figure is rendered menacing by an extrinsic circumstance, in this case the fact that he carries a large bomb on his person at all times in order that, if the police attempted to apprehend him, he would detonate it, killing himself and many bystanders. This prompts Ossipon to daydream of the Professor on an omnibus:

> Ossipon had a vision of these round black-rimmed spectacles progressing along the streets on the top of an omnibus, their self-confident glitter falling here and there on the walls of houses or lowered upon the heads of the unconscious stream of people on the pavements. The ghost of a sickly smile altered the set of Ossipon's thick lips at the thought of the walls nodding, of people running for life at the sight of those spectacles. If they had only known! What a panic! (50–51)

The reverie depicts the Professor as overlooked and insignificant object: his body is so negligible it has disappeared, and he is represented only by his glasses. This is then compared to the dreadful spectacle he would constitute if the whole context was apparent. Ossipon smiles inwardly at this thought, though at other points he finds the Professor troubling, inflicting Ossipon with a "sense of moral and even physical insignificance" (50).

At the very close of the novel, the narrative returns to the Professor and his status as terrible detail. His pronouncement of his aim of a world of merciless domination by the strong is counterpointed again with his physical feebleness:

> "And what remains?" asked Ossipon in a stifled voice.
> "I remain—if I am strong enough," asserted the sallow little Professor, whose large ears, thin like membranes, and standing far out from the sides of his frail skull, took on a suddenly deep red tint. (SA 240)

The very final lines of the novel, moreover, insist upon this juxtaposition of feebleness and menace:

> He walked frail, insignificant, shabby, miserable—and terrible in the simplicity of his idea calling madness and despair to the regeneration of the world. Nobody looked at him. He passed on unsuspected and deadly, like a pest in a street full of men. (246)

The catalogue of the Professor's humble qualities and the dash delay the introduction of what it is clear by now must inevitably come—that is, the mention of the Professor's latent threat. The shift into abstract terms at the very end with "pest" and "men" recalls Verloc and the fly and, as there, it suggests the abstract quality of the aesthetic object. Thus the spectacle with which Conrad leaves the reader is that of the Professor as an aesthetic object which is explicitly both insignificant and terrible, "unsuspected and deadly."

This is not where the connection between the Professor and Schopenhauer's sublime ends. Viewed as an object, he is a sublime detail, but he also illuminates Schopenhauer's theory as it carries into other areas. *The World as Will and Representation* claims that the "explanation of the sublime can indeed be extended to cover the ethical—namely, what is described as the sublime character" (*WWR* 1: 206). The sublime character is defined by a consistent exercise of an ability to remove oneself from individual willing, and therefore to take an impartial view of life. For Schopenhauer, "Such a character springs from the fact that the will is not excited here by objects certainly well calculated to excite it, but that knowledge retains the upper hand" (*WWR* 1: 206). This attitude, therefore, is marked not only by a distance from the hardships and frustrations of life, but by taking a broader or higher view of existence. Thus the sublime character "will look less at his own individual lot than at the lot of mankind as a whole" (*WWR* 1: 207). The Professor fits many aspects of Schopenhauer's description of the sublime character. His claimed lack of interest in individuals is particularly striking. He takes the broadest possible view of the world:

> I am not taking my cue from the Red Committee. I would see you all hounded out of here—or arrested for that matter—without turning a hair. What happens to us as individuals is not of the least consequence. (*SA* 57).

It is little wonder that Ossipon complains to the Professor that "[y]ou are too transcendental for me" (58). The sublime character's indifference to objects that charm the will can be seen in the Professor's extreme asceticism: "I don't play; I work fourteen hours a day, and go hungry sometimes. My experiments cost money now and again, and then I must do without food for a day or two" (56). The Professor's living conditions speak clearly of his resistance to all forms of individual will: "The room was large, clean, respectable, and poor with that poverty suggesting the starvation of every human need except mere bread" (239). Indeed, he attributes his ability to carry out his illegal activities with impunity to a special case of this characteristic. He insists that the efficacy of his suicide-bomb tactic to avoid arrest is down to his character. He says "the means to make myself deadly" is in itself "absolutely nothing in the way of protection," rather "[w]hat is effective is the belief those people have in my will to use the means" (54). This is simply a more extreme example of the Professor's asceticism in that he is prepared, as is the subject of Schopenhauer's highest, tragic sublime, to ignore one of the strongest drives of the will-to-life—the drive to sustain individual life—in service of his cause. The professor is utterly convinced that he represents an extraordinary character: "In the last instance it is character alone that makes for one's safety. There are very few people in the world whose character is as well established as mine" (54).

Of course, the Professor does not correspond precisely to the sublime character as Schopenhauer conceives it. For all that his asceticism and detachment resemble Schopenhauer's description, he appears rather as a dark parody of the sublime character. He lacks the benevolent selflessness that makes this character a really ethical one. Schopenhauer describes the character as one who "will observe [other men's] faults, and even their hatred and injustice to himself, without being thereby stirred to hatred on his own part. He will contemplate their happiness without feeling envy" (*WWR* 1: 206). This quality is one which is decidedly alien to the Professor. All his seeming asceticism hides a slavishness to more profound urgings of his will, specifically his desire for recognition. In an ironic comment on the Professor's quasi-Nietzschean proclamations, he is fundamentally in the throes of a sense of *ressentiment* against society. His terroristic career was arrived at after a series of jobs at which the Professor felt himself treated unfairly: "His struggles, his privations, his hard work to raise himself in the social scale, had filled him with such an exalted conviction of his merits that it was extremely difficult for the world to treat him with justice" (60). His asceticism and detachment are arrived at not from a saintly renunciation of desire, but by the failure of his attempts at social climbing. The professor's case is taken as an example of how revolutions are prepared for "by personal impulses disguised into creeds," and how "even the most ardent of revolutionaries are perhaps doing no more but seeking for peace in common with the rest of mankind—the peace of soothed vanity, of satisfied appetites, or perhaps of appeased conscience" (65). The mention here of satisfied appetites strongly suggests that the professor, for all his asceticism, has not by any means attained a true indifference to the will.

In accordance with this, the Professor, rather than impassively contemplating the world, wants desperately to change it. He dreams of radically remaking society according to the demands of his own individual will. Thus, with Ossipon, he toasts "the destruction of what is" (SA 242). He wants to create in the place of the existing world a one "like a shambles," which will satisfy his narcissism by ultimately doing away with everything else (240). He says that "the great multitude of the weak must go, then the only relatively strong. [. . .] First the blind, then the deaf and the dumb, then the halt and the lame—and so on" until only "I remain—if I am strong enough" (240). The Professor ultimately appears as a parody of the sublime character. He may seem to have renounced the cravings of will-bound desire, only for these cravings to reappear in a deeper and more disturbing way. He may pronounce himself indifferent to hardship and external circumstances, but in fact he feels slights so keenly that he wants to remake the whole world so that it accommodates him. As with the Professor's physical feebleness, then, his petty motives reflect Conrad's ironic commentary. Just as great menace can be produced by a mere detail, so a minor personal interest can produce an excessively threatening character.

Autonomy versus Will

As we saw above, Schopenhauer's theory of the sublime hinges on the object's appearing in opposition to the individual will. The sublime experience involves a turning away from this relationship in favor of aesthetic contemplation of the object. As Schopenhauer says, the sublime is obtained:

> [F]irst of all by a conscious and violent tearing away from the relations of the same object to the will which are recognized as unfavourable, by a free exaltation, accompanied by consciousness, beyond the will and the knowledge related to it. (*WWR* 1: 202)

The sublime experience for Schopenhauer thus speaks of a second-order agency, which allows the subject to raise itself freely above the will. This is even clearer in Schopenhauer's discussion of tragedy. He claims that pleasure in tragedy "belongs not to the feeling of the beautiful, but to that of the sublime; it is, in fact, the highest degree of this feeling" (*WWR* 2: 433). In this "highest degree" of the sublime, we become aware of our capacity to resist even some of our strongest desires:

> [T]hat aspect of the world is brought before our eyes which directly opposes our will. At this sight we feel ourselves urged to give up willing and loving life. But precisely in this way we become aware that there is still left in us something different which we cannot possibly know positively, but only negatively, as that which does *not* will life. (2: 433)

Schopenhauer thus retains the logic of the Kantian sublime. The object, along with the expected relationships of desire-bound willing, is found to underdetermine the reaction of the subject. This underdetermination is then held to negatively reveal an excess on the part of the subject, as Schopenhauer puts it, a "something different" (2: 433). This excess is clearly a descendent of Kantian autonomy. Schopenhauer's will is coextensive with, indeed it is fundamentally identical to, the natural world. Its promptings in the form of our own phenomenal desires are thus heteronomous in the Kantian sense.

Autonomy and heteronomy, however, are not the salient concepts for Schopenhauer that they are for Kant. This is because they come up against problems in his metaphysical system. For Kant, autonomy can be known negatively, and only negatively, because it is an attribute of the noumenal subject. In Schopenhauer's philosophy, as we saw, it is the will that takes the place of the noumenon, the thing-in-itself apart from phenomenal representation. Because of this, autonomy in Kant's sense cannot easily find a place in Schopenhauer's metaphysics. Schopenhauer accepts traditional arguments for causal determinism. In his *Essay on the Freedom of the Will*, he argues that human action in accordance with motives is essentially the same as mechanical causation and organic response to stimuli in being a deterministic process. While the effect of motives upon a person may seem to lack the absolute necessity of material causation, Schopenhauer insists that this is not the case. Along this scale of causality differences can be seen, but these do not affect the fundamental nature of the process: "The cause is more complicated, the effect more heterogenous, but the necessity by which it takes place is not smaller by even a hair's breadth" (Schopenhauer 39). Thus, the complexity and the immediacy of the relation between cause and effect account for the apparent difference between mechanical and human actions. Likewise, Schopenhauer accounts for the apparent distinction between response to stimuli and other forms of thought by the analogy of connecting wires. A psychological motive, then

> [o]nly has the advantage of a longer conducting wire, by which expression I want to convey the idea that it is not, like mere perceptual motives, bound to a certain proximity in space and time, but can act across the greatest distance, the longest time, and through a mediation of concepts and thoughts in a long concatenation. (37)

Thus, for Schopenhauer, as later for Huxley, human agents might be considered in fact to be kinds of automata. He states in *The World as Will and Representation* that the human race "presents itself as puppets that are set in motion by an internal clockwork" (*WWR* 2: 358). Thus for Schopenhauer, the phenomenal world is characterized by unbroken causality. Yet this is not accompanied by the potential for freedom in the noumenal realm. Instead, it is an expression of the heteronomy of the will, which underlies all of reality. Schopenhauer does define freedom as an attribute of our "inner being," which is an expression of the will, such that even "a stone projected through the air" can be truthfully said to be free (1: 126). This is a definition of freedom very different to the Kantian one, one which crucially does not imply an ability to be independent of natural causality or the will. So where in Kant's staging of the sublime, we find "courage to measure ourselves against the apparent all-powerfulness of nature," and thereby to act in accordance with the moral law, Schopenhauer's version is distinctly more passive (*CJ* 144—45). In describing gradations of the sublime affect, Schopenhauer says of the landscape of the empty plane, which is the most subtle on his spectrum of sublime vistas, that it is "a summons to seriousness, to contemplation, with complete emancipation from all willing and its cravings" (*WWR* 1: 203). More intense examples of the sublime only emphasize the degree to which the subject tears itself away from the natural negative response of the will. The result is always the achievement of respite in the form of seriousness and contemplation. The freedom which is implied by the Schopenhauerian sublime, then, manifests only in a temporary and mysterious opting out of the natural world.

Perfect Detonators

The Schopenhauerian view of the inescapable natural world is pervasive in *The Secret Agent*. As we saw, Conrad was writing at a time when Schopenhauer was enjoying great popularity. This popularity coincided and merged with other aspects of the intellectual climate, particularly the concerns over humanity's place in nature discussed in the previous chapter. Some of the same scientific preoccupations are there in Conrad's text as in Wells's. Various aspects of the novel, such as the motif of bombs and detonators, and even the naming of Chief Inspector Heat, speak of a concern with entropy (Houen 50). This coincidence of interest might be one factor behind Conrad's decision to dedicate the novel to H.G. Wells. Indeed, the dedication makes oblique reference to *The Time Machine*, calling Wells "the historian of the ages to come" (*SA* 2). Conrad shares Wells's interest in the evolutionary and, particularly, physiological questions which motivated Huxley's "On the Hypothesis that Animals are Automata and Its History." Indeed, a large amount of imagery in *The Secret Agent* appeals to the discussions of automata and "mechanism" that Huxley shares with Schopenhauer's "puppets." On his return from the Greenwich bombing, Verloc is described as having "an automaton's absurd air of being aware of the machinery inside of him" (*SA* 156). Later on, he remarks to his wife when she is struck dumb by the news of Stevie's death that "[o]ne can't tell whether one is talking to a dummy or to a live woman" (203). Such uncertainty is such a general condition in the novel that Wollaeger claims that Conrad's characters are "more or less self-conscious robots" (Wollaeger 154).

Just as people seem to take on the properties of machines, machines in turn seem to take on the properties of people. The clearest example is the "perfect detonator," which it is the Professor's aim to construct. This detonator is to be an utterly predictable mechanism, but the Professor dreams of a sophistication that blurs the line between mechanical output and human action. He says that

> [t]he worst is that the manner of exploding is always the weak point with us. I am trying to invent a detonator that would adjust itself to all conditions of action, and even to unexpected changes of conditions. A variable yet perfectly precise mechanism. (53–54)

The "manner of exploding" is here a distance between cause and effect. It is this gap that the Professor wishes to eradicate. He would thereby create a seamless and unbreakable chain of causality, which ensured that the results produced were entirely determined. There are hints in the Professor's short discussion that human freedom is implicated in this prospect. The Professor's "with us" on one level probably refers to anarchists or bomb-makers in general, yet it sounds strange coming from a character as volubly convinced of his own uniqueness as is the Professor. It is an unnecessary qualifier, and thus the use of the first person plural suggests a more universal human resonance. Moreover, the Professor has immediately beforehand described the detonator in his coat as "partly chemical, partly mechanical," something that hints toward the physiological complexities of the human body (53). Immediately, the Professor clarifies that he wants "[a] really intelligent detonator" (54). What has been defined as an impenetrably deterministic system can also admit the description of "intelligent." An example of what is if not artificial intelligence, then at least an apparent artificial agency counterpoints this very statement. This example comes in the form of the Silenus Restaurant's player piano. The Professor describes the destruction that would be wrought by his own detonator on his and Ossipon's immediate surroundings, and just then, "[t]he piano at the foot of the staircase clanged through a mazurka with brazen impetuosity, as though a vulgar and impudent ghost were showing off. The keys sank and rose mysteriously. Then all became still" (54). The ghost and machine of Cartesian dualism are invoked in the first sentence. Yet the focus shifts thereafter to the keys themselves and the figurative ghost is dispensed with in favor of a mystery over the movement of the keys. Yet there is of course really no mystery here; it is only a mechanism like that which the Professor has just described. The music dies away with the realization that it is only mechanical forces that are acting. The piano makes another appearance at the very end, once again counterpointing the conversation of Ossipon and the Professor: "[T]he mechanical piano near the door played through a *valse* cheekily, then fell silent all at once, as if gone grumpy" (245). The stuttering action of the piano admits of interpretation along the lines of human moods, but of course the instrument has no such things.

Just as a mechanical piano can be misinterpreted as a conscious agent then, disturbingly, characters can misinterpret themselves in this way. This happens during the climactic event of the novel, when the realization of Stevie's fate sinks in and Winnie murders her husband. She has previously realized that she no longer has to maintain her marriage to Verloc for the sake of Stevie's material wellbeing, and she is in that sense a "free woman" (SA 201). This gives Winnie an intense subjective sense of this freedom, expressed as mastery over the material. The change is outwardly visible: "Her face was no longer stony. [. . .] Mrs Verloc's doubts as to the end of the bargain no longer existed; her wits, no longer disconnected, were working under the control of her will" (206–7). It is also inwardly felt:

> "Winnie."
> "Yes," answered obediently Mrs Verloc the free woman. She commanded her wits now, her vocal organs; she felt herself to be in almost preternaturally perfect control of every fibre of her body. (207)

The phrase "her wits now, her vocal organs" appends the physical to the mental entities, applying both to the verb "commanded." The emphasis is therefore on the seamless continuity between the two, all under Winnie's control. The following paragraph continues in the vein of short declarative sentences that have Winnie as their subject: "She was clear sighted. She had become cunning" (207). There are nine such clauses in one relatively short paragraph. Encoded in the narrative, therefore, is the idea that Winnie is exercising absolute control over herself and her actions.

Yet, just at this moment, the narrative point of view shifts abruptly away from Winnie's psychological state. In the narration of the murder itself, the only thoughts that are related are those of Adolf: "His wife had gone raving mad—murdering mad" (SA 208). Winnie's thoughts are not presented. Indeed, any suggestion of conscious agency on her part is noticeably lacking in this crucial passage. Stylistician Chris Kennedy demonstrates transitivity patterns by which the agents of all the actions narrated are various objects not identical to Winnie herself (Kennedy 88–89).[3] The phrase "[h]er right hand skimmed slightly the end of the table" (SA 207) presents the hand itself as the agent. At the moment of the murder, the passive voice produces something of the same effect: "The knife was already planted in his breast" (208). These grammatical peculiarities mark a startling shift from only two short paragraphs before, when "she" was repeatedly in the subject position. The only part of the passage in which Winnie is the agent of goal-directed action simultaneously dissolves her into the factors which produced her:

> Into that plunging blow, delivered over the side of the couch, Mrs Verloc had put all the inheritance of her immemorial and obscure descent, the simple ferocity of the age of caverns, and the unbalanced nervous fury of the age of bar-rooms. (208)

The focus is here upon remote, "immemorial and obscure," yet determining, factors. It recalls Schopenhauer's discussion of motives as distinguished from other causes only by their complexity and their potential temporal remoteness from their effects. Indeed, the very breadth of the historical background referred to in this moment, bookending humanity's whole evolutionary development, drives home her being part of an unbroken causal chain stretching back indefinitely, one which manifests the timeless striving of the will. Moreover, the mention of "simple ferocity" invokes another kind of biological determinism, since it connects with the book's subtitle "A Simple Tale" and, most directly, Stevie's developmental disability. Winnie has previously begun to show a physical likeness to Stevie: "[T]he resemblance of her face to that of her brother grew at every step, even to the droop of the lower lip, even to the slight divergence of the eyes" (208). The only thing that Winnie herself is described as doing, then, is redolent of the natural processes that have produced her. The narrative shifts, therefore, to undermine the independence Winnie had felt only moments before. Even if Winnie seemed to herself to be a "free woman" when she decided to kill her husband, the action when performed has all the mechanistic quality of a song played on the automatic piano.

"The Majesty of Inorganic Nature"

To return to the Professor, it is clear that, given the nature of the world intimated in *The Secret Agent*, his desire to entirely reorder the world through the strength of his will is a doomed one. Indeed, it may be that it is already determined transtextually that the Professor will fail. Cedric Watts discusses Conrad's short story *The Informer*, which was written around the same time as *The Secret Agent*, and published before it (Watts, *Joseph Conrad* 24–25). In this story, a character called the Professor with the same physical characteristics and explosive accessories is mentioned as perishing "a couple of years afterwards in a secret laboratory through the premature explosion of one of his improved detonators" (Conrad in Watts, *Joseph Conrad* 25). If we are to take this to be the destiny of the Professor in *The Secret Agent*, then the ultimate impotence of the iron-willed Professor is striking: the list of people who are known to be killed by his explosives includes only himself and Stevie. Even if we restrict our interpretation to *The Secret Agent* itself, we can detect a tacit admission that his ambition of constructing a "perfect detonator" will inevitably run up against predetermined failure. In the same conversation in which the Professor explains his concept of the perfect detonator to Ossipon, he nonchalantly admits its impossibility: "[T]here are more kinds of fools than one can guard against. You can't expect a detonator to be absolutely fool-proof" (*SA* 61). This admission would seem to point to the fact that foolishness can never be discounted, and therefore can at any point render the perfection of his mechanism moot. In the impossibility of a really perfect detonator, therefore, the Professor must face his own inability to move the world entirely according to his will.

Despite his grandiosity, the Professor does seem aware of this. This awareness manifests in the discomposure he feels when regarding the mass of humanity. He harbors a numbing fear of the urban crowd, which he regards as an overwhelming collection of matter which has its own inertia: "The resisting power of numbers, the unattackable stolidity of the great multitude, was the haunting fear of his sinister loneliness" (*SA* 76). What provokes the Professor's anxiety is the prospect that he ultimately has no means by which to make any action upon them:

> The thought of a mankind as numerous as the sands of the seashore, as indestructible, as difficult to handle, oppressed him. The sound of exploding bombs was lost in their immensity of passive grains without an echo. (242)

Important here is that the crowd is discussed in terms reminiscent of the mathematical sublime in nature. The description dwells upon ideas of natural "immensity" and it is clear that the object is by virtue of this magnitude impalpable, "difficult to handle" (242).

This is one of a number of street scenes in the novel in which urban vistas suggest both the vastness of nature and human continuity with it. Another example comes very early on, as Verloc is travelling to his appointment with Vladimir. Verloc progresses through a series of street scenes:

> Before reaching Knightsbridge, Mr Verloc took a turn to the left out of the busy main thoroughfare, uproarious with the traffic of swaying omnibuses and trotting vans, in the almost silent, swift flow of hansoms. Under his hat, worn with a slight backward tilt, his hair had been carefully brushed with respectful sleekness; for his business was with an Embassy. And Mr Verloc, steady as a rock—a soft kind of rock—marched down a street which could in every propriety be described as private. In its breadth, emptiness and extent it had the majesty of inorganic nature, of matter that never dies. (*SA* 11)

Verloc's journey here charts a gradual transition from the familiar busy urban street to a solitude in which nature's majesty is to be encountered. However, there are several aspects of the passage that are in tension with this trajectory. Both the busy thoroughfare and the private street are alike in that they are described according to their non-living matter. The bustle of the former street is represented not by the crowd of people but by the mechanical means of their conveyance: omnibuses, vans, and hansoms. Moreover, Verloc himself does not experience this "majesty." The description of the street is firmly in the voice of the narrator and not Verloc's. Furthermore, he is included in the material presence: the narrator's parenthesis "a soft kind of rock," expands the stock phrase "steady as a rock" into a serious consideration of Verloc's material nature. Far from admitting dissimilarity between man and stone, the narrator's qualification only highlights Verloc's continuity with matter. Later in the passage, the human is explicitly reduced to the material: "[A] thick police constable, looking a stranger to every emotion, as if he too were part of inorganic nature, surging apparently out of a lamp-post, took not the slightest notice of Mr Verloc" (12). In a similar move, what initially appears as a figurative description of a subjective state is paused over and suggested to be more like a literal truth. The policeman's lack of emotion, like Verloc's steadiness, is initially represented by analogy with "inorganic nature." Yet the narrator adds that he was "surging apparently out of a lamp-post." What was initially figurative finds an unexpected corroboration in the policeman's seeming continuity with the matter of the street.

In their Schopenhauerian resonances, these urban scenes have much in common with the knitting machine in Conrad's letter to Cunninghame Graham (*CLJC* 1: 425). As in Schopenhauer's universe, this ultimate reality is unfeeling, restless, and purposeless. Human life is troublingly continuous with the rest of the universe. The knitting machine subsumes all of life and, presumably, the very narrator of Conrad's imaginative anecdote: "It knits us in and it knits us out" (1: 425). It admits of no place for human independence to be situated. It causes events to happen without it being in anyone's power to change them; as Conrad says, "You cannot with any special lubrication make embroidery with a knitting machine [. . .] You can't interfere with it. The last drop of bitterness is in the suspicion that you can't even smash it" (1: 425). With its industrial machinery, its "chaos of scraps of iron," it is an updated version of the clockwork for which Schopenhauer reached (1: 425). In fact, it is reminiscent of the Mancunian cotton mills in whose prodigious production of cloth Carlyle found his industrial sublime, as well as the "World-Steamengine," which for him signified blind necessity (Carlyle 3: 278). This is compounded by the fact that the language of sublime spectacle dominates the description. The opening instruction to spectate is strident: "[B]ehold!—it knits" (1: 425). The sentence, "[i]t is a tragic accident—and it has happened," begins by signalling the fearful absurdity represented by the machine.[5] Immediately, however, the bare fact of its presence is reiterated. The anticlimactic "it has happened" constitutes an aporia in the rhetorical sense, its failure to elaborate further effectively repeats the initial "behold!" The spectator is figured, moreover, as being overwhelmed. The sentence, "I am horrified at the horrible work and stand appalled," appeals to the classic sublime ambivalence in that the subject is repulsed and fearful, but evidently also fascinated (1: 425).

The knitting machine appears as an ancestor of the kinds of description of nature found in *The Secret Agent*'s street scenes. In this can be seen a reaching for a rhetoric of the natural sublime. They are ambivalently fascinating, and their "immensity" and "majesty" are prominent (*SA* 242; 11). This is undoubtedly a very different mode of sublime to that focusing on charged details. Nevertheless, both can be read as aspects of a consistent treatment of the Schopenhauerian sublime. Both kinds of object relate to Schopenhauer's worldview: the charged details of the novel, as Stallman says, "manifest reality" in its absurdity (Stallman 244). Likewise, the urban vistas of *The Secret Agent*, like the knitting machine, offer a glimpse of the will considered as mechanistic nature. Moreover, each mode of sublime highlights a fault line in Schopenhauer's theory, where it throws up unexpected and ambiguous consequences. The use of insignificant details as sublime objects picks up how Schopenhauer's insistence on subjective considerations as definitional for the sublime allows any object whatsoever to participate in it. This is a striking divergence from the sublime tradition, one which Schopenhauer does not state outright and on which he seems to equivocate. On the other hand, the vistas that find the sublime in the very mechanistic quality of nature and in the continuity of the human with it pick up how Schopenhauer theorizes a "free exaltation" above the will, even though it is unclear within his system where this freedom might come from (*WWR* 1: 202). In both cases, Conrad exploits these philosophical fault lines to produce versions of the sublime marked by irony, instances that subvert various expectations surrounding the experience. The charged detail brings the sublime (associated with the terrifying and elevated) into contact with the seemingly harmless and mundane. For their part the street scenes, like the knitting machine, find the sense of the sublime (associated with a sense of underdetermination by nature) in the very contemplation of that nature's all-encompassing determinism. This ironizing of the sublime is perhaps the supreme irony in a text that is saturated with ironies, from the subtitle's "Simple Tale" belying its dizzying complexity to the fact that the most revolutionary action in the plot, the nationalization of fisheries, comes about through the efforts of the Home Secretary Sir Ethelred and his civil servant, the "revolutionary" Toodles (Watts, *Joseph Conrad* 24). Conrad, indeed, saw irony as central to his achievement in *The Secret Agent*. His "Author's Note" of 1920 attests this:

> Even the purely artistic purpose, that of applying an ironic method to a subject of that kind, was formulated with deliberation and in the earnest belief that an ironic treatment alone would enable me to say all I felt I would have to say in scorn as well as in pity. (*SA* 251)

The use of irony is perhaps in one sense a way to keep explicit political statement at arm's length. Nevertheless, the "ironic method" viewed with regard to Conrad's treatment of the sublime carries a broader philosophical import. If any action will ultimately be undercut by the inescapability of nature and the will, then the response must be to embrace the irony that this creates.

Dionysus in Soho

In this way, *The Secret Agent* probes Schopenhauer's sublime in a way comparable to Friedrich Nietzsche's 1872 *The Birth of Tragedy*. Like Conrad's novel, this text combines Schopenhauerian metaphysical assumptions with criticism of his theory of the sublime. As Christine Battersby puts it, in *The Birth of Tragedy*, Nietzsche "struggles to express an attitude that is fundamentally non-Schopenhauerian within a vocabulary and a metaphysical scheme that he takes over from Schopenhauer" (Battersby 166). The book posits a fundamental reality that resembles Schopenhauer's will and is disposed towards producing suffering. It also suggests art as a remedy for this bleak state of affairs. However, Nietzsche rejects Schopenhauer's characterization of this remedy as an opting out of will-bound activity. As Nietzsche says in his "Attempt at Self-Criticism," published with the 1886 edition, "How alien to me at that time was precisely this whole philosophy of resignation!" (Nietzsche 10).

Nietzsche's critique starts in Schopenhauerian terms with an opposition between knowledge and action, with knowledge associated with passivity and action with will-driven suffering:

> Knowledge kills action; action requires one to be shrouded in a veil of illusion [...] it is not reflection, it is true knowledge, insight into the terrible truth, which outweighs every motive for action, both in the case of Hamlet and in that of Dionysiac man. (Nietzsche 40)

An insight into the "terrible truth" of the universe would not only include the recognition that suffering is our lot in life, but necessarily also the conclusion that there is in fact nothing we can do to alter the state of things and our actions have already been determined by this very repugnant reality. The sense of volition is thus part of that "veil of illusion," which is negated by true knowledge. The consequent inactive state here described bears comparison with some of Conrad's described instances of insight into reality. In his letter to Cunninghame Graham, Conrad can only "stand appalled" at the spectacle of the knitting machine, and the rest of his description is, as described above, preoccupied with the impotence felt in its presence: "[Y]ou can't even smash it" (*CLJC* 1: 425). Similar to this is the Professor's reaction to the crowd. The thought of the numerousness of humanity and the threat it poses to his purpose "oppress[es] him" (*SA* 242). Finally he is unable to look at the crowd and still go on, so at the novel's close we have him "averting his eyes from the odious multitude of mankind" (246). Nietzsche holds that this knowledge was familiar to the Greeks and is represented in a myth concerning the satyr Silenus, who is one of Dionysus's companions (Nietzsche 22–23). In the myth, King Midas asks Silenus to tell him the most excellent thing for human beings. The satyr gives the startling response that "[t]he very best thing is utterly beyond your reach not to have been born, not to *be*, to be *nothing*. However, the second best thing for you is: to die soon" (Nietzsche 23). The wisdom of Silenus thus becomes shorthand for pessimistic insight. References to Silenus lurk in the periphery of *The Secret Agent*. The club, which the anarchists frequent and in which Ossipon and the Professor have their long conversation, is, with its mechanical piano, a setting charged with darkly ironic commentary on the foreground. It is therefore fitting that the establishment should be named the "Silenus Restaurant" (*SA* 55). Elsewhere, a cab driver converses to Stevie about the many hardships that life as a cab driver entails

> like Virgil's Silenus, who, his face smeared with the juice of berries, discoursed of Olympian Gods to the innocent shepherds of Sicily, he talked to Stevie of domestic matters and the affairs of men whose sufferings are great and immortality by no means assured. (132)

The explicit allusion here is to Virgil's *Eclogue* VI (265n), but it is nonetheless the case that, as in Nietzsche, Silenus is here called upon to represent a conveyor of terrible truths about the nature of life.

Thus, for Nietzsche as for Schopenhauer, the wisdom of Dionysus's companion has the effect of producing inaction. However, he asserts that there is a way to respond to this through what he calls the Dionysiac impulse. This impulse is a drive towards artistic creativity and is represented by the chorus in Attic tragedy:

> Art alone can redirect those repulsive thoughts about the terrible or absurd nature of existence into representations with which man can live; these representations are the *sublime*, whereby the terrible is tamed by artistic means, and the *comic*, whereby disgust at absurdity is discharged by artistic means. (Nietzsche 40)

Significantly, the Dionysiac is not the same as the "veil of illusion" Nietzsche mentions. Through the Dionysiac, we "can live" with the truth of Silenus. Action, therefore, is known and accepted to be ultimately futile but it is willingly, even joyfully, pursued nonetheless. The cruel irony of life is embraced. It is just this sort of response to Schopenhauer's pessimism that Conrad shows signs of vindicating. The comic aspect, which defuses disgust at absurdity, is evident in the parting shot of the knitting machine passage: "I'll admit however that to look at the remorseless process is sometimes amusing" (*CLJC* 1: 425).

The case regarding Conrad's relationship to Nietzsche is somewhat similar to that of his relationship to Schopenhauer. Conrad certainly knew of Nietzsche and the name finds scattered mention in Conrad's correspondence. This is mostly in relation to the philosopher's amoralism, his "mad individualism" (*CLJC* 2: 188). Nevertheless, what can be known of the precise character of Conrad's engagement with Nietzsche depends largely on inference from the novels. George Butte finds the references to Silenus in *The Secret Agent* to strongly indicate a source in *The Birth of Tragedy*. He argues from the grim overtones that are carried by the naming of the anarchists' beer hall after Silenus that Nietzsche's is "the one book in which Conrad could plausibly have come across this rare version of the Silenus motif" (Butte 157). He therefore concludes that Conrad most likely read *The Birth of Tragedy* in its French translation (161). Butte characterizes Conrad's treatment of Nietzsche as deeply ambivalent; Conrad uses the Silenus motif but does not in general follow Nietzsche's thesis. Butte believes Ossipon to be the character closest to the ideal of the Dionysiac, but to be ultimately only a "pointed parody," a "papier-mâché Dionysus" (164). For him, "Conrad's relation to Nietzsche is then a mixed and unstable one," being constituted of "a conversation and a quarrel" (168). The ambiguity of Conrad's relationship to Nietzsche is in fact if anything greater than Butte supposes. Conrad, of course, had little time for Nietzschean ethics, and this can be seen in the Professor's incoherent "mad individualism." Nevertheless, if there is a parody of the Dionysiac in Ossipon, there is also a much more compelling and sympathetic Dionysiac figure in the Assistant Commissioner of Police. This character upholds Conradian virtues in a distinctively Dionysiac way. Where the grim irony of reality undermines the Professor, it works in favor of the Assistant Commissioner.

The relevant passage narrates this character's journey towards Verloc's Brett Street shop after his meeting with the Home Secretary. On this expedition the Assistant Commissioner apprehends the urban scene with its grim implications. The streets through which he travels are shabby and seedy: "His descent into the street was like the descent into a slimy aquarium from which the water had been run off. A murky, gloomy dampness enveloped him" (SA 117). This repulsive sliminess is a particularly unpleasant instance of "inorganic nature"; its description recalls both the language of the mathematical sublime and the potential of such a spectacle to be stultifying:

> He advanced at once into an immensity of greasy slime and damp plaster interspersed with lamps, and enveloped, oppressed, penetrated, choked and suffocated by the blackness of a wet London night, which is composed of soot and drops of water. (119)

The catalogue of attributive verbs here belabors the "immensity" and oppressiveness of the scene that the Assistant Commissioner confronts. It also enacts the threat of immobility by delaying the flow of the sentence too long for comfort; the sentence at this point becomes stuck in an empty, echoing space produced by the semantic near-redundancy, along with the assonance of "enveloped, oppressed, penetrated" and the rhyme of "penetrated" and "suffocated." As in other examples of urban journeys in the novel, the human is presented as continuous with the material environment. Indeed, the people whom the Assistant Commissioner passes seem to be little more than inert appendages of their surroundings:

> [T]hese people were as denationalised as the dishes set before them with every circumstance of unstamped respectability. Neither was

their personality stamped in any way, professionally, socially or racially. They seemed created for the Italian restaurant, unless the Italian restaurant had been perchance created for them. But that last hypothesis was unthinkable, since one could not place them anywhere outside those special establishments. (118—19)

Moreover, the Assistant Commissioner himself has become continuous with the environment. Almost immediately after entering the streets, he is "enveloped" by the dampness (117). Shortly afterwards we are told that "when he emerged into the Strand out of a narrow street by the side of Charing Cross Station the genius of the locality assimilated him" such that he "might have been but one more of the queer foreign fish that can be seen of an evening about there flitting around the dark corners" (117). The Assistant Commissioner's continuity with the surroundings is thus signaled by his entry into the aquarium metaphor. All this is very reminiscent of the street scene earlier in the novel in which Verloc, like the patrolling policeman he passes, is included in its material majesty. Importantly, however, unlike Verloc, the Assistant Commissioner is conscious of this fact; the above observation on the Italian restaurant is one that the Assistant Commissioner "made to himself" (118). The meditation is thus rendered a piece of free indirect discourse and the sentence fragment coming shortly after, "And he too had become unplaced" thus signals that the Assistant Commissioner recognizes his own continuity with this street scene (118).

Yet, in the face of all this, the Assistant Commissioner feels a Dionysiac joy. Far from being crushed by futility he is positively enjoying himself. He is perhaps not quite an artist but, as an officer discontented with the bureaucratic role in which he has found himself, the practical detective work upon which he has embarked has a similar connotation of unleashed creativity. It is in this endeavor that he finds a respite from the terrible truth of Silenus:

> He felt light-hearted, as though he had been ambushed all alone in a jungle many thousands of miles away from departmental desks and official inkstands. This joyousness and dispersion of thought before a task of some importance seems to prove that this world of ours is not such a serious affair after all. (119)

Most importantly, even though he recognizes that he has become enveloped by his surroundings, a "pleasurable feeling of independence possess[es] him" (119). Just as in Nietzsche, the inescapable deterministic truth is known, but an ironic, contrary sense of freedom is embraced nonetheless: "He had a sense of loneliness, of evil freedom. It was rather pleasant" (118).

This Dionysiac experience is key to the kind of agency that Conrad ultimately valorizes, of which the defining feature is self-conscious irony. Besides, perhaps, the unfortunate Stevie, the Assistant Commissioner is the closest thing to a moral agent which *The Secret Agent* contains. One strong indication of this is his frequent comparison to Don Quixote. The Assistant Commissioner has "a long, meagre face with the accentuated features of an energetic Don Quixote" (*SA* 92). As he sets out to interview Verloc he is described as "looking like the vision of a cool, reflective Don Quixote" (117). Chief Inspector Heat, by contrast, is "not quixotic" (161). Cedric Watts discusses the identification that Conrad felt with the figure of Don Quixote, drawing on statements in *A Personal Record* and other texts. As Watts states,

> Many of [Conrad's] patently honourable characters can be seen as quixotic either because their values are anachronistic or incongruous, given the nature of the environment in which those values operate, or because their idealism had the quality of a delusion or monomania. (Watts, *Preface to Conrad* 70–71)

The Assistant Commissioner is far from being delusive or monomaniacal. He is nevertheless an honorable character. He refuses to have the innocent Michael is arrested arbitrarily at the behest of Chief Inspector Heat. In this way he holds to a belief in the rule of law even in the murky world of revolutionary intrigue. Both Vladimir and the Professor would like to see liberal norms destroyed and replaced with the arbitrariness of a police state. Vladimir tells Verloc that "[t]his country is absurd with its sentimental regard for individual liberty" (*SA* 23). Vladimir's view corresponds almost exactly to the Professor's, as expounded to Ossipon:

> To break up the superstition and worship of legality should be our aim. Nothing would please me more than to see Inspector Heat and his likes take to shooting us down in broad daylight with the approval of the public. Half our battle would be won then; the disintegration of the old morality would have set in in its very temple. (58–59)

Yet neither of these characters is likely to have their wishes realized. The Assistant Commissioner is instrumental in exposing Vladimir's hand in the Greenwich bombing. At the close of the novel he is pondering a "crusade," which he explains to Vladimir as "the clearing out of this country of all the foreign political spies, police, and that sort of—of—dogs" (176; 179). The breakdown of the rule of law into open conflict between revolutionaries and state forces is pushed a step back through the Assistant Commissioner's activities.

Crucially, the Assistant Commissioner can do this because he is uniquely able to see the broader context and, indeed, the irony of situations. Ludwig Schnauder argues that his "probity [. . .] is seriously undermined by the way his ostensibly moral decision not to arrest Michaelis is revealed to be based not by ethical, legal or professional principles but by petty private interests"—that is, his desire not to upset the lady Patroness and ultimately his wife (Schnauder 242). He does, as Schnauder puts it, "the right thing for the wrong reasons" (219). On this count, he certainly fails as a Kantian moral agent. Yet more important is that the Assistant Commissioner is, as Schnauder admits, aware of this fact. He is capable of "some derisive self-criticism" on this count (Schnauder 218–19; SA 90). He is particularly alert in general to the ironies of his situation, and "consider[s] himself the victim of an ironic fate" (90). It is ultimately this capacity that allows him to navigate the ironic world of *The Secret Agent*, and, even if he recognizes that his motives are imperfect, to do the right thing.

The novel is one in which myriad different spheres overlap and undermine one another, from the Verloc family's shop to the Silenus Restaurant and the House of Commons. These spheres interact to produce the incredibly complex intrigue. They interlock like Stevie's drawings of

> [c]ircles, circles, circles; innumerable circles, concentric, eccentric; a coruscating whirl of circles that by their tangled multitude of repeated curves, uniformity of form, and confusion of intersecting lines suggested a rendering of cosmic chaos, the symbolism of a mad art attempting the inconceivable. (SA 36)

These drawings, although ironically given no notice by any other character in the novel, seem to express the nature of its plot, as well as the view of reality as a "cosmic chaos," which Conrad shares with Schopenhauer and Nietzsche. Each particular sphere, then, is liable to be rendered ironic by another that stands behind or cuts across it. In his appreciation of his "ironic fate," the Assistant Commissioner is perfectly able to observe this broader context. He can thus see better than any other character the nature of the intrigue in which he has found himself, something which is stated clearly when, speaking to the Home Secretary in the Palace of Westminster, he makes the ambiguously metafictional statement that "[f]rom a certain point of view we are here in the presence of a domestic drama (175). The Dionysiac sublime is therefore central to the Assistant Commissioner's construction as a subject. He is aware of the mechanistic reality that "assimilate[s] him," but is not paralyzed by this knowledge. This ironic sublime allows the Assistant Commissioner to see what is going on and to recapture some sense of independence and moral freedom.

The Secret Agent is thus a paradoxical and skeptical treatment of political agency that leads into a philosophical reflection on the psychology of freedom. In this capacity, it elaborates a sophisticated comment on the nature and import of the sublime affect. Conrad draws out the implications of Schopenhauer's development, extending the possibilities of the sublime object such that the seemingly insignificant detail can partake in the affect. In this, he reflects a longstanding process of subjectivizing the sublime, something which will reach its fullest extent in the dreamscapes of the Freudian uncanny. Here this contributes to the aesthetic of ironic sublimity that is central to *The Secret Agent*. Conrad thus embodies fictionally the tensions inherent in Schopenhauer's theory as the latter retains the category of the sublime while eschewing Kant's metaphysics of autonomy. However, Conrad does not do this merely to savage or to ridicule the sublime. He is, after all, fascinated by the structures of consciousness that produce it. Instead, analogously to Nietzsche, Conrad presents a necessary if fundamentally paradoxical sense of freedom that is aesthetically apprehended.

CHAPTER 5

Journeys through Nighttown

"Circe," "The 'Uncanny,'" and the Inhabited Subject

The curtain that falls on the Soho of *The Secret Agent* rises again to reveal a scene that at first seems remarkably similar. Yet instead of Conrad's Assistant Commissioner, now we find two other figures passing through two different red-light districts. In his essay on the uncanny of 1919, Freud relates a singular experience as happening to him "one hot summer afternoon" in the unspecified past (SE 17: 237). In the anecdote, he finds that he has wandered into a quarter of "a provincial Italian town," one "of whose character [he] could not long remain in doubt," a red-light district (17: 237). Freud has difficulty escaping the place and finds himself twice arriving back on the same street. It is with a sense of relief, we are told, that he finally manages to leave the area behind. In a work published three years later, Joyce's Leopold Bloom likewise finds himself, in the night after another hot summer's day, wandering through such a district. In Bloom's case, the area is Dublin's "nighttown," the notorious Monto neighborhood (U 408). In both of these cases, the wandering protagonists are confronted with sublime objects of a different type than those found in *The Secret Agent*. The sublime here takes the form of an oneiric undecidability, which infuses the world of everyday objects, in which they confront an ambiguous dreamscape that is both frightening and compelling. Neither protagonist, moreover, feels the Assistant Commissioner's "evil freedom." Instead they face a challenge to the very coherence of the autonomous subject.

A Circean Aesthetic

It might appear somewhat unusual to restrict my analysis only to the fifteenth episode of *Ulysses*, known as the "Circe" episode. After all,

135

it would seem inappropriate to focus on a single chapter of *The Secret Agent*, say, or *The Time Machine*. However, there are good reasons to restrict my discussion in this way. The episodes of *Ulysses* enjoy greater claim to being considered separately than does the usual novel chapter. Often the episodes differ radically in form from the rest of the text. Particularly in the later chapters of *Ulysses*, Joyce's experimentation produces episodes that are formally idiosyncratic. The pastiches in the "Oxen of the Sun" episode, for example, and the "Ithaca" episode's catechism renders these chapters as different from one another as they are from "Circe" with its stage directions and theatrical dialogue. The difference extends beyond formal conventions, with the strange hallucinatory events of "Circe" being unlike anything seen in the rest of the book. Given that this reading pays particular attention to precisely these characteristics, it is appropriate thus to discuss "Circe" as a text, even while bearing appropriately in mind its status as an episode within *Ulysses*.

In some ways this approach reflects more recent criticism on the episode. Older criticism on "Circe" tended to use it primarily to illuminate those larger wholes of which it was a part—that is, *Ulysses*, or even Joyce's whole oeuvre.[1] However, more recent criticism has tended to focus upon its particularity, redirecting attention towards the idiosyncrasies, formal and otherwise, of the episode.[2] In Andrew Gibson's terms, "what has moved to the top of the critical agenda is the question of how to describe a distinctively Circean aesthetic" (Gibson 15). Gibson published this statement in 1994, yet contributions to criticism of "Circe" still turn on recognizably aesthetic terms, addressing themselves to and attempting to define the unique qualities of the episode. In this vein, Derek Attridge suggested "Pararealism," and Cheryl Temple Herr "difficulty," as defining features of "Circe" in 2013 and 2014 respectively. My claim is that at least an important part of the Circean aesthetic is captured by the category of the uncanny as it is described in Freud's essay. Such a claim is not entirely new; there is a widespread but understated consciousness that the uncanny is relevant to the episode. Steven Connor mentions "the uncanny animation by language of inanimate or dead objects" (Connor 124). Daniel Ferrer states that when considering the character of the episode, "[t]he word *"Unheimliche"* springs to mind" (Ferrer 127). However, as in these instances, the uncanny is generally mentioned in passing or used adjectivally. There are few studies that read "Circe" alongside Freud's formulation of the uncanny in a sustained way, the better to establish its important presence in the episode's unique aesthetic.[4]

Part of the reason for this could be that there are certain possible objections to such a reading that immediately present themselves. These objections take two forms: to associate the uncanny with "Circe" may be inaccurate, or it may be trivial. To take first of all the charge of inaccuracy, it must be admitted that it is certainly inaccurate to say that "Circe" is written under the direct influence of Freud's "The 'Uncanny.'" Joyce does not seem to have read the essay, and he was in general scathing about Freudianism (Ellmann 524). Moreover, it may be that the uncanny feeling, which forms Freud's subject matter, is not present in the episode. Perhaps "Circe" is ridiculous rather than frightening. Without a doubt, there are humorous elements to be found in "Circe" related to the freewheeling absurdity of its goings-on. The hallucinations tend towards wild exaggeration; for example, at the height of Bloom's hallucinatory political career there is constructed a "new Bloomusalem," which is "a colossal edifice with a crystal roof, built in the shape of a pork kidney, containing forty thousand rooms" (U 458). The tendency to exaggeration combines with comic misunderstandings, as is the case with Stephen's reference to "the ends of the world," prompting, as is discussed below, a particularly confused and bizarre passage (475). Alongside this there occur characteristic Joycean puns and witticisms. Bella Cohen, for example, when dominating a feminized Bloom, becomes "Bello," uniting the Italian masculine noun ending and the English "bellow" (497). Joyce himself mentioned laughter among his possible correspondences for moly, the herb mentioned in the Circe episode of *The Odyssey*. Moly, he says, can be "laughter, the enchantment killer" (Joyce 144). Perhaps, then, the bizarre goings-on of the episode are simply comedic. To focus on the uncanny in "Circe" would therefore be to miss the point, or at least to minimize the humor that ultimately prevails.

Alternatively, perhaps the uncanny in "Circe" is too obviously present. There is a notable prevalence of ghosts and of the undead. Cohen demands of Bloom to be entertained with "smut or a bloody good ghoststory or a line of poetry," and while the first and third of these are much in evidence, it is the second genre that arguably dominates the episode (U 504). Ghoulish elements include the appearance of a hobgoblin and a procession of skeletal horses (476; 533). Perhaps the most ghastly turn of events comes when a dog transforms into Paddy Dignam's corpse:

(*The beagle lifts his snout, showing the grey scorbutic face of Paddy Dignam. He has gnawed all. He exhales a putrid carcasefed breath. He grows to human size and shape. His dachshund coat becomes a brown mortuary habit. His green eye flashes bloodshot. Half of one ear, all the nose and both thumbs are ghouleaten.*) (447)

This extreme grotesquery shades into other familiar themes of the uncanny: repetition, the return of the repressed, and, most broadly, the conjunction of the strange and familiar. Dignam's appearance in the above example is exemplary of "that class of the frightening which leads back to what is known of old and long familiar" in that he emerges out of the ordinary material of the street dog (SE 17: 220). Furthermore, Dignam's appearance leads back to what is narratively familiar in that his funeral has been related earlier in the novel. Other revenants are to be seen and, indeed, the return of the repressed is a clear preoccupation of "Circe." It is no accident that the street dog mentioned above is referred to at crucial moments as "the retriever" (U 416; 558). Stephen's deceased mother makes an appearance, prompting this exchange:

> STEPHEN (*Horrorstruck*): Lemur, who are you? What bogeyman's trick is this?
> BUCK MULLIGAN (*Shakes his curling capbell*): The mockery of it! Kinch killed her dogsbody bitchbody [sic]. (539–40)

Repetition is piled upon itself here: not only does Stephen's mother, and the conversation that Stephen had about her with Buck Mulligan in the opening episode of the book, return, but the resurrection of Dignam earlier in "Circe" is invoked in Mulligan's reference to "her dogsbody" (539). At the close of the episode, Bloom's son Rudy appears as "a fairy boy of eleven, a changeling" (565). The changeling, of course, is another representative of the *outré* embedded within the familiar. The preponderance of the fantastic and grotesque, and the emphasis on well-known things that have been forgotten or repressed, are legitimate instances of the uncanny in the episode. However, they are also fairly well trodden characteristics of its content. If to say that "Circe" is uncanny is only to say that it includes instances of supernatural and frightening things and of the return of the repressed, then little light indeed is shed by applying this category to the episode.

For all their merits, however, these objections need not ultimately deter a closer look at the uncanny in the episode. They are, after all, contradictory. There is indeed humor in "Circe," but to insist that this is its defining feature is to disregard the seemingly obvious presence of uncanny elements, those elements which lead critics to acknowledge the uncanny in passing. As is often the case in "Circe," no clear line can be drawn between what is funny and what is frightening in the episode. It is sufficient to say that the episode's grotesquery is not simply a joke. This is obvious when taking into account laughter as it is heard in the episode. Gibson in his discussion appears to gesture towards identifying the episode as fundamentally comedic when he calls laughter the "one major consistency in 'Circe'" (Gibson 25). Yet, he is aware that it is not to be taken unequivocally, calling it "a complex laughter, and still in need of further analysis and investigation" (25). Indeed, his characterization shows signs of how the uncanny is even here involved. His characterization is disconcerting: "A huge, monstrous gust of laughter sweeps right the way through the chapter" (25). Indeed, there is more laughter in "Circe" than there are jokes, and this laughter can be quite humorless. Lynch, in response to one of Stephen's pronouncements, lets forth a "mocking whinny of laughter" (U 475). Lipoti Virag's laughter at Bloom is similarly aggressive and is rendered as a cackle: "(*He crows derisively*) Keekeereekee!" (484). Moreover, the aforementioned hobgoblin introduces himself as "l'homme qui rit," referring to the Victor Hugo novel of the same name, and quite possibly to its 1909 film adaptation, both of which involve a character whose face is mutilated into a constant grin (476). Laughter seems, therefore, not necessarily to be something that defuses and nullifies the uncanny enchantments, but often to be involved with them, uncanny itself.

On the other hand, if supernatural occurrences and returns of the repressed were all that related to the uncanny in the episode, then reading it in these terms might indeed be a shallow exercise. This is not the case, however. The elements cited above are accompanied by more precise connections between Joyce's chapter and Freud's theorizing of the uncanny. I argue that these connections point towards common concerns, which are present in both texts—that is, both are investigations of the subject confronted with its fragmentation and its animation by unconscious forces. This commonality of concern is demonstrable despite Joyce's professed dislike of Freudianism. To read the Circean aesthetic as one of the uncanny need not be tired or superficial, then. Rather, it shows how the episode is a cogent interrogation of just what preoccupied Freud in theorizing the uncanny feeling.

The Old, Animistic Conception

Freud's general statement of his theory is that the uncanny is "that class of the frightening which leads back to what is known of old and long familiar" (*SE* 17: 220). This "general contention," however, is not Freud's culminating one (17: 247). He elaborates that the uncanny leads back to the familiar in two interrelated ways. The uncanny experience occurs "when infantile complexes which have been repressed are once more revived by some impression, or when primitive beliefs which have been surmounted seem once more to be confirmed" (17: 249). The latter case has less often occupied Freudian critics, but it has a profound role in the workings of nighttown. The "primitive beliefs which have been surmounted" to which this latter refers are identified specifically as "animistic" ones (17: 249). This animism is elsewhere described in greater detail; Freud explains that "the old, animistic conception of the universe" was "characterised by the idea that the world was peopled with the spirits of human beings" (17: 240). The world of Joyce's nighttown is a thoroughly animistic one, one in which spirits invest every level of being. There are animals that have human spirits. The aforementioned dog, which Paddy Dignam temporarily inhabits, is an example. Another might be the moth that sings as it flies, declaring "[l]ong ago I was a king" (*U* 486). There are also objects that become metonymically charged with human capacities. Stephen carries on a conversation with Lynch's cap, and the language of fan signals is enlisted to have Bella's fan represent her (496). The spirits that inhabit the object world of "Circe" are often not explicitly those of identifiable human beings. Objects nevertheless still frequently act as if they were animate. During Bloom's fall from his messianic favor we see a "deadhand" write on the wall, and a speaking holly bush (468). The gas jet in Cohen's brothel is particularly animated. It wails in answer to Mhanananan Mac Lir's speech and reacts to Stephen's swinging of his ashplant with a "Pwfungg!" (542). Indeed, it is hinted that it is a conduit though which spirits enter the surroundings:

KITTY (*Peers at the gasjet*): What ails it tonight?
LYNCH (*Deeply*): Enter a ghost and hobgoblins. (473–74)

Such an infestation of spirits is alluded to shortly afterwards in Zoe's comment that "the devil is in that door" (493). Perhaps the most obviously animistic figure is the nymph in the picture on Bloom's bedroom wall. Bloom treats the nymph as if it were itself semi-divine: "I was glad to look on you, to praise you, a thing of beauty, almost to pray" (510). The nymph is, of course, already an animistic figure, being a spirit associated with certain natural objects, but in this case it is the representation itself that is animated.

The animistic worldview is associated by Freud with a catalogue of beliefs that follow from it. These are "the omnipotence of thoughts," "the prompt fulfilment of wishes," "secret injurious powers," and "the return of the dead" (*SE* 17: 247). Occurrences that seem to fit under any of these categories are taken unconsciously as confirmations of the reality of animism and therefore give rise to an uncanny feeling (17: 247–48). We have already seen the many instances of the return of the dead. Moreover, the belief in "omnipotence of thoughts" and the closely related "prompt fulfilment of wishes" are much in evidence. Wishes and associations are constantly running away to create their own effects in the world. Stephen's offhand reference to "the ends of the world" is misinterpreted by Florry Talbot to refer to the biblical eschaton, prompting a series of events, including the return of Elijah (*U* 475). Zoe's mocking wish, upon hearing Bloom's professed dislike of smoking, that he "make a stump speech out of it" leads quickly to a political fantasy, which turns into a messianic one (452). This involves Bloom becoming Lord Mayor of Dublin and constructing the "new Bloomusalem" before undergoing a precipitous fall from favor (452–70). The sequence concludes with Zoe's dismissively advising Bloom to "[t]alk away til you're black in the face" (470). Yet this thought has already had its effect before it is articulated by Zoe. Bloom has just been burned at the stake; the stage direction immediately before reads "Bloom becomes mute, shrunken, carbonised" (470)—that is, Bloom's face is black and he has ceased to talk. This anticipatory effect points to another way in which the omnipotence of thoughts manifests itself in the chapter. Some unvoiced or implicit thoughts have effects in the world through becoming concretized metaphors. The canine that follows Bloom through the chapter, which is variously referred to as many different kinds of dog, is a concrete embodiment of the metaphor that Bloom is being 'dogged' by memories, something which is said outright at one point when Bloom is described as "dogged by the setter" (430). This phrasing, while making the implicit metaphor explicit, in turn implies the further metaphor that Bloom is being 'beset.' Another example of such a literally treated metaphor is borrowed from Bloom's speculations earlier in the book involving Ponchielli's piece *Dance of the Hours*:

(From a corner the morning hours run out, goldhaired, slim, in girlish blue, waspwaisted, with innocent hands. Nimbly they dance, twirling their skipping ropes. The hours of noon follow in amber gold. Laughing linked, high haircombs flashing, they catch the sun in mocking mirrors, lifting their arms.) (535–36)

This appeals to the conceptual metaphor that treats the passage of time as spatial movement and by extension intervals of time as moving through space. It partakes of a common way of thinking about the hours of a day passing. This widely used but generally implicit metaphor occurs in a concrete form across the "stage" (or perhaps the "screen") of the episode.

The dramatic form of the episode reinforces this sense of an animistic world. The convention of entering spoken lines underneath character names gives anything to which a line is attributed in some sense the status of a character. It is hard to avoid the conclusion that some objects are deliberately promoted by this means. Take, for example, the following:

> (*Two cyclists, with lighted paper lanterns awsing [sic], swim by him, grazing him, their bells rattling.*)
> THE BELLS: Haltyaltyaltyall.
> BLOOM (*Halts erect stung by a spasm*): Ow. (414)

The stage direction by itself would be sufficient to explain Bloom's "Ow," and indeed if this were a script for the stage no more would need be given. Yet the bells are given a speaking part and so they appear on the page in a position equivalent to that of Bloom. The sheer variety of such speaking parts in the episode is huge, and everything from household objects to The End of The World, embodied as "a twoheaded octopus in gillie's kilts, busby and tartan fillibegs," is treated as a character in this way (477). Moreover, these objects appear to be speaking for themselves and are not filtered through any particular character's consciousness. They have, it seems, minds of their own.

Oneiric Worlds

These aspects of the world of "Circe," the ever-present animism and its attendant belief in the omnipotence of thoughts, lead to an effacement of the distinction between external objects and mental images. The episode thus becomes akin to a long, confused hallucination or a nightmare. The form of "Circe" is crucial to this. Its particular form could perhaps best be described as that of a one-act play. All of the text that appears is identifiable as either a stage direction, a character's name, or a piece of dialogue. The consistent following of these conventions ensure that no definite demarcation can be found between physical or mental phenomena. Yet the events of the episode seem to occupy many different ontological levels. A mundane event like Bloom's taking stewardship of Stephen's money may be compared to, say, the construction of the "new Bloomusalem." It is nevertheless impossible to draw a clear line between what may be attributed to mental representation and to any putative realist substrate. There are, for example, no scene changes between those occurrences that seem more realistic and those that seem more fantastic. Gibson asserts the failure of a critical project to separate definitively what supposedly really happens from what is imagined (Gibson 9–10). The passage that describes a sadomasochistic encounter between Cohen and Bloom is a prime example. There are some aspects of the passage that suggest that Cohen has become a man, Bello, and Bloom a woman. Other aspects suggest that this state of affairs is imaginary or figurative. The whole passage seems certainly fantastic, but to dismiss it wholesale as such would be to miss the point, since this would not address why there seem to be competing ontological levels at play even within the fantasy. At the level of stage direction, the character name Bella has been replaced by the masculine equivalent Bello. This is not only a matter of stage direction, however. Other characters' dialogue begins to address Cohen in masculine terms and to speak of Bloom using feminine pronouns:

> FLORRY (*Hiding her with her gown*): She didn't mean it, Mr Bello. She'll be good, sir. (U 499)

Yet we cannot categorically say that Bloom and Cohen have switched genders. The swap is not treated quite consistently. Bloom, even as others address Cohen as "sir," calls her/him "Empress!" and begs "Don't be cruel, nurse! Don't!" (497; 499). Nevertheless, even he is not consistent in addressing Cohen in feminine terms. He slips into ambiguity on the point:

> BLOOM (Bows): Master! Mistress! Mantamer! (504)

It is ultimately undecidable, then, at which level the reversal of gender has happened between Bloom and Cohen. It is not possible in this extended sequence to say for certain which aspects of their interaction are to be granted any privileged status.

This complication and effacement of the difference between the physical and the psychological can be found throughout the text of "Circe." It happens, for instance, even within the stage directions. As Ferrer puts it, "[T]here is no difference of level between '*Enter a ghost and hobgoblins*' and '*Enter the milkman*'" (Ferrer 132). These statements are both equivalent in being stage descriptions and, moreover, share the same curtly descriptive tone. They nevertheless vary widely in the reality that might intuitively be ascribed to the actions they describe. The dreamlike strangeness of nighttown's phantasmagoria, then, is rendered almost impossible to distinguish from the familiar solid world.

Another example of this is the treatment of Bloom's copious costume changes. Bloom at various points in the chapter is described as appearing in an entirely new guise. Of course, given the lack of scene changes, the transitions between these often happen while Bloom has been "onstage." As David Galef comments in his article on fashion in "Circe," these changes "defy all sense" (Galef 423).[4] It must be concluded that Bloom's costume is something like an endlessly transforming hallucination. These costume changes follow a logic of memory and free association: they reflect the psychological situation in which Bloom finds himself. Nevertheless, each time he is described anew, his change of costume is presented as a solid *fait accompli*. Indeed, many of the descriptions approach an obsessive degree of detailed precision. Bloom at one point is described as follows:

> (*In youth's smart blue Oxford suit with white vestslips, narrowshouldered, in brown Alpine hat, wearing gent's sterling silver waterbury keyless watch and double curb Albert with seal attached, one side of him coated with stiffening mud.*) (U 417)

In this case, Bloom is talking to his father, Rudolf Virag, explaining some childhood misdemeanors involving mud puddles. His costume has changed entirely and instantly to reflect this association. The outfit thus carries implication of nostalgia; it is, as Galef calls it, a "signifier of bygone days" (Galef 421). Nevertheless the attention to detail here is exhaustive, and it is reminiscent of the lists of the later "Ithaca" episode. Bloom's disguises, then, even though they may be transitory hallucinations, mere mental images, are as carefully and solidly realized as introductory descriptions in a realist play or novel.

Thus, essential to the particular aesthetic of "Circe" and bound up with its idiosyncratic form and its baroque content is the presentation of a world in which it is impossible to distinguish what is to be considered real. Marilyn French notes the "objective" quality of the form: "[A]lthough Circe is written in the most objective of literary modes, drama, it is in this episode that the objectively real is most difficult to discern" (French 186). This formal strategy marks "Circe" out from other parts of *Ulysses* in which free indirect discourse blurs the line between mind and object. It is certainly true that what happens in, for instance, Stephen's mind and in his surroundings becomes difficult to distinguish in some of the stream-of-consciousness sections of the novel, but never do mental contents become so clearly and solidly a part of the surroundings as when they are laid out on the stage of this episode.

The uncanny aesthetic of "Circe," then, culminates in a vision of an undecidable dreamscape. This finds an extraordinary echo in some features of the narratives in Freud's own text. Though far less baroque than "Circe," the passage in "The 'Uncanny'" in which Freud finds himself in a nighttown of his own has a similarly unsettling sense of being a waking dream. It is worth quoting the passage in full. At the relevant point in the essay, Freud is discussing the uncanny effect of repetition:

> From what I have observed, this phenomenon does undoubtedly, subject to certain conditions and combined with certain circumstances, arouse an uncanny feeling which, furthermore, recalls the sense of helplessness experienced in some dream states. As I was walking, one hot summer afternoon, through the deserted streets of a provincial town in Italy which was unknown to me, I found myself in a quarter of whose character I could not long remain in doubt. Nothing but painted women were to be seen at the windows of the small houses, and I hastened to leave the narrow street at the next turning. But after having wandered about for a time without enquiring my way, I suddenly found myself back in the same street, where my presence was beginning to excite attention. I hurried away once more, only to arrive by another *détour* at the same place yet a third time. Now, however, a feeling overcame me which I can only describe as uncanny, and I was glad enough to find myself back at the piazza I had left a short while before, without any further voyages of discovery. (SE 17: 237)

This passage ostensibly describes a real experience of Freud's, yet its narration has a dreamlike quality over and above that occasioned by the repetition. Freud mentions that recurrences can evoke a sense of helplessness reminiscent of dream states. He does not make this idea's connection with the following story explicit, yet it hangs over its telling. There are other aspects that make this narrative feel like one of the many dream descriptions which appear in Freud's writings. Specific markers of place names and times are omitted in favor of broad narrative strokes and generic signifiers. There is precious little to connect the events with the real world. Instead we find Freud wandering in a nondescript, empty town. The anticlimactic finish also suggests some of the absurdity of dream narratives.[5] Robin Lydenberg views these elements as hedging the uncanniness of the narrative:

> [T]he narrator maintains an aloof and controlling distance which partially contains and diminishes the episode's uncanny power. Freud's narrative choices reinforce this diminishment in several ways. He is lost not in some threatening metropolis but merely in a "provincial town" where disorienting foreignness is kept to a manageable scale. (Lydenberg 1075)

Certainly, Freud's is not the most disturbing story ever committed to paper, yet Lydenberg goes too far in identifying these distancing features with a diminishment of its power. Rather, it is the very distance upon which Freud insists, the story's unreal quality, which stands out. For example, if the episode happened in a major metropolis, then the place would be more likely to be named or could at least be narrowed down to a few possible locations. The thorough ambiguity of the "provincial town," on the other hand, is so vague as to seem almost unlike a real place. The case here, in fact, is the inverse of that which applies to Bloom's costume changes. The latter's mutability and the associative logic that they follow, mean they are intuitively assumed to be hallucinations, but the descriptions treat them as solid reality. In Freud's anecdote, by contrast, we are told that the occurrence is a real happening, but the vague and slippery narration treats it as a dream. Lydenberg continues,

> The story concludes with a variation on the conventional form of narrative closure in which events are framed as a dream or hallucination from which both protagonist and reader awaken into reality (or, in this case, into the piazza). This framing device serves to limit the uncanny expansion the Italian experience calls up. (1075)

Lydenberg correctly identifies this narrative "awakening," but understates how this awakening jars with the fact that the story is after all meant to be a real incident. It is the fact that we wake up that is itself surprising and uncanny. This unexpected awakening only calls attention to the ambiguity that marks out the anecdote. The story presents itself within the text of the essay as a waking dream, one which the reader is not expecting to have and has no reason to anticipate.

Omnipotence and Helplessness

The uncanny as Freud expounds it is therefore a useful category to bring to bear on the aesthetic of "Circe." Light is shed on both Joyce's and Freud's texts by their juxtaposition. Of profound importance to the episode is its dramatization of the animistic worldview and the concomitant beliefs in the omnipotence of thought and in the prompt fulfilment of wishes. In this way "Circe" gives prominence to some of the less commented-upon aspects of Freud's theory. In doing so, moreover, it dramatizes some of the underlying logic of the Freudian uncanny, in that the psychological logic of this surmounted, narcissistic worldview clashes with the solid, "objective" reality of the world implied by the dramatic form. The uncanny thus reveals the connection between the animism of nighttown and some of the episode's characteristic formal qualities, those expressed in Freud's comment that "an uncanny effect is often and easily produced when the distinction between imagination and reality is effaced" (SE 17: 244). This also allows a reading of some of Freud's own narrative procedures in his own red-light district anecdote. Yet in revealing these connections, a puzzling aspect of Freud's account is also thrown up. As we saw, an important part of the animistic worldview was what Freud calls the omnipotence of thoughts, the belief that things can really be accomplished just by thinking about them or wishing for them. However, Freud's Italian anecdote centers on the "sense of helplessness," which he experiences (17: 237). The feeling of the uncanny, then, according to Freud, can accompany both a feeling of omnipotence and of helplessness, of both power and lack thereof.

This is a strong ambivalence in Freud's account; it is difficult to see how someone who makes the judgment "So, after all, it is *true* that one can kill a person by the mere wish!" might have the same feeling in common with someone who experiences a "sense of helplessness" (17: 248; 237). If omnipotence and helplessness are simply predicated of the same subject then the contradiction is acute. It is less puzzling, however, if the "omnipotence of thoughts" is taken to apply specifically to thoughts—that is, if it implies that some thoughts have a kind of omnipotence of their own distinct from that of the ego which feels helpless in dream states. The ambivalence implies, then, an uneven distribution of agency within the subject. This concern with a fragmentation of the subject points towards the issues that shape the essay. "The 'Uncanny'" is fundamentally concerned with competing conceptions of the subject and its relationship with nature. Particularly emphasized are those that oppose the tradition of the modern autonomous subject. The most frequently mentioned of these is, of course, animism. Animism can be taken as a prime example of a worldview that contrasts with the one implied by modern subjectivity. For Freud, as we saw, animism is "characterised by the idea that the world was peopled with the spirits of human beings" (17: 240). In place of a contrast between the realm of human moral freedom and deterministic nature, animism presents a very differently conceived kind of human realm which stretches across all levels of being.

Freud of course does not endorse animism as a worldview. Its presence is nonetheless revealing, because the worldview that Freud does endorse shares important similarities with it. This is the one he takes his own psychoanalytic theory to imply. Freud considers this theory to be a departure from the tradition of modern subjectivity as radically different to it as animism and to have profound consequences for how human beings understand themselves with reference to the natural world. Accordingly, in the *Introductory Lectures on Psychoanalysis*, he describes it in grandiose terms:

> In the course of centuries the naïve self-love of men has had to submit to two major blows at the hands of science. The first was when they learnt that our earth was not the centre of the universe but only a tiny fragment of a cosmic system of scarcely imaginable vastness. This is associated in our minds with the name of Copernicus, though something similar had already been asserted by Alexandrian science. The second blow fell when biological research destroyed man's supposedly privileged place in creation and proved his descent from the animal kingdom and his ineradicable animal nature. This revaluation has been accomplished in our own days by Darwin, Wallace and their predecessors, though not without the most violent contemporary opposition. But human megalomania will have suffered its third and most wounding blow from the psychological research of the present time which seeks to prove to the ego that it is not even master in its own house, but must content itself with scanty information of what is going on unconsciously in its mind. (SE 16: 283–84)

What Freud here talks about in terms of "wounds" to the "megalomania" of humanity are discoveries that the relationship between it and nature are different to what was previously assumed. In both the case of the Copernican revolution and the theory of evolution, the developments are ones that dispel the assumption that humans have some kind of unique relationship to the rest of the universe, either by being situated at its center or by being specially created apart from the rest of organic life. What these developments meant for humanity per se, then, Freud suggests psychoanalysis means for the individual ego. It is neither privileged nor unique because the individual consciousness is shaped by parts of the self that are as alien to it as the rest of the universe is.

This view's consequences for the idea of the autonomous subject surface in Freud's discussions of free will. In *The Psychopathology of Everyday Life*, Freud presents an account of how an illusory sense of ourselves as autonomous subjects comes about. He argues that it is our most unimportant and arbitrary thoughts and decisions that seem the most free, but that this does not mean that they are, in actual fact, free. Instead, the feeling tells us only that they are determined by causes that are unconscious and thus not apparent to us. He says that

> it is precisely with regard to the unimportant, indifferent decisions that we would like to claim that we could just as well have acted otherwise: that we have acted of our free—and unmotivated—will. According to our analyses it is not necessary to dispute the right to the feeling of conviction of having a free will. If the distinction between conscious and unconscious motivation is taken into account, our feeling of conviction informs us that conscious motivation does not extend to all our motor decisions. *De minimis non curat lex*. But what is this left free by the one side receives its motivation from the other side, from the unconscious; and in this way the determination in the psychical sphere is still carried out without any gap. (SE 6: 254)

So arbitrary and seemingly free decisions invariably receive their motivation from the unconscious. This is not only true of arbitrary decisions, however, which are unusual only in that their unconscious determinants are, as it were, closer to the surface. For Freud there are in fact no examples of decisions independent of the unconscious. Early in the *Introductory Lectures on Psychoanalysis*, Freud tells his audience that "you nourish the illusion of there being such a thing as psychical freedom, and you will not give it up. I am sorry to say I disagree with you categorically over this" (SE 15: 49). In a later lecture, Freud reiterates this point even more emphatically, saying that the "faith in undetermined psychical events" is "quite unscientific and must yield to the demand of a determinism whose rule extends over mental life" (15: 106). If there is no such thing as an undetermined psychical event, then at some point in any decision the unconscious will have stepped in. This is the view that is propounded in *The Interpretation of Dreams*, where Freud states that

> the unconscious must be assumed to be the general basis of psychical life. The unconscious is the larger sphere, which includes within it the smaller sphere of the conscious. Everything conscious has an unconscious preliminary stage; whereas what is unconscious may

remain at that stage and nevertheless claim to be regarded as having the full value of a psychical process. (5: 611–12)

The only difference between the aforementioned arbitrary choices and ordinary thought is that the unconscious "preliminary stage" occurs immediately before the decision is taken and so appears as a gap in reasoning. The unconscious determinants of behavior, implied in the former case, are nonetheless always at work within the mind.

It is in this context that the "sense of helplessness" that Freud reports in his Italian anecdote, can be understood (*SE* 17: 237). This feeling is prompted by the suggestion that his apparently free actions are in fact the inevitable outworking of unconscious determinants. This is particularly apparent if we take into account Freud's position in *The Psychopathology of Everyday Life*. Freud presents his returns to the street as chance occurrences: "[A]fter having wandered about for a time without enquiring my way, I suddenly found myself back in the same street [. . .] I hurried away once more, only to arrive by another *détour* at the same place" (17: 237). These returns, then, are the result of arbitrary decisions: Freud has not asked the way, but has simply "wandered about," presumably deciding on the spur of the moment which direction to go. Yet according to Freud's own statements these seemingly undetermined choices must betray the causation of the unconscious. A libidinal interpretation of Freud's actions in the narrative seems obvious (Rabaté 77). Freud himself connects his returning to the street with the repetition compulsion; the anecdote is employed by Freud as a demonstration of the uncanny effect of "repetition of the same thing" (*SE* 17: 236). In both these cases, unconscious motives determine Freud to return to the red-light district despite his desire to avoid it. The construction "I found myself" betrays narratively Freud's doubtfulness as to his own agency upon this unexpected arrival: his agency shrinks until his role is only that of finding out what has happened (17: 237).[6] Freud's sense of helplessness in the Italian town, then, is a brief puncturing of his ego's sense of mastery. He feels for a short while that no matter what he does he cannot escape the red-light district. This feeling is merely a recognition that the seemingly free and indifferent choices he makes in his attempts to navigate away from the place are not, in fact, under his control at all.

Living Dolls

It is clearer, then, why animism is a preoccupation in "The 'Uncanny.'" It is for Freud closely related to the uncanny because it bears a surprising resemblance to what he considers the feeling's real source.

Animism is in a sense a mirror image of Freud's own psychoanalytic worldview. Both break down the distinction between the realms of the human and natural. In animism, the realm of the human extends across the whole world, inhabiting it such that nothing is exactly nature in the modern sense. Psychoanalysis reverses this relation. The unconscious is for Freud continuous with the natural world. It is, as Alfred Tauber puts it, "grounded in the biological" (Tauber 96). The repetition compulsion, which Freud alludes to in the Italian anecdote, has a fundamental origin that is "probably inherent in the very nature of the instincts" (SE 17: 138). He ultimately traces the compulsion back to the nature of organic matter in general, saying that it is "the expression of the inertia inherent in organic life," something he suggests is linked back to the law of entropy (18: 36; 38). Given that the unconscious is ever-present in human mental life, then the uncanny consists in a recognition of a state of affairs wherein nature extends fully into the realm of the human. In the psychoanalytic double of animism, it is nature that inhabits the human subject.

It is therefore appropriate that the double is very closely associated with the uncanny feeling (SE 17: 234). In discussing it, Freud lists several psychological roles that the double may have. One is as a representation of the immortal soul as "preservation against extinction" (17: 234). Another is a function of the faculty of self-observation, an alienated part of the mind "which we become aware of as our 'conscience'" (17: 235). Finally, however, Freud suggests that the double may be a product of the belief in free will. He explains:

> There is also all the unfulfilled but possible futures to which we still like to cling in phantasy, all the strivings of the ego which adverse external circumstances have crushed, and all our suppressed acts of volition which nourish in us the illusion of Free Will. (17: 236)

The double in this guise can be thought of as a representation of a hypothetical self. Believing that the future is open, we reinforce this by imagining a double of ourselves having taken a different course of action. The figure of the double in this way serves comfortingly to connote our freedom. It "nourishes the illusion" of free will just as the double as immortal soul both signifies and reinforces belief in a life after death (17: 236).

Of course, this is not the end of the matter. The double is claimed to be frightening and not comforting. Freud's explanation of this stems from the doubling already established between animistic and psychoanalytic worldviews. This is because the double as the symbol of an independent self can be transformed into a threat to it. This is implicit in Freud's account of how the double in general becomes a figure of fear. The double was originally an "energetic denial of the power of death," something which springs "from the primary narcissism which dominates the mind of the child and of primitive man" (17: 235). This is, however, a prelude to the double's transformation into an uncanny object: "[W]hen this stage has been surmounted, the 'double' reverses its aspect. From having been an assurance of immortality, it becomes the uncanny harbinger of death" (17: 235). This process, the reversal of aspect, is the general account that Freud offers for the phenomenon of the uncanny double. He sums up his discussion of the double thus:

> When all is said and done, the quality of uncanniness can only come from the fact of the double being a creation dating back to a very early mental stage, long since surmounted—a stage, incidentally, at which it wore a more friendly aspect. The 'double' has become a thing of terror, just as, after the collapse of their religion, the gods turned into demons. (17: 236)

Freud, however, does not enumerate all the consequences of this account for the several possible significances of the double in this earlier mental stage. Importantly, the logic in the case of the double as guarantor of freedom is identical to the case of the double as guarantor of immortality. The belief in free will, after all, must give way in Freud's worldview just as much as the belief in a life after death. Thus, if the double has a "friendly aspect" in that it reinforces the sense of freedom, its reversed aspect will undermine that sense. It will, in short, become a symbol of the unconscious, which has usurped the autonomous subject's mastery of its own house. Thus, if the double is uncanny because it can connote the dread of impending death, so is it uncanny also because it inspires that very feeling of helplessness which took hold of Freud in his Italian anecdote.

In this sense, the double shares a great deal with the automaton or "living doll." Both are figures that appear indistinguishable from live people, and both serve to highlight the subject's inhabiting by natural forces. The double does this through the "reversal of aspect," which has it undermine rather than reinforce free will. The automaton, for its part, undermines the sense by being under the control of a hidden mechanism. The figure of the automaton exists somewhat peripherally in Freud's essay. He seems initially to downplay the role of automata as objects of very pronounced uncanny effect. The theme of objects that seem to be living but that are in fact inanimate is one raised by the earlier essay on the uncanny to which Freud responds, Ernst Jentsch's "On the Psychology of the Uncanny." After his extended lexical analysis of the term "Unheimliche," Freud moves on to considering instances of objects that arouse the uncanny feeling. He uses Jentsch's essay as a starting point:

> Jentsch has taken as a very good instance "doubts whether an apparently inanimate being is really alive; or conversely, whether a lifeless object might not be in fact animate"; and he refers in this connection to the impression made by waxwork figures, ingeniously constructed dolls and automata. To these he adds the uncanny effect of epileptic fits, and of manifestations of insanity, because these incite in the spectator the impression of automatic, mechanical processes at work behind the ordinary appearance of mental activity. (SE 17: 226)

Jentsch mentions E.T.A. Hoffmann as an author who effectively employs this sort of intellectual uncertainty and Freud takes this mention to refer to Hoffmann's story "The Sandman." Freud thus offers an interpretation of this story that, he claims, shows that Jentsch's emphasis on the automaton or living doll is misguided. "The Sandman" may indeed include an automaton that is doubtfully animate. However, for Freud, the uncanny effect of the story is produced instead by very different thematic elements. After a description of the events of the plot, Freud concludes that there is "no doubt" that the uncanny is related "to the idea of being robbed of one's eyes" (17: 230). He says that Jentsch's theory of "[u]ncertainty whether an object is living or inanimate, which admittedly applied to the doll Olympia, is quite irrelevant in connection with this other, more striking instance of uncanniness" (17: 230). By extension, Freud claims that it is the Sandman figure's association with castration that is the ultimate cause of the uncanny feeling (17: 232). Whatever uncanny effect Olympia has, it seems, is overshadowed. Freud in an extended footnote goes even further, reinterpreting the figure of Olympia with little regard to Jentsch's account. Olympia, he claims, is "a materialisation of Nathaniel's feminine attitude towards his father in infancy" (17: 232n). Freud thus begins his discussion of typically uncanny objects with a seeming rejection of Jenstch's account of the automaton.

    The issue, however, re-emerges both discursively and narratively. Soon after the discussion of "The Sandman," Freud makes a more sympathetic reference to Jentsch's theory of the "living doll" (SE 17:

233). Unlike in the preceding analysis, he does not attack Jentsch's account but instead amends it. He points out that "the idea of a 'living doll' excites no fear at all; children have no fear of their dolls coming to life, they may even desire it" (17: 233). In admitting the uncanniness of the living doll, Freud gestures towards the connection of the automaton with the double. The living doll is originally an unthreatening idea that becomes threatening after childhood belief in it has subsided. That is to say that it corresponds to the logic of the double's reversal of aspect. Later on in the essay, Freud returns to Jenstch's examples. This time it is the related "uncanny effect of epilepsy and madness" that is discussed (17: 243). Of these, Freud says that "[t]he layman sees in them the working of forces hitherto unsuspected in his fellow-men, but at the same time he is dimly aware of them in the remote corners of his own being" (17: 243). This links Jentsch's examples of "epilepsy and madness" to the uncanny coincidences in the Italian anecdote. Both awaken in the subject an awareness of these hidden psychic forces. The uncanny effect of the automaton, then, is a strong theme running through Freud's argument, albeit one that is mainly insinuated or mentioned in passing. More than this, the living doll finds its way into Freud's Italian narrative. One of the few details that Freud mentions about the narrow street to which he returns is that "nothing but painted women were to be seen at the windows of the small houses" (17: 237).[7] Robin Lydenberg comments on the aspects of the women that seem to render them unlike living people. They are "framed by windows that display and immobilise them," and appear "like painted dolls enclosed in miniature domestic spaces" (Lydenberg 1076). Moreover, the reference to windows recalls the neighbor's "glass door" through which Hoffmann's protagonist, Nathaniel, originally observed the doll Olympia in Hoffmann's tale (Hoffmann 147). Like Olympia, these figures are peripheral to the main focus of Freud's story, but their uncanniness is nonetheless difficult to ignore.

Circe's Spell

The fragmentation of the autonomous subject and its inhabiting by unconscious forces is also very much present in Joyce's episode. Just as "Circe" shows spirits animisticaly inhabiting the whole world, it also thematizes the natural and instinctual inhabiting the human. Like in Freud's anecdote, there are living dolls seen through windows: "*Gaudy dollwomen loll in the lighted doorways, in window embrasures, smoking birdseye cigarettes*" (U 429). The metaphor of the prostitute as doll is here made entirely explicit, and the reference to cosmetics with its implication of artifice appears also. Moreover, as in Freud's text, the appearance of the women in liminal spaces such as doorways and windows serves to "display and immobilise" them and renders it difficult to know for certain if they are really women or dolls (Lydenberg 1076). This sense is reinforced by the action of the figures: the fact that they "loll" could speak of their being animate but languorous, or being inanimate dolls hung or propped. The fact that they are described as smoking specifically "birdseye" cigarettes points to a different but related motif. As well as living dolls, human animals abound in "Circe." Animals, of course, are not inanimate, but the living doll and the human animal both represent ways in which the domain of the human is blurred with that of nature. There are, as mentioned above, many instances of animals speaking like humans, such as the dog that becomes Paddy Dignam and the singing moth. There is, too, a "covey of gulls" whose cries suggest a parody of human speech: "Kaw kave kankury kake" (U 430). More often, however, human characters are described in animal terms. Late in the chapter, Cohen is dismissed by Bloom as "mutton dressed as lamb" (517). He goes on to state that her "eyes are as vapid as the glass eyes of your stuffed fox," an image that brings together the blurring of human and animal with the motif of the doll (517). For her part, Bella responds by calling Bloom a "dead cod" (517). Bloom's grandfather, Lipoti Virag, is perhaps the most extreme example of the tendency. The stage directions present him as a veritable menagerie. In the space of four pages he is described as having "weasel teeth" and a "yellow parrotbeak," as well as "turkey wattles" and a "glowworm nose" (482–85). He speaks "in a pig's whisper" or "crows derisively" (484). Importantly, Lipoti Virag is an amateur sexologist, and the link between sex and the animal is central to the episode. Most telling, perhaps, is the appearance of this motif in a description of Zoe:

> (*She leads him towards the steps, drawing him by the odour of her armpits, the vice of her painted eyes, the rustle of her slip in whose sinuous folds lurks the lion reek of all the male brutes that have possessed her.*)
> THE MALE BRUTES (*Exhaling sulphur of rut and dung and ramping in their loosebox, faintly roaring, their drugged heads swaying to and fro*): Good! (472)

The drive towards sexual gratification is here represented by the human becoming animal. Zoe's previous clients are figured as "male brutes" who leave a "lion reek" (472). In the episode's usual procedure, moreover, this figure materializes in the brutes themselves appearing as characters. The metaphorical connection between animal imagery and libido is much wider in the episode. After all, it corresponds to Odysseus's adventure with Circe, the sorceress who used her power to turn his crew into pigs. The setting of the episode in a brothel figures this threatening power as the sexual urge, something that transforms rational humans into beasts.

Closely related is the thematization of sexually transmitted disease. The preoccupation with symptoms recalling those of syphilis serves as a reminder of hidden and ultimately physical determinants of movement and even thought. Important here is Florry's mention of "locomotor ataxy" (*U* 489). This is a reference to locomotor ataxia, a symptom of syphilis that causes the loss of voluntary muscular control. A depiction of a similar condition is included at the very outset of "Circe." There happens past a character who has lost a great deal of control over his movements: "*A deafmute idiot with goggle eyes, his shapeless mouth dribbling, jerks past, shaken in Saint Vitus' Dance*" (408). This description, coming as it does at the very beginning of "Circe," can be read as a statement on what is to come. Frank Budgen reports that Joyce linked the episode itself with syphilitic symptoms, so that "[t]he rhythm is the rhythm of locomotor ataxia" (Budgen 234). As discussed above, the form of "Circe" places great emphasis on undecidable mental images, and this is also part of the thematization, since hallucinations are a notorious symptom of advanced syphilis. The representation of hallucination on the stage drives the action of an important influence on "Circe," Ibsen's play "Ghosts." Syphilis, then, is another aspect of the inhabiting of the subject by extrinsic factors. It is a physical cause, being a disease of the body. Yet it usurps the place of volition and thought. In the case of locomotor ataxia, this is in the motion of the limbs, in which voluntary movement is overridden. The principle here is the same as in Jentsch's and Freud's discussion of "epilepsy and madness," which renders visible the "working of forces hitherto unsuspected" (*SE* 17: 243). Syphilis also makes its presence felt mentally, in the realm of perception, where a physical pathology produces mental images.

Almost everything about "Circe" is marked by the loss of control. The hallucinatory passages are conspicuously unmoored from the conventions of realism. Indeed, their very excess appeals to the logic Freud discusses in *Psychopathology of Everyday Life* and which reappears in the Italian anecdote in "The 'Uncanny'"—that is, the baroque hallucinations are often set off by arbitrary or unimportant things. As we saw above, it is only Zoe's seemingly arbitrary choice to use the phrase "stump speech," and Stephen's seemingly arbitrary reference to "the ends of the world," accidentally misunderstood by Florry, which produce the political and apocalyptic sequences respectively (452; 475). The fact that these trivial causes lead to the most seemingly disproportionate results gives the extraordinary welter of "Circe" its freewheeling quality. Moreover, just as in the Italian anecdote, the very arbitrariness of the causes seems to underdetermine the consequences. This underdetermination suggests an unconscious layer; the hallucinations work instead by unseen or implicit rules of association or motive forces that take over where conscious rules are not applied.

Yet, to say that the form of "Circe" embodies the inhabiting of the self by external forces is an understatement. In fact, the episode dramatizes the dissolution of the unitary autonomous subject far more starkly than even Freud does. Charles Ko discusses this tendency with reference to Joyce's reading of F.W.H. Myers. Myers provided what was likely Joyce's first exposure to psychoanalytic ideas (Ko 743). Myers presents a radically fragmented self, an "occulted, multiply porous and potentially telepathic consciousness existing beneath the surface or 'supraliminal' mind" (743). In this model, information can pass between subliminal and supraliminal, and also subliminally between individuals (745). This outlook radically challenges the boundaries of the self, such that "[o]ne is not merely a multiplicity of subliminal selves, but potentially and telepathically, always already a multiplicity of other selves and other texts" (746). This is linked with "Circe" in that the events of the episode break "logical," "interpersonal," and "narratological" boundaries (746). In this way, the sheer all-encompassing reference of the episode is itself implicated in its model of the self. References are taken from all corners of culture and all parts of *Ulysses* and are presented together without regard to distinctions of inside or out.

Its eclectic content thus combines with the episode's dramatic form, in that the melting away of boundaries is facilitated by its ontological levelling effect. Material internal to the protagonists' minds, such as Bloom's memories of his father or Stephen's of his mother, are presented as independent of the characters themselves. Hélène Cixous sums up the effect, saying Bloom "passes into the street which passes into Bloom. He opens the door opens him and enters the brothel which prostitutes him" (Cixous "At Circe's" 387). The protagonists in "Circe" confront alienated parts of their own selves on the same ontological level as themselves. The fragmentation of the self is also thematized in the form of Bloom's constant costume changes. These insinuate his lack of self-similarity, certainly temporally, in that they continually alter throughout the chapter, but also psychologically, in that like the hallucinations they give solid external form to assorted elements of Bloom's own psyche. This is something Cixous also picks up on, pointing out that Bloom "de-compartmentalizes, identifies himself with a cohort of sub-blooms, flowers, super-blooms, successive booloohooms" (393). "Circe," then, offers an extreme image of how psychoanalysis, whether theorized by Myers or by Freud, challenges the modern tradition of the subject.

The Uncanny and the Sublime

It might seem that the uncanny, as described in Freud's essay and played out in "Circe," has little to do with the sublime. In fact, it seems in certain senses a negation of it. The uncanny, unlike the other iterations of the sublime discussed in previous chapters, appears not to be a way of staging the post-Kantian conception of the autonomous human with respect to nature. Even Schopenhauer, whose position was in many ways close to Freud's, does not make such a departure. Schopenhauer, as we saw, viewed nature as inhabiting the individual in the guise of the will. Yet his theory of the sublime was still based upon the Kantian model of the subject exercising autonomy over the realm of nature—that is, Schopenhauer described the sublime as revealing a possible independence of the subject from the will, even though, as we saw, this can be achieved only mysteriously, passively, or, in the case of the responses of Nietzsche and Conrad, ironically. By contrast, "The 'Uncanny'" seems to stage a dissolution of the modern self, to dismantle once and for all the distinction between human and nature on which this post-Kantian sublime is built.

Yet for all this, the connections between the uncanny and the sublime tradition seem compelling. There is a striking coincidence in iconography between Freud's and Joyce's texts and *The Secret Agent*. There are similarities in setting, of course: all of them are at least partially set in the streets of red-light districts. Other touches, too, are suggestively similar: the animated gas jet in Cohen's brothel corresponds to the ominously purring gas jet that presides over the scene of Verloc's murder in *The Secret Agent* (SA 154). Moreover, in both Conrad's novella and in those texts that relate to the uncanny, automata become a recurring motif. Verloc is described at one point as a self-aware automaton (156). Perhaps the most striking example of this is the pianola or player piano, which features prominently in Cohen's Brothel in "Circe" and in the Silenus Restaurant of *The Secret Agent*. An anecdote related by Frank Budgen is particularly reminiscent of scenes involving Ossipon and the Professor in Conrad's novel:

> Sitting with Joyce in a little café in the Rue de Grenelle our conversation was interrupted by the fierce pounding of an electric piano garnished with coloured lights.
> "Look!" said Joyce. "That's Bella Cohen's pianola. What a fantastic effect! All the keys moving and nobody playing." (Budgen 234)[8]

The obsession with automata in *The Secret Agent* seems in some ways like a proto-uncanny. Coupled with this, there is also the emphasis on trivial details becoming charged with menace, something implicit in Schopenhauer, but emerging as a major theme of "The 'Uncanny.'" *The Secret Agent*'s investment with the sublime, of course, comes from its response to German romanticism and its legacy in the form of Schopenhauer and Nietzsche. Freud's essay is similarly steeped in this background. Freud mentions with approval Schelling's characterization of the uncanny as everything "that ought to have remained secret and hidden but has come to light" and much of his discussion relates to this statement (SE 17: 225). Matt Ffytche, who traces the source of the comment to Schelling's "Philosophy of Mythology" lectures, remarks that this text is one that discusses the rituals of the cult of Dionysus (Ffytche 159). It therefore anticipates and may well have influenced Nietzsche's *The Birth of Tragedy* (158–59). Freud and Nietzsche are thus responding to a common source in texts of German romanticism, and are describing in their own ways a sublime object that is associated with something threatening and primitive. Thus what is "secret and hidden" in Schelling's original discussion is close to what Nietzsche took to be the Dionysiac impulse, and which Freud interprets instead according to his own theory of the unconscious.

Freud's only use of the term "sublime" in the essay also points to this context. This is because it speaks of the sublime's absorption into the concept of the beautiful or of the aesthetic in general and this is a feature of the treatment of the sublime in German idealism. As was discussed in the previous chapter, Schopenhauer's particularly subjective theory of the sublime involves bringing it and the beautiful closer together. This is part of the shift discussed by Paul Guyer of the sublime "ultimately being absorbed into a cognitive interpretation of the beautiful" in German philosophy (Guyer, "German Sublime" 105). It is likely this development that leads to Freud artificially distancing the uncanny from the sublime. In the preamble to his discussion, Freud makes the contention that aesthetics generally does not concern itself with negative feelings like fear:

> As good as nothing is to be found upon this subject in comprehensive treatises in aesthetics, which in general prefer to concern themselves with what is beautiful, attractive and sublime—that is, with feelings of a positive nature—and with the circumstances of the objects which call them forth, rather than with the opposite feelings of repulsion and distress. (SE 17: 219)

It is not easy to tell what precisely Freud means by the sublime as he uses it here in passing. He nonetheless clearly includes it as an example of the concerns of aesthetics as such, which is held to be interested only in positive feelings and the corresponding objects. Indeed, the similarity of the two terms that precede it, "beautiful, attractive," seems to hint that Freud is giving a list of different but effectively equivalent terms, which he holds that aestheticians use to describe their invariably positive subject matter. There could hardly be a clearer instance of the absorption of the term "sublime" into the aesthetic in general than its use here as a near-synonym for "beautiful." The concern with positive feelings shown by this unipolar aesthetics leaves, for Freud, a large gap in that it does not address feelings that are not, or not simply, positive. In theorizing the uncanny, Freud sees himself as addressing this lacuna. The uncanny "is undoubtedly related to what is frightening—to what arouses dread and horror" (17: 219). It is not, however, straightforwardly so. After his lexical study of the term, Freud states that "*heimlich* is a word the meaning of which develops in the direction of ambivalence, until it finally coincides with its opposite, *unheimlich*" (17: 226). The term "*heimlich*" has, in the preceding discussion, been connected to what is pleasantly familiar (17: 223). That "unheimlich develops in the direction of ambivalence" is a fact that proceeds from Freud's contention that the uncanny is "that class of the frightening which leads back to what is known of old and long familiar" (17: 220). The uncanny, therefore, is frightening, but its frightening quality is impossible to disentangle from the very different quality of familiarity. Despite the fact that Freud rejects the term sublime, the uncanny very much occupies its territory: the latter is conceived in opposition to the aesthetics of positive feeling and concerns itself instead with an ambivalent affect. Critics have been quick to point out the inappropriate distinction Freud makes between the sublime and uncanny in these terms.[9] Andrew Smith points out the lineage of the sublime as a negative feeling, citing those authors who most highlight the negative part of the sublime and its consequent ambivalence. He states that "for Kant the sublime takes on a negative quality," and that Freud "also appears to offer a negative version of the sublime, because it is associated with 'unpleasure,' which is similar to Burke's understanding of sublime terror" (A. Smith 149). Harold Bloom makes this point more stridently, saying that Freud's statement "blandly ignores the long philosophical tradition of the negative Sublime" (Bloom, *Agon* 101). If anything, then, Freud's hasty distinction between the sublime and uncanny in fact draws attention to their similarities.

The uncanny's deeper links with the Kantian sublime become apparent in its treatment of ambivalence. In Kant, the ambivalent feeling occasioned by the object implies an excess on the part of the subject, such that the usual relationship with the object underdetermines the subject's response. The same dynamic is at play in Freud's description of the uncanny. The uncanny object is neither straightforwardly frightening nor familiar but ambivalently both. In both cases the ambivalence, the feeling of familiarity when considering something frightening, or the feeling of fear when confronting something familiar, indicates the presence of an excess on the part of the subject. This excess, for Freud, is unconscious content. His general conclusion states that the uncanny occurs when "infantile complexes which have been repressed" are revived, "or when primitive beliefs which have been surmounted seem once more to be confirmed" (SE 17: 248). In the case of "epilepsy or madness," the uncanny effect is produced by evidence of forces that the subject is "dimly aware of [. . .] in remote corners of his own being" (17: 252). That there is a structural resemblance between Kant and Freud on the presence of implicit aspects of the subject is not surprising. It is, after all, in the idealist followers of Kant that the concept of the unconscious has its origin (Ffytche 2). More specifically, the unconscious and the noumenal subject in Freud's and Kant's theories respectively perform similar roles (Pettigrew 76). Here again, Schopenhauer's identification of the thing-in-itself with the will is an important intermediary. Andrew Smith goes so far as to call the sublime "the prototype of the very theoretical basis which underpins psychoanalysis in the first place" (A. Smith 32). It is Harold Bloom who most strongly links Freud with the sublime. He claims that the uncanny is "the only major contribution that the twentieth century has made to the aesthetics of the sublime" (Bloom, *Agon* 101). Bloom renders Freud an out-and-out romantic, locating a connection with the sublime in Freud's mention of the omnipotence of thought:

> Uncanniness is traced back to the narcissistic belief in "omnipotence of thought," which in aesthetic terms is necessarily the High Romantic faith in the power of the mind over the universe of the senses and of death. (102)

However, as we have seen, this is a partial interpretation in that the feeling of helplessness is also uncanny. Inasmuch as the belief in omnipotence of thoughts is an example of a primitive belief that has been surmounted, it is only uncanny in that it indicates the continued influence of unconscious material, not the unbounded power of the mind.

So the uncanny resembles a version of the Kantian sublime, but an inverted one. Where in Kant's theory it is the positive aspect of the feeling that is underdetermined, in that ordinarily threatening objects cause it, in Freud's uncanny it is the negative part of the experience that is excessive—that is, the objects associated with the uncanny are not obviously dangerous or threatening. Indeed, Freud points out that the figure of the living doll is not necessarily frightening (SE 17: 232). The fear, then, is what needs explanation in the uncanny. When considering what is implied by these affective excesses, another reversal is visible. For Kant the excessive positive aspect of the feeling comes from the subject's potential freedom with reference to the object. For Freud, however, the fear in the uncanny comes from the fact that it makes us aware of the forces that, despite us, ultimately determine and dominate our mental life, making freedom illusory.

Surmounting

Yet even these contrasts do not tell the whole story of the uncanny's relationship to the Kantian sublime. There is another tendency in Freud's theory which is in fact not so much an inversion of Kant's sublime, but in fact more like a variation of it. It is not to be found, as Bloom suggests, in an interpretation of animism that compares it to high romantic ideas. Instead, alongside the discussions of animism and Freud's explicit commitment to a scientific-determinist psychoanalytic view, the essay contains assumptions that are much more in line with Kantian ethics. These assumptions are most visible in Freud's view of psychoanalysis not as metapsychology but as therapeutic practice. David Edward Rose and Alfred Tauber have both argued that psychoanalysis as a clinical practice depends heavily on the patient's assumed capacity for autonomy. The aim of the psychoanalytic method, they claim, is to free the patient from the harmful domination of the unconscious and this implies a kind of independence of the ego with reference to it. The importance of this commitment to freedom in the psychoanalytic cure is summed up by Ffytche. He comments upon how Freud's conception of normal mental life is embedded in a gendered set of values that emphasizes autonomy:

> There is no doubt that, as a therapeutic practice, psychoanalysis was meant to strengthen the powers of independence in the individual. Although Freud's remarks on what constitutes psychical health are actually few and far between, where male patients are concerned he invariably raises the issue of overcoming dependency, submissiveness or passivity—by implication, the normal individual is able to handle his own affairs, according to the demands of "reality." (Ffytche 230)

Freudian psychoanalysis, then, aims to guide the patient away from domination and towards autonomy. Rose claims that the Freudian cure does not make conceptual sense within the mechanistic model of the hard determinist:

> The patient's role in the [psychoanalytic] process is to become aware of the wish which he or she finds repugnant and to re-evaluate it. But, if the organism is nothing but a collection of drives and their conflicts, and deliberation is in fact an illusion, in what sense can the ideas be "revaluated"? (Rose 27)

Rose therefore argues that the role played by the patient as a conscious agent is essential, saying that "Freud's most telling discovery" was "the concept of responsibility for one's wishes and drives, the transcending of them and their selection—in short, acts of will—are by far the most effective way to a cure" (27). This aspect of psychoanalytic practice, therefore, cannot be reconciled with the scientific positivism of Freud's metapsychology:

> The goal of analysis is for the patient to become aware of and be able to articulate his motivating desire and the cure resides in judging either the course of action or the desire itself appropriate or inappropriate. In recognizing one's responsibility, one becomes freer. The presentation of Freud's theory of mind could offer no room for such an approach, and it is difficult to see how analysis fits with the bigger, scientific story he wishes to tell. (30)

The most extensive treatment of this issue is Tauber's. He regards the "paradox of a free willed reason coupled to deterministic unconscious forces" as the "basic unresolved tension" of Freud's thought (Tauber 21). Like Rose, he notes that psychoanalysis depends upon escaping the determination of the unconscious:

> Insofar as Freud devised psychoanalysis to break the causal chain of instinctual drives so they might come under the rational control (as opposed to repression) of the ego, and thus free choice—as opposed to psychological determinism—might be achieved, a gap opened before him [. . . .] Freud never explained how the leap from one domain (natural causation) to the other (moral freedom) might be accomplished. (138)

Tauber therefore goes further, interpreting this part of Freud's project as an unacknowledged fellowship with Kant's philosophy. Freud's and Kant's systems, he says, "share a deep philosophical kinship: an ethics of freedom that must be based on reason's independence and capacity to judge itself" (139). For all his talk of the illusion of free will, then, there is a way in which Freud is invested in a notion that resembles Kantian autonomy, one in which the self exercises its independence from the inclinations that stem from natural causation as manifested in the unconscious.

This view is represented in "The 'Uncanny'" in the form of what Freud calls "surmounting." Surmounting occurs when an individual partially or completely abandons erroneous beliefs or ways of thinking in favor of ones that more adequately represent reality. Freud introduces the concept during his discussion of the animistic worldview. Our relationship with animistic beliefs, he claims, is one of incomplete surmounting:

> Let us take the uncanny associated with the omnipotence of thoughts, with the prompt fulfilment of wishes, with secret injurious powers and with the return of the dead. The condition under which the feeling of uncanniness arises here is unmistakable. We—or our primitive forefathers—once believed that these possibilities were realities, and were convinced that they actually happened. Nowadays we no longer believe in them, we have surmounted these modes of thought; but we do not feel quite sure of our new beliefs, and the old ones still exist within us ready to seize upon any confirmation. (SE 17: 247)

Things are surmounted, then, when a more rational appreciation of reality is adopted. It is not the case, for instance, that the dead return, or that wishes can have physical effects by themselves. Freud therefore adopts the term "surmounting" as a way to characterize our outgrowth of narcissistic attitudes, which are ultimately incompatible with the reality principle. This is even more explicit in Freud's discussion of the double as an assurance of immortality. He claims that ideas of the double as a "preservation against extinction" have "sprung from the soil of unbounded self-love, from the primary narcissism which dominates the mind of the child and of primitive man," before adding that "when this stage has been surmounted, the 'double' reverses its aspect" (17: 235). This narcissism is for Freud an unconscious belief: "[O]ur unconscious has as little use now as it ever did for the idea of our own mortality" (17: 242). Surmounting therefore involves the process of adapting ourselves to reality and simultaneously freeing ourselves from the domination of the unconscious, a process that for Freud is the path to a normal mental life. In that incorrect beliefs give way, even if partially, to more accurate ones, surmounting must resemble the deliberation that Rose mentions as a prelude to the exercise of will. The similarity of this process to that of the psychoanalytic cure is striking. Importantly, surmounting is different from repression. Freud takes care to distinguish the two as relating to the uncanny associated with infantile complexes and the uncanny associated with primitive beliefs:

> We might say that in the one case what has been repressed is a particular ideational content, and in the other the belief in its (material) reality. But this last phrase no doubt extends the term "repression" beyond its legitimate meaning. It would be more correct to take into account a psychological distinction which can be detected here, and say that the animistic beliefs of civilised people are in a state of having been (to a greater or lesser extent) *surmounted* [rather than repressed]. (17: 249)[10]

It is not simply the case that the kind of content involved is different in cases of repression and of surmounting. Rather, the difference in content speaks of these being very different processes. Unlike repression, for instance, surmounting is conceived as a process that can at least potentially be stable and complete. It offers, if it is carried out thoroughly enough, immunity to the uncanny: "[A]nyone who has completely and finally rid himself of animistic beliefs will be insensible to this type of the uncanny" (17: 248). Thus, just as in the result of a successful psychoanalysis, surmounting is different from, and preferable to, repression. This is because it confers on the subject a permanent and stable freedom from continuing symptoms of unconscious content. Moreover, like the cure, it is achieved through rational deliberation and the subject's choosing to endorse beliefs that better allow it to navigate reality.

It is when the relationship of surmounting to Kantian freedom is considered that Freud's uncanny can best be compared with the sublime and its ambivalence towards agency seen in the clearest light. For Kant, the sublime allows us to infer our own freedom to act according to reason outside of nature's causation. Freud's uncanny, by contrast, allows us to infer our ability to surmount narcissistic ways of thinking and therefore discloses our ability to bring reason to bear on the contents of the unconscious. This is an aspect of the theory that is not emphasized by Freud, who presents the finding of an object uncanny as a crisis of surmounting. Nevertheless, the discovery of an implicit ability to surmount is essential to the uncanny as Freud conceives it. At one point he offers an approximation of the cognition at work in a judgement of the uncanny:

> As soon as something actually happens in our lives which seems to confirm the old, discarded beliefs we get a feeling of the uncanny; it is as though we were making a judgement something like this: "So, after all, it is *true* that one can kill a person by the mere wish!" (17: 247–48)

The implicit statement here expresses both the surmounted belief and simultaneously the fact of its surmounting. The statement's tone of surprise, its italics and exclamation mark attest to the latter. To paraphrase Freud, the "after all" is the token of surmounting.[11] Thus, as soon as we become aware of the narcissistic belief, we become aware that we have, if unsteadily, surmounted it. The uncanny, then, is an instance in which an object calls forth primitive unconscious material that frightens the subject, but it also negatively demonstrates the subject's ability to surmount, to become free of, this material just as Kant's sublime negatively demonstrates our autonomy as moral beings. Yet there is an extra twist to the uncanny compared to Kant's sublime. While the uncanny does reveal the possibility of surmounting, it does so only when it is incomplete. If we had, as Freud suggests is possible, surmounted the primitive beliefs so completely as to be immune to the uncanny, then it would be impossible to have this aesthetic awareness of the fact that we had surmounted them: the surmounting would be invisible. The uncanny therefore intimates the possibility of surmounting, but it simultaneously emphasizes those cases in which surmounting is provisional and unstable. It is this aspect, most of all, which explains why the uncanny is such a tricky concept, marked by myriad ambivalences. It also explains why the essay "The 'Uncanny'" is itself such a bizarre one.

Sigmund Astray

Any reading of "The 'Uncanny'" must take into account its singular stylistic features. Many critics have commented on the evasive rhetorical maneuvers that Freud employs. This widespread feeling is what Hélène Cixous articulates when she says that "this long text of Freud employs a particularly disquieting method to track down the concept Das Unheimliche" (Cixous, "Fiction" 525). This makes the piece, ostensibly a theoretical essay on aesthetics, seem to be "less a discourse than a strange theoretical novel" (525). Prominent among such features of the text is Freud's apparent loss of agency with respect to his subject matter. Freud at various times makes reference to a lack of control over his discourse. This is apparent at the very outset of the essay, which Freud begins: "It is only rarely that a psycho-analyst feels impelled to investigate the subject of aesthetics" (SE 17: 219). Why Freud "feels impelled" to do so on this occasion, and which force is doing the impelling, is not made clear in the ensuing text.[12] What is clear is that Freud opens with an implicit disavowal of agency; he tells the reader that he "feels impelled," just as he will later feel helpless in the Italian anecdote (17: 219). Further into the essay, there occurs a section in which Freud musters possible doubts that a reader may have regarding his theory. This is done initially with some considerable explanation of each potential doubt. Two paragraphs in, however, the list begins to spin out of control. Freud pours forth a long paragraph of objections, of which the following quotation is representative:

> Who would be so bold as to call it uncanny, for instance, when Snow-White opens her eyes once more? And the resuscitation of the dead in accounts of miracles, as in the New Testament, elicits feelings quite unrelated to the uncanny [. . .] And once more: what is the origin of the uncanny effect of silence, darkness and solitude? [. . .] And are we after all justified in entirely ignoring intellectual uncertainty as a factor, seeing that we have admitted its importance in relation to death? (17: 246–47)

The multiplicity of objections here is emphasized by the liberal use of conjunctions, generally at the start of sentences: "Then, too"; "Or again"; "And once more," (17: 246). No time is spent expanding upon these counterarguments or signaling possible rebuttals. Instead, Freud's mastery of his subject matter is seemingly lost in this flood of objections. Following this, Freud considers throwing up his hands and leaving the issue to the aestheticians: "We might say that these preliminary results have satisfied *psychoanalytic* interest in the problem of the uncanny, and that what remains probably calls for an *aesthetic* enquiry" (17: 247). However, Freud ultimately presses on with a discussion of the uncanny in fiction. The sense, which existed from the outset, that the subject matter is not quite under Freud's control nevertheless persists. Just before the end of the essay there is another similar protestation on his part. After discussing the peculiarly directive power of the storyteller over the audience, Freud says that "[w]e have drifted into this field of research half involuntarily, through the temptation to explain certain instances which contradicted our theory of the causes of the uncanny" (17: 251–52). Thus the fusillade of objections discussed above has, it seems, deflected Freud, "half involuntarily" from his argument. Freud's volition is thus in question all through his discourse, as evidenced by the similarity of this statement on the final page to the mention of mysterious impulsion in the very opening sentence. The doubt that he casts over his mastery of his own topic is a persistent feature of the rhetorical strategy in this most unusual disquisition.

Critics have come up with a great many accounts of the essay that address these factors. Each offer interpretations to the effect that Freud, in Robert Young's phrase, "finds himself [. . .] caught up in the very processes he seeks to understand" (Young 93).[13] This is true, but not straightforwardly so. The twists and turns and seeming befuddlement on the part of Freud's voice should not be taken too quickly at face value. They are elements of what can be understood as a staging of the uncanny at the discursive level. Freud, in effect, dramatizes himself as the narrator of the essay. The uncanny, as Freud theorizes it, depends upon a surmounting that is unsteady and partial, and when writing about the uncanny, Freud takes on this unsteadiness. In the Italian anecdote, Freud bolsters his own authority to talk about the uncanny by describing an incident in which he had a strong experience of it. To do this, then, it is necessary to present a moment of personal embarrassment and ineffectuality in narrative form. Freud's repeated claims of discursive befuddlement can be read as just such a self-dramatizing maneuver. There is good reason to think that Freud felt such a move was necessary. Near the beginning of the essay he protests his unsuitability for the task of theorizing the uncanny. He has, he says, very little feeling for it: "The writer of the present contribution, indeed, must plead guilty to a special obtuseness in the matter, where extreme delicacy of perception would be more in place" (*SE* 17: 220). What is implied is that Freud has rendered himself immune to the uncanny by surmounting it in the way he subsequently discusses. The paradox here is that the very thorough theoretical understanding that gives him the ability to theorize the uncanny, threatens to deprive him of that very ability. He therefore continues:

> It is long since he has experienced or read anything which has given him an uncanny impression, and he must start by translating himself into that state of feeling, by awakening in himself the possibility of experiencing it. (17: 220)

This, as Smith points out, is an extraordinary claim. Freud "suggests the possibility of entering a state of uncanniness rather than simply encountering it" (A. Smith 149). Despite the tone found elsewhere in the essay, Freud here betrays a remarkable confidence in his ability to theorize the uncanny. Yet he cannot be too confident in asserting this ability because, as we saw, the subject must be made ambiguously uncertain of its own independence of the unconscious in order to feel the uncanny. Therefore, in surmounting it enough to theorize it, Freud must protest his own helplessness. It is important to note that here Freud talks about himself in the third person as "the writer," a construction that finds an echo in his comment that he "found himself" back in the Italian street (*SE* 17: 237). Here, too, Freud is adopting a persona, one who throughout the essay is presented as victim of the uncanny. Thus he is "impelled" to investigate the subject, he is led into "half involuntar[y]" digressions and courts total theoretical failure. Regardless whether Freud in fact is in total control of his brief at these points, he presents himself in the guise of author as being, just as he was in the provincial Italian town, lost and helpless.

Bloom's Moly

As drastic as Freud's staging of the uncanny is, it is nothing to "Circe." As was mentioned above, the form of the episode embodies much of the worldview of the uncanny. The hallucinatory content and dramatic form combine to produce the effect of the dissolution of the subject. The episode does not betray even Freud's lingering commitment to a Kantian model of autonomy and the self. For this reason, it seems a difficult task to understand the episode in anything like the same terms. Here character is apparently demoted from its position in the narrative. Center stage is instead held by associations, allusions, jokes, and parodies. Yet it would not be correct to say that the episode is not invested in a certain model of subjectivity, or even a certain model of freedom. Indeed, it is even invested in a relationship to the sublime, if a largely parodic one.

The episode's engagement with models of the self is visible in the behavior of Stephen Dedalus. Stephen is committed to a romantic kind of subjectivity, insisting on his own individuality and autonomy. His reaction to the above-mentioned appearance of his deceased mother is an example. Stephen falls into denial:

> STEPHEN (*Horrorstruck*): Lemur, who are you? What bogeyman's trick is this? (*U* 539)

The apparition asks him, as his mother did on her death bed, to pray. Stephen reacts to its exhortation that he "repent!" with his characteristic defiance (541). He slips into vehement declarations of autonomy. He exclaims his famous "*Non serviam!*" and desperately challenges all the forces that threaten to master him: "No! No! No! Break my spirit all of you if you can! I'll bring you all to heel!" (541). He then flourishes his ashplant and runs from Cohen's brothel. What he finds in the street is another kind of alien force, and his reaction to it is much the same. He bumps into a pair of pugnacious soldiers, Private Compton and Private Carr. Much as he fell into denial when confronted with the apparition of his mother, so Stephen stays resolutely in denial about the danger that this street altercation poses. He rebuffs Bloom's attempts to caution him:

> BLOOM (*Elbowing through the crowd, plucks Stephen's sleeve vigorously*): Come now, professor, that carman is waiting.
> STEPHEN (*Turns*): Eh? (*He disengages himself.*) Why should I not speak to him or to any human being who walks upright on this oblate orange? (*He points his finger.*) I'm not afraid of what I can talk to if I see his eye. Retaining the perpendicular. (547)

Stephen insists on standing up to the soldiers and to the institutional powers they represent. He antagonizes them further with another declaration to the effect that he will not serve: "(*He taps his brow.*) But in here it is I must kill the priest and the king" (548). In his frequent declarations, and in his shaking off grasps and his running from buildings, Stephen thus spends much of the episode attempting to deny that the world around him, either internally in the form of memory or externally in the form of political power, has any hold on him.

Yet, of course, in the nighttown of "Circe," the hollowness of this attitude becomes particularly apparent. Stephen's outspoken assertions of autonomy are rendered doubtful in various ways. The memories against which he is struggling in this episode are particularly potent ones for him. The nighttown locale is the same as that in which the character had his first sexual experience, visiting a prostitute in *A Portrait of the Artist as a Young Man*. Also, the painful memory of his mother has been troubling Stephen since the uncomfortable conversation had with Buck Mulligan in the book's first episode. These memories in fact seem to come close to overwhelming Stephen. Uniquely in the episode, Stephen's loss of composure is commented upon by nearby characters who do not seem to be involved in the hallucination. Thus, when the apparition of his mother makes its first appearance, Florry comments "Look! He's white." (U 540). His violent reaction leads Lynch to attempt to restrain him (542). The fact that Stephen is sent running from the brothel in fear casts doubt about how much he can indeed bring to heel those powers that oppress him. Likewise, his defiant pose in conversation with Privates Compton and Carr is only so much bravado. Immediately after he reproves Bloom's warnings and talks of "retaining the perpendicular," Stephen's inebriation undermines him:

(He staggers a pace back.)
BLOOM (Propping him): Retain your own. (547–48)

This confrontation ends with Stephen having been knocked out by Private Carr. Stephen ends up "prone" and "stunned" (558). Despite his protestations, then, Stephen is tossed about by alien forces and finishes the episode barely conscious.

Yet, as the seeming chaos of nighttown seems to expose the failure of one model of the subject, it does perhaps suggest a possible alternative. This alternative model is centered around the treatment of Bloom in the episode. Bloom is far from the traditional subject of the sublime. In fact, some of the hallucinations savagely parody this kind of subjectivity and the gendered aspects of the sublime in particular. Nevertheless, Bloom's treatment does affirm a certain kind of response to the challenge of the uncanny. Of all Bloom's hallucinations, perhaps the most memorable is the long sadomasochistic sequence. During this passage, "*Non serviam!*" is emphatically reversed for Bloom. Cohen visits various forms of violence on him with his acquiesence. Cohen twists the feminized Bloom's arm, "grabs her hair violently and drags her forward," and "quenches his cigar angrily on Bloom's ear" (U 499; 501). Besides these actions, Cohen threatens other, more theatrical and gruesome, punishments (499). Throughout this, Bloom puts up only feeble defense. Moreover, Cohen explicitly deprives Bloom of any independence: "(*He places a ruby ring on her finger.*) And there now! With this ring I thee own. Say, thank you, mistress," a command with which

Bloom complies (504). Bloom is threatened, indeed, with becoming one of the living dolls:

> BELLO (*Points to his whores*): As they are now, so will you be, wigged, singed, perfumesprayed, ricepowdered, with smoothshaven armpits. Tape measurements will be taken next your skin. You will be laced with cruel force into vicelike corsets of soft dove coutille, with whalebone busk, to the diamond trimmed pelvis, the absolute outside edge, while your figure, plumper than when at large, will be restrained in nettitght frocks, pretty two ounce petticoats and fringes and things stamped, of course, with my houseflag, creations of lovely lingerie for Alice and nice scent for Alice. (502)

The specter of domination, of uncanny helplessness, invests the litany Cohen here delivers. The intermingling of artificial and animate comes to the fore once again. The list focusses obsessively on non-living materials: fabrics, cosmetics, and garments. Yet these are to be brought into such close contact with Bloom that he will, it seems, lose his status as a living being at all. The best example of this is the mention of the "diamond trimmed pelvis" (502). This refers ostensibly to a part of the aforementioned corset, but, coming immediately as it does after the mention of "whalebone," it carries with it the disturbing implication that Bloom's pelvis might be accessorized in this way. Bloom is seemingly to become transformed inside and outside into a piece of artifice. The uncanniness of the living doll is even embodied grammatically. The cluster of words at the beginning of the speech "wigged, singed, perfumesprayed, ricepowdered," might initially seem to be verbs in the past tense but turn out to be used attributively as adjectives modifying "they" (502). The grammatical wrongfooting caused by apparent verbs turning out merely descriptive conveys a sense of the strange artificiality of Cohen's inanimate "dollwomen."

This hallucination is the opposite of a staging of the autonomous individual. It involves instead the most extreme subjection. Nevertheless, in the mixture of emotions that are in play, it resembles the affective structure of the sublime. Lisa Rado points out the "affective similarities between [the] descriptions of masochistic bondage and the commonly held emotions associated with sublime transport" (Rado 51). Despite the suffering inflicted upon him, Bloom evidently feels a positive aspect to the experience, at least initially. He is "enthralled" by Cohen's "magnificence" and "hugeness," the language here overlapping with the themes of scale, grandeur, and ecstasy so prominent in descriptions of the sublime (U 498). Shortly before this sequence, Virag has declared that "[f]rom the sublime to the ridiculous is but a step!" (484). Given this, the echoes of the sublime in the Bella/Bello passage can be read as suggesting an irreverent parody, pointing out how close the sublime can be to masochism. The scene also implicates the longstanding gendered associations of the sublime. For much of its history, the sublime was implicitly associated with masculinity. This is perhaps most obvious in Burke, where both the object and subject of the sublime were associated with maleness. Although disputed by figures such as Mary Wollstonecraft, Burke's gendering had an extensive influence. Kant's early work echoed Burke on this point, with his *Observations on the Feeling of the Beautiful and Sublime* stating that the "fair sex has just as much understanding as the male, but it is a *beautiful understanding*, whereas ours should be a *deep understanding*, an expression that signifies identity with the sublime" (Kant, *Observations* 78). Even in Kant's later works, the sublime subject was implicitly male (Battersby 60). This is something he shares with Freud. Barbara Claire Freeman argues that Freud expresses a view of gender that was previously articulated in the Kantian sublime. For Freeman, Freud's idea of normal feminine sexuality depends upon the recognition and acceptance of lack, and this is "strikingly congruent" with "the imagination's perception of its own inadequacy" in the process of the Kantian sublime (Freeman 73). A part of the parodic treatment of the sublime in "Circe," then, is an undercutting of its masculine associations. Bloom's androgyny is highlighted at crucial points. As was discussed, the Cohen sequence involves an undecidable switching of gender. Before this, Bloom is examined by a team of physicians and pronounced "bisexually abnormal" and "'a finished example of the new womanly man" (U 165). Most significantly, in this passage Bloom is diagnosed with "hypsospadia." As Rado points out, this term combines "hypospadia," a condition that causes male genitals to resemble female genitals in some respects, with the term "hypsos," the original Greek term as used in Longinus's treatise, which is translated as "sublime" (Rado 44–45). The word, then, unites an idea of the sublime and the suggestion of hermaphroditism. This is consistent with the treatment of Bloom in the chapter. His experiences present him as on many fronts a subversion of the sublime subject as male, unitary, and autonomous.

For all this, however, Bloom is not undermined in the way that Stephen is. After the sadomasochistic hallucination, Bloom is able to meet Cohen eye to eye, acting with a quiet confidence. He procures the talismanic potato Zoe took from him: "(*Gently.*) Give me back the potato, will you?" (U 518). His new mien even earns the admiration of the erstwhile fearsome Bello: Bella says "(*Admiringly.*) You're such a slyboots, old cocky. I could kiss you" (520). Most of all, Bloom is effective in taking care of Stephen. Although he does not prevent Stephen's being knocked out, without his presence Stephen would have been in considerably worse shape. Cohen tries to extort money from Stephen, threatening to call the police (543). Bloom, however, manages to warn her off, employing information he learned earlier in the episode about Cohen's son in Oxford (544). Similarly, after his altercation with the soldiers, members of the watch threaten to take Stephen's name and address, something that would lead at least to a scandal. Bloom again smooths things over, and does it in an unassuming way, enlisting the help of passerby Corny Kelleher (561). Karen Lawrence holds that the goings-on of the episode are not decisive events, but rather "suggestions to the reader" about the characters (Lawrence 159). Certainly, the thorough dispensing with narrative conventions of realism does serve to demote the importance of incident as such. Nevertheless, what is suggested throughout "Circe" about the character of Bloom is that he exemplifies qualities appropriate to an alternative model of subjectivity.

One way of conceiving this is with reference to the Homeric resonance of the chapter. The particular qualities that Bloom displays can be related to the idea of "moly." In *The Odyssey*, moly is the herb Odysseus uses to render himself immune to Circe's sorcery, and so avoid being transformed into a swine. In Joyce's correspondence with Frank Budgen, he speculates at some length on what in the episode could correspond to moly. After his initial ideas about moly being "laughter," Joyce returns to the subject (Joyce 144). In this further discussion, aspects of character are prominent:

> Moly is a nut to crack. My latest is this. Moly is a gift of Hermes, god of the public ways and is the invisible influence (prayer, chance, agility, presence of mind, power of recuperation) which saves in the case of accident. (Joyce 147)

Prominent in this list are character traits, and these traits correspond to a great degree with Bloom's. Bloom at one point dwells explicitly upon how one of these qualities has saved him in the case of an accident. He reflects upon a tram that nearly hit him at the beginning of the episode, saying "[m]ight have lost my life too with that magongwheeltracktrolleyglarejuggernaut only for presence of mind" (U 429). These clues all suggest the model of agency that allows Bloom to retain his independence in nighttown. These qualities, "power of recuperation," "presence of mind," and "agility," are all continuous with the Ulyssean cunning Bloom displays elsewhere in the novel. "Circe," for Lawrence, is "a stunning image of Bloom's ability to survive," something which "we have seen all day" (Lawrence 163).

There are a couple of reasons that the kind of qualities that moly represents constitute an appropriate response to the subjectivity implied by the uncanny. The first concerns the combination of chance and presence of mind, particularly as it relates to noticing trivial matters. A good example of this is found immediately after the sadomasochistic sequence with Cohen. This is the passage that finds Bloom confronted by the nymph, who plays the role of an idealized femininity and has Bloom cringing in shame before her:

THE NYMPH (*Loftily*): We immortals, as you saw today have not such a place and no hair there either. We are stonecold and pure. We eat electric light. (*She arches her body in lascivious crispation, placing her forefinger in her mouth.*) Spoke to me, heard from behind. How then could you...
BLOOM (*Pacing the heather abjectly*): O, I have been a perfect pig. Enemas too, I have administered. (U 514)

This, situation, however, does not last; the scene reaches a turning point shortly afterwards:

THE NYMPH (*Eyeless, in nun's white habit, coif and huge winged wimple, softly, with remote eyes.*): Tranqilla convent. Sister Agatha. Mount Carmel, the apparitions of Knock and Lourdes. No more desire. (*She reclines her head, sighing.*) Only the ethereal. Where dreamy creamy gull waves o'er the waters dull.
(*Bloom half rises. His back trousers' button snaps.*)
THE BUTTON: Bip!
[...]
BLOOM (*Coldly*): You have broken the spell. The last straw. If there were only ethereal where would you all be, postulants and novices? Shy but willing like an ass pissing. (516)

Bloom seizes upon the bathos of the burst trouser button as an opportunity to reassess the assumptions, roles, and relations implied in the hallucination. In order to interrogate the nymph's idealized femininity, Bloom musters instead his experience of married life with his unfaithful wife, Molly: "(*Calls after her.*) As if you didn't get it on the double yourselves. No jerks and multiple mucosities all over you. I tried it. Your strength and our weakness. What's our studfee?" (517). Molly represents a very much embodied femininity: she is neither idealized, nor doll-like, and her name is, incidentally, one letter away from that of moly. Bloom is able, then, to bring this experience to bear in pointing out the contingency of the roles that are implied by the figure of the nymph. It should not be passed over, however, that it is the chance occurrence of Bloom's trouser button snapping that breaks the nymph's hold over him, a small, trivial event that Bloom takes as his opportunity. For Freud, as we saw, trivial things that fall beneath the notice of the ego are directly determined by the unconscious. This leads to their potential to produce uncanny effects, as in his Italian wanderings. It is Bloom's presence of mind that guards against this. Rather than failing to notice trivialities, or alternatively, being discomfited by the hidden forces potentially revealed by them, Bloom notices them and is sensitive to their implications. In this way, the "invisible influence" of the unconscious is treated not as a threat, but is associated with the saving herb.

This is the attitude that Bloom displays throughout the episode. When arbitrary decisions or chance occurrences provoke baroque hallucinations, Bloom does not attempt to deny or resist them. In contrast to Stephen lashing out at the vision of his mother, Bloom is an active participant and makes the most of his attention to his surroundings. Related to this is the "agility" that Joyce identifies (Joyce 147). Bloom is not so much physically agile but able to adapt himself to situations. It is this ability that is suggested in Bloom's costume changes. Most characters in "Circe," even if they are outlandishly dressed, tend to retain the same costume. This, as we saw, is not the case for Bloom, who spends the episode passing through a huge range of different costumes. This is, as Lawrence would have it, an "image" of Bloom's particular agility. This agility, moreover, takes the form of an ability to deal with the subject implied by the uncanny, the subject inhabited by the unconscious. Each of the costumed Blooms, after all, are versions of himself that are inhabited by, or even inhabiting, a certain unconscious content.

This, then, is the fundamental contrast between "Circe" and "The 'Uncanny'" as stagings of the subject. Freud stages himself, in the Italian anecdote and as author of the essay, with an unspoken commitment to a kind of autonomy fitting within the tradition of the post-Kantian sublime. In the essay this is bound up with his own ability to rationally surmount the uncanny. Yet his theory means that he can only do this unsteadily and ambivalently. He must present himself as a subject in a certain kind of crisis of autonomy. Joyce, for his part, stages Bloom not as a masculine subject clinging to unity and independence, but as androgynous and already fragmented, myriad versions of the same person. For just this reason, he is a subject ideally suited to navigate nighttown.

Conclusion

The Sublime beyond the Uncanny

With "The 'Uncanny,'" we come to a threshold. Freud's essay can be interpreted as a culmination or terminal point of the sublime. Indeed, general accounts of the sublime's development after romanticism often find its destination in the uncanny. Harold Bloom regards it as "the only major contribution that the twentieth century has made to the aesthetics of the sublime" (Bloom, *Agon* 101). This statement is striking for its exclusivity: the uncanny is the century's only development, and it came early in that century. Elsewhere, Bloom calls the uncanny "our modern form" of the sublime, once again suggesting that there is no aesthetic of the sublime to be found today, only its uncanny descendant (Bloom, *The Sublime* xv). This view is reflected in other sources. Both Andrew Smith and David Ellison put the uncanny at the latter end of their itineraries of the post-romantic sublime. It is a fairly widely held view, then, that the uncanny as theorized by Freud is in some way an end point of the sublime tradition. It is this view that I wish here to examine. Reflecting on the history of the sublime drawn in the foregoing chapters both reinforces this view in some ways and in some ways complicates it. The uncanny investigated in the previous chapter provides an important stage in this history, and in some ways might be considered a point of exit from the post-Kantian sublime. It represents the culmination of a number of tendencies that develop throughout the texts studied. However, the idea that the uncanny simply provides a conclusion to the story of the sublime should be resisted. The sublime's renewed presence in philosophical discourse in the late twentieth century shows that this is too neat a conclusion. Jean-François Lyotard's "Answering the Question: What is Postmodernism?" is a text that acknowledges the drift in conceptions of the subject that took place since Kant's formulation, but which nevertheless still embraces the sublime as a structure or grammar of staging the autonomous subject.

The first thread that runs through the texts in this study is the use of the sublime to articulate ever more problematic relationships between the human and the natural. This starts from an immediately post-Kantian view of the human as locus of moral autonomy independent of natural determination, the view that, as Schiller put it, "[a]ll other things must; the human being is the entity that wills" (Schiller 70). Even though Marx and Engels were scathing of Kant, neither they, nor Carlyle, seriously question the central importance of freedom as a distinguishing characteristic of human beings and their sublimes instead concern the hampering or realization of this freedom at a societal level. Wells, in his post-Darwinian moment, has a darker view. While his nonfiction is optimistic, *The Time Machine* depicts a world in which the mastery of nature, assumed by the mid-century authors, is shown as illusory. The staging of the sublime Wells employs in the novel reveals the breaking down of the distinctions he later attempts to maintain between the human and natural. The final two chapters show nature striking ever closer to home on an individual level. Conrad was influenced by the same scientific discourses as Wells, but more so by Schopenhauer's pessimistic strain of German idealism. For Conrad as for Schopenhauer, the true reality of the human self is as continuous with the rest of an absurd cosmos, something that threatens a fate of suffering and ineffectuality. This process then culminates in Freud's "The 'Uncanny,'" where the very self-similarity of the subject is called into doubt. Freud's uncanny raises the possibility of a worldview far different from the Kantian one. Here the human subject is "not even master in its own house" (SE 16: 283–84). It is devoid of unity and integrity and its naive understanding of itself as separate from nature is undermined by nature's unaccountable "inhabiting" of the self.

As the background assumptions of these various authors have nature striking closer and closer to the subject, so there is a parallel movement in the way their sublime manifests itself. Carlyle, followed by Marx and Engels, makes the first move. These authors reposition the iconography of the sublime to fit their emphasis on social and political issues. Thus the traditional objects of the sublime become a source of imagery, used to illuminate the power of the industrial world, as in Carlyle's comparison of Manchester with Niagara Falls. *The Time Machine* finds a sublime in nature that is subtly but even more profoundly different. The objects of Wells's sublime are natural, but are distinctive in that they are theory laden—that is, they are not aspects of nature as ordinarily seen, but are filtered, as it were, through the findings of thermodynamics and geology. Thus the Time Traveller describes a landscape lit by the final glow of a dying sun, or his vision of deep time passing before his eyes. Where the objects of the sublime in *The Time Machine* are filtered through particular scientific theories, those in *The Secret Agent* are filtered through any number of subjective circumstances. Drawing from Schopenhauer's aesthetics, potentially any object that confronts Conrad's characters, be it a buzzing fly, an upturned hat, or a feeble elderly man, can become an object of the sublime. This process, too, reaches its apogee in the uncanny narratives of Freud and Joyce. Here the emphasis on the subjective is so strong that there may not need to be an object as such at all. Situations count, as do dreams and hallucinations. Those objects that do evoke the uncanny themselves, doubles and living dolls, stand in for obscure and unacknowledged parts of the self.

The texts in the previous chapter therefore see the culmination of two linked tendencies that develop through these iterations of the sublime. They also present in various ways a profound challenge to the sublime tradition. The sublime in "Circe" appears perverted and parodied as a kind of masochism, and both Joyce's chapter and Freud's essay hint towards a model of the subject radically different from those held by the post-Kantians. For all that the uncanny is a culmination of the sublime, then, it seems to move away from it. Yet there is another thread in all these versions of the sublime, one which runs through the uncanny and beyond it. This is found in the way that the sublime works between philosophy and literature, the way it lends itself to thinking the subject dramatically. This was implicit in Kant, whose theory of the sublime essentially involves a kind of staging, an implicit imagining of the subject as a moral hero overcoming nature. This was built upon by Schiller, who found the sublime in artworks, like the Laocoön group, that play out this confrontation. Marx and Engels powerfully evoke the sweep of modern history as a background against which the proletariat emerges and Wells stages a hero grappling physically and cognitively with the world in all its temporal extent. As the subject becomes more problematic, so an appeal to literary categories becomes even more important. Conrad's response to pessimism is ultimately irony, staging a hero in the Assistant Commissioner whose prime virtue is that he is all too aware of the text he is in. To explain the uncanny, Freud ultimately makes himself a character in his essay, both in his strange Italian anecdote, and in the turns and protestations of his discursive voice. Finally, Leopold Bloom navigates nighttown and ultimately maintains his own sense of self precisely through portraying himself again and again in myriad different costumes and roles. For all the differences, Bloom returns to the act of imagining the possibilities of the self, something implicit from the third *Critique*.

More than anything else, it is this tendency that causes writers to keep returning to the sublime. It is at play in the second great flourishing of overt philosophical interest in the later twentieth century. This revival was in large part kickstarted by Lyotard's use of the sublime in his essay "Answering the Question: What is Postmodernism?" Lyotard signals his awareness of some of the issues that mark "The 'Uncanny.'" He prefaces his discussion of the Kantian sublime by saying that it must be submitted "to that severe reexamination which postmodernity imposes on the thought of the Enlightenment, on the idea of a unitary end of history and of a subject" (Lyotard 73). Among other things, then, Lyotard recognizes that, in an intellectual moment well after the uncanny, the traditional conception of the autonomous subject that was the basis of the Kantian staging cannot be taken for granted. This caveat surfaces again when Lyotard writes that in "the tradition of the subject, which comes from Augustine and Descartes, and which Kant does not radically challenge," the ambivalent feeling of the sublime "develops as a conflict between the faculties of a subject" (77). Lyotard deals with this question by moving his discussion from being in terms of faculties to being in terms of his Wittgenstein-influenced language games. Indeed, the two seem to be treated somewhat interchangeably. He says that the sublime should not be expected to "effect the last reconciliation between language games (which, under the name of faculties, Kant knew to be separated by a chasm)" (81).

Yet beyond the substitution of language games for faculties, Lyotard's account of the sublime is very readily recognizable from the kind of treatments seen in the foregoing chapters. He utilizes the classic affective structure, insisting the "the real sublime sentiment" is "an intrinsic combination of pleasure and pain," that the sublime will "please only by causing pain" (Lyotard 81; 78) Crucially, the excessive positive part of this ambivalence is associated with the potential for autonomy. It is "the increase of being and the jubilation which result from the invention of new rules of the game, be it pictorial, artistic, or any other" (80). This is autonomy in the literal sense of self-given laws, rules of conduct not given by any outside entity. For the writer or artist, "the text he writes, the work he produces are not in principle governed by preestablished rules" (81). These rules are self-given, so it is a case of "working without rules in order to formulate the rules of *what will have been done*" (81). This is in the sphere of art, but it is also implied to hold in "any other" game. It is opposed to realism, which is a kind of formulaic representation in accordance with "preestablished rules." There are hints of Kantian distinctions between autonomy and heteronomy here too. Lyotard presents realism as not truly aesthetic in the Kantian sense because it appeals to interest. The language of appetite and desire marks its discussion. Realism works in one-party states as a creature comfort when "the 'correct' images, the 'correct' narratives, the 'correct' forms" can "find a public to desire them as the appropriate remedy for the anxiety and depression that public experiences" (75). In liberal capitalist societies, realist works communicate "the endemic desire for reality with objects and situations capable of gratifying it" (75). Tellingly, Lyotard goes on to give as an example of realism pornography, something that obviously links his talk of desire and gratification with sensuous interest as Kant would understand it (75).

Realism therefore seems to distinguish autonomy from nature in its internal manifestation as sensuous interest. Yet in the essay there is also an external figure that fulfills the same function in what Lyotard calls "techno-science" (76). This is the correlative to artistic realism in that it does not tolerate self-generated rules, excluding all but an intersubjective consensus. Thus the "objects and thoughts which originate in scientific knowledge and the capitalist economy" impose upon art "the rule that there is no reality unless testified by a consensus between partners over a certain knowledge and certain commitments" (77). The dominance of techno-science, then, leaves no room for individual autonomy; it is "the massive subordination of cognitive statements to the finality of the best possible performance" (76–77). If this is not nature itself in the Kantian sense, then it is clearly a variant of the development of the concept. It is ultimately descended from the alienated world of capitalism, which for Marx and Engels is not nature, but is nonetheless reified as if it is and that thus serves to mitigate human autonomy. Lyotard even mentions the "mephistophelian functionalism" of science and technology, echoing the *Manifesto*'s imagery of sorcery out of control (76). So there are themes here very familiar from the sublime tradition as we have seen it. It is not Lyotard's conception of the autonomous subject as such that is the common factor with the other uses of the sublime, since he is at pains to signal that he is aware of the problems with naively using a Kantian model of the subject. Rather, the point is that Lyotard's discussion of the sublime concerns the potential of art and literature for staging the conflict between human and nature, heteronomy and autonomy, and thus for staging human freedom in general.

While Lyotard talks about subjecting the Kantian sublime to a "severe reexamination" of its assumptions about the subject, he is far from the first to do this (73). In fact, this reexamination has been going on throughout the nineteenth and early twentieth centuries through a complex series of engagements between literature and philosophy. The interest in the sublime that Lyotard heralded was an emergence back into explicit discussion of something that had been happening consistently in a less overt, but no less engaged, way since the third *Critique*. The sublime had persisted between philosophy and literature, exercising a kind of gravitational pull on both. The sublime became what happens when art attempts to think through a certain conception of human distinctiveness and spontaneity by setting it in conflict with non-human forces, and conversely what happens when philosophy tries to articulate a certain dynamic relationship between the human and non-human. Inasmuch as what it means to be free and autonomous as a modern self has been a constant question, the sublime has never left.

Notes

Chapter 1

1. For another recent study that reads the post-romantic sublime with the subject, albeit with a different set of theoretical concerns and in relation to a different set of texts, see Steven Vine's *Reinventing the Sublime*.

Chapter 2

1. The German uses "kurz," or "mit einem wort" (*MEW* 4: 462; 465).
2. The sense is the same in the German, as in this case the phrase is "mit einem wort" (4: 465).
3. At least in the English version; the German has "die modern große Industrie" (*MEW* 4: 463).
4. The German edition has in place of "far surpassing" "ganz andere" (*MEW* 4: 465). Terrell Carver's alternative translation renders this "quite different," which loses the explicit sense of supersession, yet retains and strengthens the emphasis on the qualitative difference and thus perhaps the obscurity of the wonders (Carver, "Re-Translating" 1998 16).
5. This account echoes Richard Klein's reading of the sublime in *Capital*. Using a Kantian structure, he argues that money, in its guise as gold, is a sublime object (Klein 37).
6. Engels's German review has "Gespenst," translated here as "spectre" (MEW 1: 528). The word is "chimera" in Carlyle's original and Engels prefers this slightly more evocative term to the closer German "Schimäre" (Carlyle 3: 255; Oxford-Duden 1004). The vagaries of precisely translating

this term from English to German and back led to Helen MacFarlane's famous "frightful hobgoblin" (Carver, "Re-Translating" 62n).
7. Terrell Carver argues that Engels was profoundly influential on the text, going so far as to claim that "Marx's effort on the text was essentially, though rather heavily, editorial" (Carver, *Marx and Engels* 86). Despite this, he claims that "Marx was responsible for the narrative flow of the *Manifesto* in its final version" (86). Stedman Jones is less certain of this particular account of the division of labor. He suggests that "Engels may have participated in the final draft. These are matters of surmise" (Stedman Jones, "Introduction" 70n).
8. Tristram Hunt's biography of Engels exemplifies this approach, saying of Marx's writing of the final draft, "In [Engels's pet subjects'] place he offered the kind of rhetorical flights that Engels could never master" (Hunt 146). Indeed, Berman does not mention Engels at all in the context of the *Manifesto*'s authorship, speaking exclusively of "Marx's vision" (Berman 102).
9. Kirwan, indeed, goes so far as to claim that it "has turned out to be an enduring nineteenth-century contribution" in the form of the Hollywood film (Kirwan 127).
10. Allen Wood, for instance, has argued that none of Marx's statements on the importance of economic conditions prevents him from being a metaphysical libertarian (Wood 112).
11. While the English translation gains in traces of Carlyle's rhetoric, it can obscure somewhat this general Hegelian coloring. A great many terms that denote bourgeois power in the English translation, such as "sway" here, as well as "rule" and "upper hand," (*MECW* 6: 489–95) appear in the German as "Herrschaft" (*MEW* 4:467–72), which is the term translated "Lordship" in Hegel's *Phenomenology*.

Chapter 3

1. For a fuller discussion of the uses and implications of the term's alchemical resonances, see Christine Battersby's *The Sublime, Terror and Human Difference* (Battersby 105).
2. This interest in the sublimity of the night sky is something to which Wells returned. Wells in *God, The Invisible King* makes mention of Kant's famous "starry vault above" (Wells, *Invisible King* xiv). Furthermore, the chapter in *The First Men in the Moon* entitled "Mr. Bedford in Infinite Space" describes the experience of the protagonist adrift in a spacecraft. He is so impressed by its vastness that he begins to feel himself an entirely depersonalized, noumenal subject (Wells "Men" 570–75).

3. Sherrie Lyons, incidentally, attributes this interest in the young Huxley to Carlyle's influence in popularizing German culture (Lyons 26).
4. A commentary on the interrelation of Newtonian science and the eighteenth-century sublime can be found in Anne Janowitz's article "'What a Rich Fund of Images Is Treasured up Here': Poetic Commonplaces of the Sublime Universe."
5. The explanation I give here owes much to Richard Klein's useful one (Klein 34).
6. In this, my argument can be understood to be somewhat related to Patrick Parrinder's in *Shadows of the Future*. There, Parrinder argues that the date of the future destination is arrived upon by the operation of two timescales laid on top of one another, one geological or evolutionary and measured in hundreds of thousands of years, and one historical and measured in centuries (Parrinder 42). However, far from making the date less arbitrary, if Parrinder is right it shows that the date has the irresolvable tension between the comprehensible timescale and the incomprehensible deeply encoded within it.
7. The comparison with Kant's mathematical sublime illuminates commentary on the sublime in *The Time Machine* and in science fiction in general. Michael Page discusses the sublime as characterizing this time travel passage. He asserts that "Wells brings the sublime visionary cognition of the Romantics into the post-Darwinian world," finding in this the first instance in science fiction of the "sense of wonder" (Page 157). This sense involves, fundamentally, a "sudden dislocation of scale, a shift to a new position along the enormous span between cosmos and microcosm" (Clute in Page 157).
8. Parrinder here highlights that Wells is addressing the philosophical issue of universals, something Wells held to be the defining question of philosophy (Wells, *Invisible King* viii). That the aesthetics of the sublime, particularly Kant's mathematical sublime, are relevant to the problem of universals is shown in depth by Frances Ferguson's *Solitude and the Sublime*, which discusses these themes under the name of "the question of individuation" (Ferguson viii).
9. It is just before this explanation that the Time Traveller exclaims "Confound Kant!" in reply to an attempt at interjection from the Psychologist (Wells, *Definitive Time Machine* 176). This is most likely meant as a rejection of the idea of time being only a phenomenal category, but that in itself suggests a rejection of Kantian ideas of noumenal freedom.
10. Frank McConnell, speaking of the relation between the Time Traveller and the narrator of the epilogue, says that "[t]he two voices of

The Time Machine [...] encapsulate between them that elementary tension between cosmic determinism and freedom of the will that we have seen at the heart of all speculation about the future of mankind" (McConnell 88).

Chapter 4

1. Critics have found much evidence of familiarity with Schopenhauer in Conrad's novels. Mark Wollaeger calls Schopenhauer "Conrad's favorite philosopher" (Wollaeger xv). William J. Scheick calls *Heart of Darkness* "quite possibly [...] Conrad's most pronounced experiment in Schopenhauerian aesthetics" (Scheick 115). Nic Panagopoulos studies Schopenhauer's and Nietzsche's influence on Conrad's Major works from *Lord Jim* to *Under Western Eyes*.
2. There is certainly comparison to be made between Poe's stories and this passage. Not least of the similarities is that Heat here encounters the Professor, a very different sort of "Man of the Crowd." The similarity between the "essence of all crime" and the "perfect anarchist" is suggestive.
3. Here Schopenhauer is particularly close to Freud's "The 'Uncanny,'" in which essay Freud too describes how numbers can acquire a terrible aspect in certain subjective circumstances (SE 17: 237–38).
4. This is discussed in more depth by Ruth Kolani, who draws out the ethics implied by Conrad's style. She argues that responsibility is difficult to locate due to a lack of agents: "In effect, nobody does anything in the novel; things just happen" (Kolani 89).
5. As was seen above, the tragic for Schopenhauer is the highest degree of the sublime (WWR 2: 433).

Chapter 5

1. Early psychoanalytic critics such as Mark Shechner emphasized in their discussion the supposedly privileged access that "Circe" gives to Joyce's unconscious (Shechner 101). Other critics discuss "Circe" as being a central event in the development of *Ulysses*'s plot (Maddox 116).
2. Karen Lawrence, for instance, argues that the prevalence of anticlimaxes in the episode's hallucinations "undercuts the idea of crisis and radical change" (Lawrence 161–62).
3. In one exception, the concept is treated at greater length in Michael Bruce McDonald's "'Circe' and the Uncanny, or Joyce from Freud to Marx," a reading that applies Marxian commodity fetishism to the episode (McDonald 65).

4. Galef's article culminates in a comparison between Joyce and Carlyle's Teufelsdröckh in their sartorial preoccupations (Galef 429).
5. This is something that is also true of the anti-climaxes that Lawrence perceives in "Circe" (Lawrence 161–62).
6. The relevant phrase is "fand ich mich" in the original (Freud 1947 249).
7. The German "geschminkte" is slightly less ambiguous in its reference to makeup than the English translation "painted," but the focus is nevertheless squarely on the artificiality of the women's appearance (Freud 1947 249).
8. This link is commented upon by Paul Saint-Amour in his recent article on the pianola in "Circe" (Saint-Amour 30). He notes that in both texts the mechanical pianos come to stand metonymically for their surroundings (29–30).
9. Alongside those discussed here may be mentioned Hertz and Ellison. A useful discussion of this critical tendency is given in Masschelein (Masschelein 132–33). Relevant also is Seigbert Prawer, who discusses the uncanny in terms of Rudolf Otto's Kantian-derived category of the numinous (Prawer 15).
10. The phrase here in square brackets is not mine, but appears in Strachey's translation.
11. Or "doch" in the original (Freud 1947 262).
12. Freud writes "verspürt [...] den Antreib zu" in the original (Freud 1947 229).
13. These critics offer different accounts of which aspect of the process this might be. Some see these factors within Freud's psyche. Sarah Kofman traces it back to the death instinct (Kofman 160–61). A different explanation is offered in various ways by Hertz and Bloom, who see Freud as beset by anxieties about priority (Hertz 113). Elizabeth Wright represents another community of critics who bring literary concerns to the fore in their reading of the essay's rhetoric (Wright 146). This view reads the literariness of the essay as working against Freud's professed theoretical motive, and thus causing the text to escape his grasp. Thus Lydenberg discusses the "destabilising literariness of narrative" as it marks the essay (Lydenberg 1072). Nicholas Royle reads a Derridean logic of the supplement in the essay (Royle 16). These various interpretations, then, cluster around the idea that the essay is, as Ellison puts it, "self-deconstructing," and that there is an identifiable aspect either in Freud's psychology or in the nature of writing that, try as he might "vitiate[s] Freud's efforts to control his own text" (Ellison 52).

Works Cited

Primary

Literary Works

Carlyle, Thomas. *Sartor Resartus*. Oxford: Oxford U P, 2008. Print.
———. *Thomas Carlyle's Works*. 18 vols. London: Chapman and Hall, 1904–1906. Print.
Conrad, Joseph. *The Secret Agent*. Ed. Introd. Michael Newton. London: Penguin, 2007. Print.
Joyce, James. *Ulysses* (1922 text). Ed. Jeri Johnson. Oxford: Oxford U P, 1993. Print.
Wells, Herbert George. *The Time Machine*. Ed. Patrick Parrinder. Notes. Steven McLean. London: Penguin, 2005. Print.

Philosophical or Theoretical Works

Freud, Sigmund. *The Complete Standard Edition of the Works of Sigmund Freud*. 24 vols. Trans. James Strachey. London: Hogarth Press, 1953–1974. Print.
———. *Gesammelte Werken*. Vol. 12. Ed. Anna Freud. London: Imago Publishing, 1947. Print.
Kant, Immanuel. *Critique of the Power of Judgment*. Trans. Paul Guyer. Cambridge: Cambridge U P, 2000. Print.
———. *Kritik der Urteilskraft*. Berlin: Georg Reimer, 1908. Print.
———. *Observations on the Feeling of the Beautiful and Sublime*. 2nd ed. Trans. John T. Goldthwait. Berkeley: U of California P, 2003. Print.
———. *Practical Philosophy*. Trans. Mary J. Gregor. Cambridge: Cambridge U P, 1996. Print.

Lyotard, Jean-François. "Answering the Question: What is Postmodernism?" *The Postmodern Condition: a Report on Knowledge*. Trans. Geoff Bennington and Brian Massumi. Manchester: Manchester U P, 1984. 71–84. Print.

Marx, Karl, and Frederick Engels. *Collected Works*. 50 vols. London: Lawrence and Wishart, 1975–2004. Print.

———. *Karl Marx, Friedrich Engels Werke*. 43 vols. Berlin: Dietz. 1956–1990. Print.

Nietzsche, Friedrich. *The Birth of Tragedy and Other Writings*. Trans. Ronald Spiers. Cambridge: Cambridge U P, 1999. Print. Cambridge Texts in the History of Philosophy.

Schopenhauer, Arthur. *The World as Will and Representation*. 2 vols. Trans. E.F.J. Payne. New York: Dover Publications, 1969. Print.

Secondary

Aldiss, Brian. "Doomed Fomicary versus the Technological Sublime." *H. G. Wells's Perennial Time Machine*. Eds. George Slusser, Patrick Parrinder, and Danièle Chatelain. Athens, Georgia: U of Georgia P, 2001. 188–194. Print.

Ashfield, Andrew, and Peter de Bolla. Ed. *The Sublime: A Reader in British Eigtheenth-Century Aesthetic Theory*. Cambridge: Cambridge U P, 1996. Print.

Ashton, Rosemary. *The German Idea: Four English Writers and the Reception of German Thought, 1800–1860*. Cambridge: Cambridge U P, 1980. Print.

Attridge, Derek. "Pararealism in 'Circe.'" *Joycean Unions: Post-Millenial Essays from East to West*. Ed. R. Brandon Kershner and Tekla Mecsnóber. Amsterdam: Rodopi, 2013. 119–25. Print.

Baillie, John. *An Essay on the Sublime, By the Late Dr. Baillie*. London: R. Dodsley, 1747. ECCO. Web. 2 Sept. 2015.

Battersby, Christine. *The Sublime, Terror and Human Difference*. London: Routledge, 2007. Print.

Beattie, James. *Dissertations Moral and Critical*. Vol 2. Dublin: n.p., 1783. ECCO. Web. 2 Sept. 2015.

Beiser, Frederick. *Hegel*. London: Routledge, 2005. Print.

———. *Schiller as Philosopher: a Re-examination*. Oxford: Clarendon, 2005. Print.

Berman, Marshall. *All that Is Solid Melts into Air: The Experience of Modernity*. London: Verso, 1983. Print.

Bloom, Harold. *Agon: Towards a Theory of Revisionism*. Oxford: Oxford U P, 1982. Print.

———. Ed. *The Sublime*. New York: Bloom's Literary Criticism-Infobase, 2010. Print. Bloom's Literary Themes.
Brady, Emily. *The Sublime in Modern Philosophy: Aesthetics, Ethics, and Nature*. Cambridge: Cambridge U P, 2013. Print.
Budgen, Frank. *James Joyce and the Making of Ulysses and Other Writings*. Oxford: Oxford U P, 1972. Print.
Burchfield, Joe D. *Lord Kelvin and the Age of the Earth*. London: Macmillan, 1975. Print.
Burke, Edmund. *A Philosophical Enquiry into the Origin of our Ideas of the Sublime and Beautiful*. Oxford: Oxford U P, 2008. Print.
Butte, George. "What Silenus Knew: Conrad's Uneasy Debt to Nietzsche." *Comparative Literature* 41.2 (Spring 1989): 155–69. *JSTOR*. Web. 22 Aug. 2015.
Cahm, Caroline. *Kropotkin and the Rise of Revolutionary Anarchism 1872–1886*. Cambridge: Cambridge U P, 1989. Print.
Cardwell, Donald Stephen Lowell. *From Watt to Clausius: the Rise of Thermodynamics in the Early Industrial Age*. London: Heinemann Educational, 1971. Print.
Carver, Terrell. Trans. *Manifesto of the Communist Party*. *The Communist Manifesto: New Interpretations*. Ed. Mark Cowling. Edinburgh: Edinburgh U P, 1998. 14–40. Print.
———. *Marx and Engels: the Intellectual Relationship*. Bloomington: Indiana U P, 1983. Print.
———. "Re-translating the Manifesto: New Histories, New Ideas." *The Communist Manifesto: New Interpretations*. Ed. Mark Cowling. Edinburgh: Edinburgh U P, 1998. 51–62. Print.
Cixous, Hélène. "At Circe's, or the Self-Opener." Trans. Carol Bové. *Boundary 2* 3.2 (Winter 1975): 387–97. *JSTOR*. Web. 5 Sept. 2015.
———. "Fiction and Its Phantoms: A Reading of Freud's *Das Unhiemliche* (The 'Uncannny')." Trans. Robert Dennomé. *New Literary History* 7.3 (Spring 1976): 525–48. *JSTOR*. Web. 24 Aug. 2015.
Colley, Ann C. *Victorians in the Mountains: Sinking the Sublime*. Farnham: Ashgate Publishing, 2010. *ProQuest*. Web. 21 Aug. 2015.
Connor, Stephen. "'Jigajiga . . . Yummyyum . . . Pfuiiiiiii ! . . . Bbbbblllll-blblblblobschb!': 'Circe's' Ventriloquy." *Reading Joyce's "Circe."* Ed. Andrew Gibson. Amsterdam: Rodopi, 1994. 93–142. Print.
Conrad, Joseph. *The Collected Letters of Joseph Conrad*. 9 vols. Ed. Frederick R. Karl and Laurence Davies. Cambridge: Cambridge U P, 1983–2007. Print.
———. *The Nigger of the "Narcissus."* Ed. Robert Kimbrough. New York: W.W. Norton & Company, 1979. Print.
Creggan-Reid, Vybarr. *Discovering Gilgamesh: Geology, Narrative and*

the Historical Sublime in Victorian Culture. Manchester: Manchester U P, 2015. *University Press Scholarship Online.* Web. 12 April 2018.

de Bolla, Peter. *The Discourse of the Sublime: Readings in History, Aesthetics and the Subject.* Oxford: Basil Blackwell, 1989. Print.

Dennis, John. *The Critical Works of John Dennis.* Ed. Edward Niles Hooker. Baltimore: Johns Hopkins Press, 1943. Print.

Eagleton, Terry. *The Ideology of the Aesthetic.* Oxford: Basil Blackwell, 1990. Print.

Ellison, David. *Ethics and Aesthetics in European Modernist Literature: From the Sublime to the Uncanny.* Cambridge: Cambridge U P, 2001. *ProQuest.* Web. 21 Aug. 2015.

Ellmann, Richard. *James Joyce.* New and Revised ed. Oxford: Oxford U P, 1982. Print.

Ferguson, Frances. *Solitude and the Sublime: Romanticism and the Aesthetics of Individuation.* London: Routledge, 1992. Print.

Ferrer, Daniel. "Circe, Regret and Regression." *Post-Structuralist Joyce: Essays from the French.* Ed. Derek Attridge and Daniel Ferrer. Cambridge: Cambridge U P, 1994. 127–44. Print.

Ffytche, Matt. *The Foundation of the Unconscious: Schelling, Freud and the Birth of the Modern Psyche.* Cambridge: Cambridge U P, 2012. Print.

Freeman, Barbara Claire. *The Feminine Sublime: Gender and Excess in Women's Fiction.* Berkeley: U of California P, 1997. Print.

French, Marilyn. *The Book as World: James, Joyce's* Ulysses. London: Harvard U P, 1976. Print.

Furniss, Tom. *Edmund Burke's Aesthetic Ideology.* Cambridge: Cambridge U P, 1993. Print.

Galef, David. "The Fashion Show in *Ulysses*." *Twentieth Century Literature* 37.4 (Winter 1991): 420–31. *JSTOR.* Web. 10 Sept. 2015.

Gibson, Andrew. Introduction. *Reading Joyce's "Circe."* Ed. Andrew Gibson. Amsterdam: Rodopi, 1994. 3–32. Print.

Guyer, Paul. *A History of Modern Aesthetics.* Vol 1. Cambridge: Cambridge U P, 2014. *Cambridge University Press Online Books.* Web. 20 April 2018.

———. *Kant and the Experience of Freedom: Essays on Aesthetics and Morality.* Cambridge: Cambridge U P, 1993. Print.

———. "The German Sublime after Kant" *The Sublime: From Antiquity to the Present.* Ed. Timothy M. Costelloe. Cambridge: Cambridge U P, 2012. 102–17. Print.

Hammond, John R. *H. G. Wells's* The Time Machine: *a Reference Guide.* London: Praeger Publishers, 2004. Print.

Hancock, Stephen. *The Romantic Sublime and Middle-Class Subjectivity in the Victorian Novel*. London: Routledge, 2005. Print.
Hegel, Georg Wilhelm Friedrich. *Aesthetics: Lectures on Fine Art*. Trans. T.M. Knox. Vol. 1. Oxford: Clarendon, 1975. Print.
———. *Phenomenology of Spirit*. Trans. A.V. Miller. Oxford: Clarendon, 1977. Print.
Herr, Cheryl Temple. "Difficulty: 'Oxen of the Sun' and 'Circe.'" *The Cambridge Companion to Ulysses*. Ed. Sean Latham. Cambridge: Cambridge U P, 2014. 154–68. Print.
Hertz, Neil. *The End of the Line*. Aurora, Colorado: Davies Group, 2009. *ProQuest*. Web. 21 Aug. 2015.
Hobsbawm, E.J.E. "Marx, Karl Heinrich (1818–1883)." *Oxford Dictionary of National Biography*. Oxford U P, 2004. Web. 3 Dec. 2013.
Hoffmann, E.T.A. "The Sandman." *Selected Writings of Hoffmann*. Ed. Trans. Leonard J. Kent and Elizabeth C. Knight. Vol. 1. Chicago: U of Chicago P, 1969. 137–67. Print.
Houen, Alex. *Terrorism and Modern Literature: From Joseph Conrad to Ciaran Carson*. Oxford: Oxford U P, 2002. Print.
Hovanec, Caroline. "Rereading H.G. Wells's *The Time Machine*: Empiricism, Aestheticism, Modernism." *English Literature in Transition 1880–1920* 58.4 (2015): 459–85. *JSTOR*. Web. 30 March 2016.
Hunt, Tristram. *Marx's General: the Revolutionary Life of Friedrich Engels*. New York: Metropolitan Books, 2009. Print.
Huxley, Thomas Henry. "Evolution and Ethics [1893]." *Collected Essays*. Vol. 9 London: Macmillan, 1894. 46–116. *Cambridge University Press Online Books*. Web. 20 April 2018.
———. "On the Hypothesis that Animals are Automata, and its History." *Collected Essays*. Vol. 1. London: Macmillan, 1894. 199–250. *Cambridge University Press Online Books*. Web. 20 April 2018.
Jacquette, Dale. *The Philosophy of Schopenhauer*. Chesham: Acumen, 2005. Print. Continental European Philosophy.
Janowitz, Anne. "'What a Rich Fund of Images Is Treasured up Here': Poetic Commonplaces of the Sublime Universe." *Studies in Romanticism* 44.4 (Winter 2005): 469–92. *JSTOR*. Web. 22 Aug. 2015.
Johnson, Bruce. *Conrad's Models of Mind*. London: Oxford U P, 1971. Print.
Joyce, James. *Letters of James Joyce*. Vol 1. Ed. Stuart Gilbert. London: Faber and Faber, 1957. Print.
Kennedy, Chris. "Systematic Grammar and its use in Literary Analysis." *Language and Literature: An Introductory Reader in Stylistics*.

Ed. Ronald Carter. London: George Allen and Unwin, 1982. 83–100. Print.

Kirschner, Paul. *Conrad: The Psychologist as Artist*. London: Oliver and Boyd, 1968. Print.

Kirwan, James. *Sublimity: The Non-Rational and the Rational in the History of Aesthetics*. New York: Routledge, 2005. Print.

Klaver, Jan M. I. *Geology and Religious Sentiment: the Effect of Geological Discoveries on English Society and Literature between 1829 and 1859*. New York: Brill, 1997. Print.

Klein, Richard. "Kant's Sunshine." *Diacritics* 11.2 (Summer 1981): 26–41. *JSTOR*. Web. 21 Aug. 2015.

Knowles, Owen. "Who's Afraid of Arthur Schopenhauer? A New Context for Conrad's *Heart of Darkness*." *Nineteenth-Century Literature* 49.1 (June 1994): 75–106. *JSTOR*. Web. 22 Aug. 2015.

Ko, Charles. "Subliminal Consciousness." *The Review of English Studies* New series 59.242 (2008): 740–65. Print.

Kofman, Sarah. "The Double is/and the Devil: the Uncanniness of *The Sandman (Der Sandmann)*." *Freud and Fiction*. Trans. Sarah Wykes. Oxford: Polity Press, 1991. 119–62. Print.

Kolani, Ruth. "Secret agent, Absent Agent? Ethical-Stylistic Aspects of Anarchy in Conrad's *The Secret Agent*." *The Ethics in Literature*. Ed. Andrew Hadfield, Dominic Rainsford and Tim Woods. Basingstoke: Macmillan, 1999. 86–100. Print.

LaValley, Albert J. *Carlyle and the Idea of the Modern: Studies in Carlyle's Prophetic Literature and Its Relation to Blake, Nietzsche, Marx, and Others*. New Haven: Yale U P, 1968. Print.

Lawrence, Karen. *The Odyssey of Style in Ulysses*. Princeton: Princeton U P, 1981. Print.

Lloyd, Tom. "High Air-Castles: Carlyle's Reactions to Schiller's Aesthetics." *Victorians Institute Journal* 12 (1984): 91–104. Print.

Longinus. "On Sublimity." *Classical Literary Criticism*. Ed. D.A. Russell and Michael Winterbottom. Oxford: Oxford U P, 2008. 143–87. Print.

Lukács, Georgy. *History and Class Consciousness: Studies in Marxist Dialectics*. Trans. Rodney Livingstone. London: Merlin Press, 1971. Print.

Lydenberg, Robin. "Freud's Uncanny Narratives." *PMLA* 112.5 (October 1997): 1072-1086. *JSTOR*. Web. 24 Aug. 2015.

Lyell, Charles. *Principles of Geology*. Vol. 1. Intro. Martin Rudwick. Chicago: U of Chicago P, 1990. Print.

Lyons, Sherrie L. *Thomas Henry Huxley: The Evolution of a Scientist*. New York: Prometheus Books, 1999. Print.

Maddox, James H. Jr. *Joyce's* Ulysses *and the Assault upon Character*. Hassocks: Harvester Press, 1978. Print.

Masschelein, Anneleen. *The Unconcept: The Freudian Uncanny in Late Twentieth-Century Theory*. Albany: State U of New York P, 2011. ProQuest. Web. 24 Aug. 2015.

McConnell, Frank. *The Science Fiction of H. G. Wells*. Oxford: Oxford U P, 1981. Print.

McDonald, Michael Bruce. "'Circe' and the Uncanny, or Joyce from Freud to Marx." *James Joyce Quarterly* 33.1 (Fall 1995): 49–68. JSTOR. Web. 25 Aug. 2015.

Mendilow, Jonathan. "Carlyle, Marx & the I.L.P.: Alternative Routes to Socialism." *Polity* 17.2 (Winter 1984): 225–47. JSTOR. Web. 21 Aug. 2015.

Monk, Samuel Holt. *The Sublime: A Study in Critical Theories in Eighteenth-Century England*. New York: Modern Language Association, 1960. Print.

The Oxford–Duden German Dictionary. 2nd ed. "chimera, n." Oxford U P, 1999. Print.

Oxford English Dictionary Online. "sublime, v." Oxford U P, June 2015. Web. 21 Aug. 2015.

Page, Michael R. *The Literary Imagination from Erasmus Darwin to H. G. Wells: Science, Evolution, and Ecology*. Farnham: Ashgate, 2012. ProQuest. Web. 22 Aug. 2015.

Paley, Morton D. *The Apocalyptic Sublime*. New Haven: Yale U P, 1986. Print.

Panagopoulos, Nic. *The Fiction of Joseph Conrad: the Influence of Schopenhauer and Nietzsche*. Frankfurt am Main: Peter Laing, 1998. Print. Anglo-American Studies.

Parrinder, Patrick. *Shadows of the Future: H. G. Wells, Science Fiction, and Prophecy*. Syracuse: Syracuse U P, 1995. Print.

Pettigrew, David E. "The Question of the Relation of Philosophy and Psychoanalysis: the Case of Kant and Freud." *Metaphilosophy* 21.1&2 (January 1990): 67–88. Print.

Plotz, John. "Crowd Power: Chartism, Carlyle, and the Victorian Public Sphere." *Representations* 70 (Spring 2000): 87–114. JSTOR. Web. 21 Aug. 2015.

Prawer, Siegbert S. *The "Uncanny" in Literature: an Apology for its Investigation*. London: Westfield College, 1965. Print.

Puchner, Martin. *Poetry of the Revolution: Marx, Manifestoes and the Avant-gardes*. Princeton: Woodstock, 2006. Print.

Rabaté, Jean-Michel. *The Cambridge Introduction to Literature and Psychoanalysis*. Cambridge: Cambridge U P, 2014. Print.

Rado, Lisa. *The Modern Androgyne Imagination: A Failed Sublime.* Charlottesvile, U P of Virginia: 2000. Print.

Reid, Thomas. *The Works of Thomas Reid, D.D.* Ed. William Hamilton. Edinburgh: MacLachlan and Stewart, 1863. Print.

Rose, David Edward. *Free Will and Continental Philosophy: the Death without Meaning.* London: Continuum, 2009. *ProQuest.* Web. 25 Aug. 2015.

Royle, Nicholas. *The Uncanny.* Manchester: Manchester U P, 2003. Print.

Saint-Amour, Paul K. "*Ulysses* Pianola." *PMLA* 130.1 (January 2015): 15–36. Print.

Scheick, William J. *Fictional Structure and Ethics: The Turn-of-the-Century English Novel.* Athens: U of Georgia P, 1990. Print.

Schiller, Friedrich. *Essays.* Trans. Walter Hinderer and Daniel O. Dahlstrom. New York: Continuum, 1998. Print.

Schnauder, Ludwig. *Free Will and Determinism in Joseph Conrad's Major Novels.* Amsterdam: Rodopi, 2009. *ProQuest.* Web. 21 Aug. 2015.

Schopenhauer, Arthur. *Essay on the Freedom of the Will.* Trans. Konstantin Kolenda. Indianapolis: Bobbs-Merrill, 1960. Print.

Shapshay, Sandra. "Schopenhauer's Transformation of the Kantian Sublime." *Kantian Review* 17.3 (November 2012): 479–511. *Cambridge Journals Online.* Web. 22 Aug. 2015.

Shechner, Mark. *Joyce in Nighttown: A Psychoanalytic Inquiry into Ulysses.* Berkeley: U of California P, 1974. Print.

Smith, Andrew. *Gothic Radicalism: Literature, Philosophy and Psychoanalysis in the Nineteenth Century.* London: Palgrave Macmillan, 2000. Print.

Smith, Roger. *Free Will and the Human Sciences in Britain, 1870–1910.* London: Pickering & Chatto, 2013. Print. Science and Culture in the Nineteenth Century.

Sorel, George. *Reflections on Violence.* Trans. T.E. Hulme. New York: AMS Press, 1975. Print.

Sperber, Jonathan. *Karl Marx: a Nineteenth-Century Life.* London: Liverlight, 2013. Print.

Stallman, R.W. "Time and *The Secret Agent*" *The Art of Joseph Conrad: A Critical Symposium.* Ed. R.W. Stallman. Lansing: Michigan State U P, 1960. 234–53. Print.

Stedman Jones, Gareth. Introduction. *The Communist Manifesto.* By Karl Marx and Friedrich Engels. London: Penguin, 2002. 3–187. Print.

———. *Karl Marx: Greatness and Illusion.* London: Allen Lane, 2016.

Sussman, Herbert L. *Victorians and the Machine: the Literary Response to Technology.* Cambridge: Harvard U P, 1968. Print.
Tauber, Alfred I. *Freud, the Reluctant Philosopher.* Princeton: Princeton U P, 2011. Print.
Taylor, Charles. *Sources of the Self: the Making of the Modern Identity.* Cambridge: Cambridge U P, 1989. Print.
Tomko, Michael. "Varieties of Geological Experience: Religion, Body and Spirit in Tennyson's 'In Memoriam' and Lyell's 'Principles of Geology." *Victorian Poetry* 42.2 (Summer 2004): 113–34. *JSTOR.* Web. 22 Aug. 2015.
Tuveson, Ernest L. "The Millenarian Structure of *The Communist Manifesto.*" *The Apocalypse in English Renaissance Thought and Literature.* Ed. C.A. Patrides and Joseph Wittreich. Manchester: Manchester U P, 1984. 323–41. Print.
Vine, Steven. *Reinventing the Sublime: Post-Romantic Literature and Theory.* Brighton: Sussex Academic Press, 2013. Print.
Watts, Cedric. *A Preface to Conrad.* 2nd ed. London: Longman, 1993. Print.
———. *Joseph Conrad: The Secret Agent.* Tirril: Humanities E-Books, 2007. *ProQuest.* Web. 22 Aug. 2015.
Weiskel, Thomas. *The Romantic Sublime: Studies in the Structure and Psychology of Transcendence.* London: Johns Hopkins U P, 1976. Print.
Wells, H.G. *A Short History of the World.* London: Watts & Co., 1929. Print.
———. *Anticipations of the Reaction of Mechanical and Scientific Progress upon Human Life and Thought.* Mineola, N. Y.: Dover Publications, 1999. Print.
———. *Correspondence of H. G. Wells.* Vol. 2. Ed. David C. Smith. London: Pickering and Chatto, 1998. Print.
———. *The Definitive Time Machine: A Critical Edition of H. G. Wells's Scientific Romance.* Ed. Harry M. Geduld. Bloomington, Indiana: Indiana U P, 1987. Print.
———. *The Discovery of the Future.* New York: B.W. Heubsch, 1913. Print.
———. *First and Last Things: A Confession of Faith and a Rule of Life.* London: Cassell and Co., 1917. Print.
———. "The First Men in the Moon." *Seven Science Fiction Novels of H. G. Wells.* New York: Dover Publications, 1934. 455–620. Print.
———. *The Future in America: a Search after Realities.* London: Chapman and Hall, 1906. Print.

———. *God, the Invisible King*. London: Cassell and Co., 1917. Print.
———. *H. G. Wells: Early Writings in Science and Science Fiction*. Eds. Robert M. Philmus and David Y. Hughes. Berkeley; London: U of California P, 1975. Print.
———. *The Sleeper Awakes: and, Men Like Gods*. London: Odhams Press, [1921?]. Print.
Wells, H.G., Julian S. Huxley, and G.P. Wells. *The Science of Life*. London: Cassell and Co., 1931. Print.
Wollaeger, Mark. *Joseph Conrad and the Fictions of Skepticism*. Stanford, California: Stanford U P, 1990. Print.
Wood, Allen W. *Karl Marx*. 2nd ed. London: Routledge, 2004. Print.
Wright, Elizabeth. *Psychoanalytic Criticism: Theory in Practice*. London: Routledge, 1989. Print.
Young, Robert. "Psychoanalytic Criticism: Has it Got Beyond a Joke?" *Paragraph* 4 (1984): 87–114. Print.

Index

Addison, Joseph, 1, 2, 108
aesthetics, 1–3, 16, 57, 79, 97, 135–36, 179; Conrad's view of, 100–1; and ethics, 7–14 passim; Freud and, 159–62, 167–68; Kant's, 8–12, 73–75, 166, 182–83; Nietzsche's, 129; Schiller's, 13–14, 39; Schopenhauer's, 17, 98, 100–4, 106, 107–110, 113–15, 117, 134, 181, 188n1
alchemy, 57, 186n1
alienation, 24, 44, 48–49, 53, 151, 157, 183
ambivalent affect, 5–7, 74, 182; in Conrad, 126; and Freud's uncanny, 160–61; in *The Communist Manifesto*, 13, 23–24, 38; in *The Time Machine*, 56–57, 92; in Schopenhauer's account, 108
America, 20, 29, 58
anarchism, 96–98, 101, 121, 128–29, 188n2
androgyny, 173, 177
animism: in "Circe," 141–42, 147, 154; in "The 'Uncanny,'" 140–41, 147–48, 150–51, 162, 164–65
apocalyptic, the: as mode of writing, 20, 35–38; sequence in "Circe," 142, 157
aristocracy, 28, 49–52, 87
Aristotle, 9
art, 3, 14, 100–1, 127, 129 182–84; mentioned, 1, 133
atoms, 78, 79, 90
Augustine of Hippo, 182
automata, 62, 119–20, 152–54, 158–59. See also consciousness; self-consciousness; "The '"Uncanny'"
autonomy: in Freud, 162–64, 176–77; as ideal of subjectivity, 4–5, 15, 180, 184; Kant's account of, 5–12 passim, 15, 38, 43, 49, 118, 134, 164, 166; in Marx and Engels, 43, 52, 88; post-Kantian articulations of, 13, 15, 39–40, 47, 49, 158, 182–83; as problematic, 135, 147, 149–54 passim, 157–58, 169–73 passim; in Schopenhauer, 118, 134, 158; in Wells, 84, 88–89, 93. See also freedom

Baillie, John, 8
Bakunin, Mikhail, 96–97

bathos, 175
Beattie, James, 8
beautiful, the, 3, 8, 12, 107–9, 159–60
Boileau, 1
Burke, Edmund, 1, 2, 8, 35–36, 108; account of the sublime, 5–6, 46, 161; gendering of the sublime, 17, 173
bourgeoisie, 8, 16, 19–31 passim, 35, 37 41–48 passim, 95, 186

capitalism, 183; in *The Communist Manifesto*, 19–26, 29, 33–36 passim, 47–49, 52–53, 57; mentioned, 86, 88
Captain of Industry, 41, 51–53, 88
Carlyle, Thomas, 20; and German thought, 13, 26–28, 31–32, 39–40, 42, 187n3; Marx's and Engels's reading of, 26–28, 30–32; motif of clothes in, 33–35, 41, 125–26, 189n4; *Past and Present*, 27, 30, 33, 39–41, 51; political opinions of, 26–28, 49–52; *Sartor Resartus*, 34, 38, 40, 50, 58, 189n4; theory of crisis, 33–35; in *The Time Machine*, 87–88; valorization of labor, 38–41, 49; mentioned, 16, 43–44, 60, 63, 180. See also *Chartism*
cash nexus, 26–28, 31, 35
categorical imperative, 62
categories of perception, 99–104, 106, 187n9. See also space; time
cathedrals, 22–23, 73
causality, 40, 42, 62, 85, 90, 101–3, 118–21, 123, 150, 164, 166
character, virtuous, 8, 40; Schopenhauer's sublime, 106, 115–17; Kantian, 8–9
Chartism, 28, 32–33, 49–51

Chartism: apocalyptic in, 35–37; echoes in *The Communist Manifesto*, 27–30, 32, 35, 58, 185n6, 186n11; political agency in, 49–52; and the sublime, 32–33, 37, 51, 53
chemistry, 57
chivalry, 17, 23, 51. See also Don Quixote
"Circe": animal imagery in, 155–56; animated objects in, 140; apocalyptic sequence, 137, 141, 157; Bella Cohen, 137, 143, 155, 158–59, 170–75; as comical, 137–39; costume changes in, 144, 146, 157, 176, 188n4; critical approaches to, 136, 137–39, 188n1–3; as dreamscape, 135, 142–45, 147, 156, 169; Florry, 141, 143, 156, 157, 171; formal characteristics of, 136, 141–45, 147, 157, 169, 174, 188n2; Kitty, 140; Leopold Bloom, 135, 137–39, 140–44, 146, 155, 157–58, 169–77, 181–82; Lynch, 139–40, 171; mentioned, 16; metaphors in, 141–42, 155–56; model of the subject in, 154, 157, 169–77, 181–82; Molly Bloom, 176; Nymph, 140, 175–76; political hallucination, 137, 141, 157; Privates Compton and Carr, 170–71; relationship to the rest of *Ulysses*, 135–36, 138, 171; sadomasochistic hallucination, 143, 171–73; stage directions in, 136, 141–43, 155; Stephen Dedalus, 137–44 passim, 157, 170–74, 176; the sublime in, 169, 172–73, 181; as uncanny, 136–45 passim; Zoe, 140, 141, 155, 156–57, 174
class consciousness, 17, 52–53
clothes: in Carlyle, 33–35, 41; in

"Circe", 144, 146, 157, 176, 182, 189n4
cognitive failure, 5–6, 59, 67–72 passim, 77, 92, 105. *See also* mathematical sublime
Coleridge, Samuel Taylor, 2
The Communist Manifesto: apocalyptic aspects of, 35–38; authorship of, 29–32, 186n7; critics on, 19–20, 25–26; depiction of capitalism, 19–26 41–42; echoes of Carlyle in, 27–30, 32, 35; echoes of Hegel in, 45, 47, 52; "melting vision," 19, 32, 47, 57, 77; mentioned, 17, 51, 63, 88, 95, 97, 183; rhetorical strategies of, 20–25, 52–53, 58; sublime imagery in, 22–24, 32, 48–49, 55–58; translation of, 30–32, 185n1–4, 185–86n6, 186n11
communism, 25–26, 28, 30, 36
communists, 52–53, 88
compatibilism, 62, 90
complementarity, 89
condition-of-England question, 26–27
Conrad, Joseph: aesthetic theory of, 100–3, 181; ethical views of, 17, 129, 132–34; *Heart of Darkness*, 95, 188n1; *The Informer*, 123; knitting machine passage, 98–99, 125–26, 128–29; *Lord Jim*, 188n1; mentioned 16, 125, 158; and Nietzsche, 96, 129–34 passim; *The Nigger of the Narcissus*, 100; *A Personal Record*, 132; philosophical views of, 98–99, 125–26, 128–30; political opinions of, 98, 127; and Schopenhauer, 99–103, 120, 125–26, 180–81, 188n1; *Under Western Eyes*, 188n1. *See also The Secret Agent*

conscience, 53, 98–99, 117, 151
consciousness, 48, 61, 83, 87, 134, 142, 157; of automata, 62; in Freud, 148–49, 163; in Schopenhauer, 106–7, 117. *See also* ego; self-consciousness; unconscious
cosmetics, 154–55, 172, 189n7
cotton, 27, 32–33, 36, 41, 49, 51
courage, 8–11, 40, 46, 119
crowds, 105, 124–25, 128, 188n2
Cunninghame Graham, R. B., 98, 125, 128

Dance of the Hours, 141–42
Darwin, Charles, 148. *See also* Darwinism
Darwin, George, 64
Darwinism, 16, 60, 63–64, 148, 180, 187n7. *See also* evolution
death, 6, 14, 98–99, 151–52, 162, 167, 189n13. *See also* life-or-death struggle
de Bolla, Peter, 2–5, 7
deep time, 64–77 passim, 82–83, 86–87, 92–93, 181, 187n6
Dennis, John, 5
Derrida, Jacques, 189n13
Descartes, René, 121, 182
desire, 40, 46, 163, 183; in Schopenhauer's philosophy, 100, 103, 116–18. *See also* inclination
determinism, 40–41, 70, 85, 88–93, 118–19, 125–26, 148–49, 162–64, 188n10
Dionysiac, 96, 128–32, 134, 159
Dionysus, 128–30, 159
disenchantment, 24, 29, 35
Don Quixote, 132
drama: in "Circe," 142–44, 147, 169; staging of the subject, 12, 14–15, 20, 38, 45–47, 53, 93, 108, 157, 168–69, 176–77, 181–83

dreams, 32–33, 145–47, 181
dreamscapes, 16, 134, 135, 145
duty, 28; in Kant, 9, 11; in Schiller, 14
Dublin, 135, 141
dynamic sublime, 6, 14, 23, 48, 107; and Hegel, 46; and Kant's ethics, 9–11

economics, 16, 24–25, 37, 42, 44–45, 49, 183, 186n10
ego, 62, 147, 148–51 passim, 162–64, 176
Engels, Friedrich: and Carlyle, 26–32; contribution to *The Communist Manifesto*, 29–32, 186n7; *The Condition of the Working Class in England*, 26–28, 31. *See also* Marx, Karl; *The Communist Manifesto*
Enlightenment, the, 182
entropy, 91, 120, 151
ethics, 1, 7–8, 15, 43, 60, 97, 132–34, 188n4; Carlyle's, 39–40, 49; Conrad's, 130; "ethical process;" 62–63, 83–84, 86; Kantian, 5, 7–12, 38, 42, 71, 107, 119, 162, 164, 166; Schopenhauer's, 115–16; Schiller's, 13–14, 180–81; virtue ethics, 9
etymology of "sublime," 57
evolution, 38, 60–64, 74, 83, 120, 123, 148, 187n6
exploitation, 21, 24–26, 35

faculties, Kantian, 6, 62, 67, 107, 182. *See also* imagination; reason; understanding
fear, 5–6, 9–10, 126; in "Lordship and Bondage," 45–48; in Schopenhauer's sublime, 109–10; in *The Secret Agent*, 106, 110, 112, 124; in *The Time Machine* 56–57, 87; in "The 'Uncanny,'" 152, 154, 160–62
femininity, 143, 153, 171, 173, 175, 176
Freud, Sigmund: *Beyond the Pleasure Principle*, 151; commitment to autonomy, 163–64, 168–69; as determinist, 149–52, 162; and gender, 153, 173; *The Interpretation of Dreams*, 149; *Introductory Lectures on Psychoanalysis*, 148–49; and Kant, 161–62, 164, 166, 169, 173; mentioned, 15–16; as narrator of "The 'Uncanny,'" 17, 135, 145–46, 150, 167–69; psychoanalytic cure, 162–66; psychoanalytic worldview, 148–49, 151–52, 158, 162, 180; *The Psychopathology of Everyday Life*, 149–50, 156; and the sublime, 159–61, 179. *See also* "The 'Uncanny'"
Fichte, Johann Gottlieb, 15, 62
fiction, 17, 168, 187n7
flooding imagery, 23–24, 26, 32, 42, 48
freedom: Carlyle's conception of, 38–43, 49, 51; Freud and, 149–52, 162–66; as human distinctiveness, 7, 13–15, 20, 38–41, 45, 53, 83, 90, 147–48, 180, 183–4; Huxley on, 61–62, 64; as illusory; 61, 85–88, 91, 96, 121–23, 149–52; Kant's conception of, 10–12, 43–44, 46, 162, 180; manifested in labor, 20, 38–41, 44–45, 52; Marx's conception of, 41–45, 52; Schopenhauer's conception of, 100, 117–19, 126; the sublime as staging of, 11–15, 39, 46–47, 53, 93, 131–32, 117–19, 126–27, 134, 162, 169,

180, 183–84; Wells on, 83–84, 88–91, 187n9, 188n10. See also autonomy, determinism
free indirect discourse, 106, 131, 144
free will. See freedom; determinism
futurity, 56, 75–76

gas jets, 140, 158
gender, 17, 143, 163, 171, 173. See also masculinity; femininity; androgyny
geology, 60, 64–69 passim
Germany: culture, 26, 32, 39, 159, 187n3; literature, 26, 28; philosophy, 27–28, 34, 39, 42–44, 49, 159, 180
German language, 31, 57, 62, 185n1–4, 185–87n6, 189n6–7, 189n11–12
ghosts, 121, 137, 140, 143, 156
gods, 40, 128, 150, 152, 174
Goethe, 39
Greenwich meridian, 102. See also *The Secret Agent*
Gregorian calendar, 74
Guyer, Paul, 11–12, 14, 108, 159

hallucination, 137, 142–46 passim, 156–58, 169, 171–72, 181
Hegel, Georg Wilhelm Friedrich, 14–15, 38; "Lordship and Bondage," 15, 20, 44–48, 52–53, 57, 186n11
Herder, Johann Gottfried, 1
heroism, 8–12, 40, 63, 85, 181
heteronomy, 5, 9, 38–40, 118–19, 183. See also autonomy
history, 15, 68, 182; in *The Communist Manifesto*, 20–22, 29–31, 35, 38, 41–42, 45, 47, 52, 181; narrated in *Chartism*, 29, 32, 35; geological, 64–66, 68, 74, 83; mentioned, 1, 44. See also deep time
history of the sublime: ancient, 5, 8, 173; apparent disappearance from aesthetics, 1–4; culminating in the uncanny, 158–55 passim, 179; cultural influence, 1–3, 37–38; eighteenth century, 1–12 passim, 16, 32–33, 37–38, 57, 66–67; late twentieth-century resurgence, 1–2, 182–84; Newtonianism, connection to, 67; post-romantic development, 2–4, 11–17, 179–81, 185n1; romanticism, 1–4, 22, 33, 159, 187n7; seventeenth century, 1, 67; shift away from traditional objects, 16, 32–33, 58–60, 180–81; subjective emphasis increasing, 108–10, 134, 181
hobgoblins, 137, 139–40, 143, 185–86n6
Hoffmann, E. T. A., 153–54
Homer, 8, 174
horror. See fear
Hugo, Victor, 139
humanity: as ethical quality, 7, 25, 27, 34, 62–64; as collective, 15–16, 56, 62–63, 82–83, 86–87, 124, 128; Marx's species-character of, 44–45. See also nature; freedom as human distinctiveness
humor, 114, 137–39
hurricanes, 23, 46
Hutton, James, 66–67
Huxley, Thomas Henry, 16, 60–64, 70, 83–84, 93, 119–20, 187n3
Huxley, Julian, 69
hypospadia, 173

Ibsen, Henrik, 156
imagination, 3, 65–69, 73–74, 147; Kantian faculty, 6, 11, 67, 72–75, 77, 92, 173
inclination, 9–12, 40, 109, 164
individual, the: and collective understandings of freedom, 15–16, 49, 63, 180, 183; in "Circe," 170, 172; in *The Communist Manifesto*, 24, 41; Freud and, 148, 163; Schopenhauer and, 100, 104, 106, 108, 113, 115–17, 158; in *The Secret Agent*, 132. See also subjectivity
industry: and Carlyle, 29–37 passim, 49, 51, 180; in *The Communist Manifesto*, 16, 20–25 passim, 41–43, 48–49, 180; and Conrad, 125; and Wells, 58, 60, 86. See also Captain of Industry; object of the sublime
insanity. See madness
irony: and Nietzsche, 129, 131–32, 158; in *The Secret Agent*, 17, 96, 116–17, 127–28, 130, 131–33, 181; and the sublime, 126–27, 134, 158

Jentsch, Ernst, 153–55, 156
Joyce, James: attitude to Freud, 137, 139; on pianolas, 159, 189n8; on moly, 174; critics on, 136, 188n1; and psychoanalysis, 137, 139, 157, 188n1; mentioned, 17, 189n4; *A Portrait of the Artist as Young Man*, 171. See also "Circe;" *Ulysses*

Kames, Henry Home, Lord, 1, 2
Kant, Immanuel: "Analytic of the Sublime," 1, 5, 11–12, 23, 46, 48, 70, 107; Carlyle's relation to, 39–40; ethical theory of, 5, 7–12, 38, 42, 71, 107, 119, 133–34, 162, 164, 166, 183; *Critique of Judgment*, 1, 5, 11–12, 16, 22; *Critique of Practical Reason*, 12, 71; Freud and, 161–66 passim, 169; *The Groundwork of the Metaphysics of Morals*, 9, 11, 44, 63; Huxley and, 62–63; Lyotard and, 182–84; Marx and Engels and, 42–45, 48, 52; metaphysics of, 38, 101, 161; *Observations on the Feeling of the Beautiful and Sublime*, 173; *Religion Within the limits of Reason Alone*, 11; Schopenhauer and, 96, 107–109, 118–19, 158; theory of the sublime, 4–7, 9–12, 13–17, 20, 22–23, 25, 26, 46, 48, 53, 67, 71–74, 78–79, 92, 104–105, 106, 108, 118, 173, 179–84; Wells and, 70–79 passim
Kelvin, William Thompson, Lord, 64, 68, 92
King James Bible, 36
King Lear, 111
Kirwan, James, 2–3, 8, 13, 37, 186n9

labor, 8; Carlyle and, 38–41, 49, 51, 63; Marx and Engels and, 24–25, 44–45, 49, 52, 63; theory of value, 39
landscapes, 119; industrial, 16, 32–33; Wells's, 55, 58–59, 65, 77, 88, 181. See also dreamscapes, streets
Laocoön, 13–14, 40, 181
Laplace's demon, 85
laughter, 137, 139, 174
life-or-death struggle, 15, 45–46
liberalism, 42, 132, 183
libido, 150, 156
literature: apocalyptic, 38; *The*

Communist Manifesto as, 19–20, 30; German, 26, 28, 39; and philosophy, 2, 16–17, 181–82, 184; *Principles of Geology* as, 66
locomotor ataxia, 156
London, 16, 86, 130
Longinus, 1, 5, 8, 173
Lyell, Charles: *The Antiquity of Man*, 68; *Principles of Geology*, 64–69, 84
Lyotard, Jean-François, 179, 182–84

Machiavelli, Niccolò, 52
madness, 103, 115, 129–30, 153–54, 156, 161
Manchester, 31–34, 35–36, 41, 58, 125, 180
Martin, John, 37
Marx, Karl: and Bakunin, 96; *Deutsche-Französische Jahrbücher*, 27; *The German Ideology*, 42–43; *Economic and Philosophic Manuscripts of 1844*, 42, 44; and Engels, 29–32; and Hegel, 44–45. See also *The Communist Manifesto*
mathematical sublime, 6, 25, 107, 124, 130, 187n7; in *The Time Machine*, 71, 74, 77–78
masculinity, 17, 143, 173, 177
masochism, 143, 171, 175; as analogous to the sublime, 172–73, 181
Mendelssohn, Moses, 1
metaphor, 31, 34–35, 61, 67, 156; rendered literal, 58, 141–42, 154–56; sublime imagery as, 16, 24, 48, 93
metaphysics, 11, 96, 98–99, 118, 127, 134, 186n10
Middle Ages, 20, 36
middle class, 24, 29, 43, 55, 95, 97, 102. See also bourgeoisie

millenarianism. See apocalyptic, the
modernity, 19, 29, 32–33, 35, 49, 53
money, 24–26, 28, 185n5; mentioned, 116, 142, 174. See also cash nexus
Monk, Samuel, 2, 108
Moore, Samuel, 30–31
moral sublime, 8–9. See also ethics
motives, 100, 102, 118–19, 123, 128, 133, 150

narcissism, 117, 147, 152, 162, 165–66
nature, 16, 180–81; as deterministic, 40, 93; human continuity with, 62–62, 86–88, 118, 123, 127, 147–52 passim, 154–55; human distinction from, 5, 15, 20, 38, 45, 93, 183; human domination of, 20, 23, 38–41, 48, 56, 83–86; Kant's view of, 6–7, 9–13, 44, 46, 158, 164, 166; Schopenhauer's view of, 96, 118–20, 127, 158; state of, 34
natural sublime, 10, 16, 71, 108; in *The Communist Manifesto*, 23, 48–49; in *Chartism*, 32–33; in *The Time Machine*, 59–60, 64, 77, 81; in *The Secret Agent*, 124–27, 130
necessity. See determinism
neo-nominalism, 77–80, 82, 89, 93
New Republicans, 17, 82–83, 89–91, 95
New Testament, 167
Nietzsche, Friedrich, 15, 131; Conrad and, 129–30, 133–34, 158, 188n1; response to Schopenhauer, 127–28; *The Birth of Tragedy*, 127–29, 159. See also Dionysiac
Niagara Falls, 32–33, 36, 49, 58, 180

Normal School of Science, 60
noumenon, 11, 99, 118–19, 161, 186n2, 187n9

object of the sublime, 5–10, 16, 22–23, 46–47, 107–10, 118, 180–81; architecture as, 22, 73–74; changing status of, 16, 22–23, 58, 108–9, 134, 180–81; deep time as, 67–68, 77, 81, 92, 180–81; details as, 111–13, 114–16, 126, 181; Greenwich bomb as, 103–5; industry as, 16, 22–23, 32–33, 180; nature as, 10–12, 14, 16, 22, 58–60, 81, 124, 180
oceans, 14, 23, 25, 29, 32, 39, 46, 65
Old Testament, 37
optimism, 41, 63–64, 81–86, 88, 91, 96, 180

pain, 13, 50–51, 90–91, 98–99, 106; as component of the sublime, 5, 67, 182
parody: of the Dionysiac, 130; of the sublime subject, 116–17, 171, 173
pessimism, 40–41, 82, 95–96, 98–99, 128–29, 180–81
philosophy, 1, 15, 39, 161; analytic, 1; Conrad and, 98–100, 126–27, 134, 188n1; Freud and, 164; German, 28, 34, 159; Huxley and, 60, 62; and literature, 2, 16–17, 181–82, 184; scholastic, 107; Wells and, 70–71, 187n8
physics, 65, 84 *See also* thermodynamics
physiology, 46, 61, 106, 120, 121
pianola, 113, 121, 123, 128, 158–59, 189n8
pleasure, 5–6, 12, 74, 118, 182
player piano. *See* pianola

Poe, Edgar Allan, 104–5, 188n2
political agency: in Carlyle, 49–52; in *The Communist Manifesto*, 52–53; in Conrad, 98–99, 134; in Wells, 82–83, 89–90
political economy, 4. *See also* economics
pornography, 183
postmodernism, 1–2, 179, 182,
power: of the bourgeoisie, 16, 24, 44, 47–48, 186n11; industrial, 58, 21–23, 180; of the mind, 162; natural, 6–7, 10, 14, 23, 46, 119, 124; political, 170; supernatural, 22, 32, 141, 156, 164
principium individuationis, 101–2
principle of sufficient reason, 101
proletariat, 17, 20, 24, 35, 42, 45–53 passim, 88; mentioned, 95, 96
propaganda by deed, 96–98. *See also* terrorism
psychoanalysis, 168, 188n1; as metapsychological worldview, 148–52, 158; pre-Freudian ideas of, 157–62 passim; as therapeutic practice, 162–65
pyramids, 22

realism, 143–44, 156, 174; in Lyotard, 183
reason, 15, 38–39, 44, 46, 82–83, 87–92 passim, 166; irrationality, 97, 113; Kantian faculty, 6–7, 12, 52, 62–63, 74, 79, 105–6, 107, 163–65
red-light districts, 135, 147, 150, 158
Reid, Thomas, 7–8
reification, 48, 183
religion, 21, 23, 24, 36–37, 71, 152
repetition, 138, 145, 150–51
repression, 138–40, 161, 164–65
revolution, 86, 88, 117, 127, 132;

in *The Communist Manifesto*, 20–22, 29, 37, 42–43, 47, 52–53
Reid, Thomas, 7–8
rhetoric, 5, 57, 76, 95–97, 168, 189n13; of *The Communist Manifesto*, 19, 20–25, 30, 37, 52–53, 58, 186n8
romanticism, 26, 161–62, 170; and the sublime, 2, 22, 33, 159, 179, 187n7

sadomasochism. *See* masochism
Saint Peter's Basilica, 73
scales of magnitude, 64, 68–77 passim, 91, 93
Schelling, Friedrich Wilhelm Joseph, 159
Schiller, Friedrich, 13–15, 38–41, 108, 180–81
Schopenhauer, Arthur, 14, 17, 96, 180–81; aesthetic theory of, 100–6; Conrad's relation to, 99, 129, 133–34; *Essay on the Freedom of the Will*, 118; ethics of, 115–17; on freedom, 118–20, 125–26; metaphysics of, 16, 99, 113, 118–19, 125–27, 161; relation to Kant, 107–9, 118–19, 158; on the sublime, 15–16, 106–120 passim, 126, 158–59; *The World as Will and Representation*, 100–1, 106–10, 115–19, 126, 188n5
science, 56, 79–80, 180–81, 183, 187n3; Conrad and, 98, 100, 103; Freud and, 148–49, 162–63 nineteenth-century developments in, 56, 58–68 passim, 93; Wells and, 17, 70–71, 77–78, 81–84, 88, 90–92; in *The Secret Agent*, 95–96, 102, 111, 120
The Secret Agent: the Assistant Commissioner of Police, 17, 104, 112, 130–34, 135, 181; "Author's Note," 97, 103, 127; Bourdin incident, 97; Chief Inspector Heat, 103–6, 113, 120, 132, 188n2; dedication to Wells, 120; depiction of the urban landscape in, 124–26, 130–31, 135; Greenwich plot, 96–98, 101–5, 110–13, 132; the Home Secretary, 103, 105, 112, 127, 130, 134; Michaelis, 132–33; narrative characteristics of, 113–15, 121–23, 131, 133, 188n4; mentioned, 17, 99, 136; motif of details in, 110–15, 117, 126; motif of mechanism in, 120–23, 158–59; motif of Silenus in, 128–29; Ossipon, 111–15, 117, 121, 124, 128–30, 132, 159; the Professor, 113–17, 120–21, 123–24, 128, 130, 132, 159, 1188n2; Stevie, 105–106 112–13, 120–21, 123, 128, 132, 133; sublime in, 96, 100, 104–106, 107, 110–17 passim, 124–27 passim, 130–32, 134, 181; Toodles, 127; Verloc, 95–96, 101–102, 110–13, 115, 120–22, 124–25, 130–33, 158; Vladimir, 95–97, 101–3, 110–11, 124, 132–33; Winnie, 110, 112, 121–23. *See also* Conrad, Joseph
self-consciousness, 82, 83, 88, 132; in Hegel, 45–47, 52; of automata, 120–22. *See also* class consciousness
self-determination. *See* autonomy
sex, 155–56, 171, 183
Silenus, 128–29, 131
Silenus Restaurant, 121, 128, 133, 158
solar extinction, 59, 64, 91–92, 181
solitude, 59, 125, 167
sorcery, 22, 32, 42, 48, 156, 174, 183

Sorel, George, 97
soul, 10, 40, 62, 151
space, 67, 85–86, 90, 98–99, 101–3, 104, 119, 142, 186n2
Spencer, Herbert, 70
spontaneity, 44, 61, 184
starry skies, 14, 16, 71, 186n2
steam engines, 22–23, 57–58, 60, 61; Carlyle and, 39–40, 88, 125
Stoicism, 62
streets, 50, 114–15, 135, 158, 169, 170; as dreamscape, 145, 150, 154, 157; as sublime landscape, 16, 124–26, 130–31
suicide, 40, 88, 116
subject, the: autonomy and, 4–5, 15–17, 180–83; challenge to unitary conception of, 135, 139, 147–49, 151–58 passim, 169, 179–83; Conrad's ideal, 130–34; Freud's conception of, 151–54, 165–67, 169; the sublime and the, 1–2, 4–7 passim, 9–12, 14–17, 105–10, 161–62, 179–81; in Joyce, 154–58, 169–77; Marx's and Engels's conception of, 38, 44–47, 49, 52–53; postmodern attitude to the, 179–83; Schopenhauer's conception of, 99–100, 105–10, 116, 118–19; Wells's ideal, 56, 81–84, 89–90
subliminal mind. *See* unconscious
subliming (chemical process), 57–58, 93
syphilis, 156

technocracy, 17, 56, 88, 90, 95
technology, 16, 33, 58, 82, 183
The Tempest, 32
Tennyson, Alfred Lord, 64
thermodynamics, 60, 64, 92, 181
terror, 5; in *The Communist Manifesto*, 26, 38, 49; in *The Secret Agent*, 106, 112; in "The 'Uncanny,'" 152, 161. *See also* fear
terrorism, 96–103 passim, 116
thing-in-itself. *See* noumenon
time, 4, 84–86, 90, 98–99, 102, 104, 106, 119, 141–42. *See also* deep time
The Time Machine: The Chronic Argonauts, 84–86; depiction of future world, 57, 59, 79–80, 86–89; descriptions of time travel, 55–57, 74–77; Eloi, 57, 59, 79, 87–88; epilogue, 64, 81–83, 93, 187n10; "further vision", 65, 75, 79, 92, 181; frame narrative of, 80–82, 187n10; linguistic skepticism in, 79–80; mentioned, 136; *New Review* version, 70, 85; Morlocks, 59, 79, 84, 86–88; scientific background of, 60–69, 180–81; the sublime in, 57–60, 70, 77, 92–93; tension with Wells's later views, 83–93 passim; Time Traveller, 55–57, 58–60, 64–65, 70, 75–77, 79–89, 92–93, 181, 187n9; Weena, 57, 87–88

Ulysses, 135–36, 144, 157, 175, 188n1; "Ithaca," 136, 144; "Oxen of the Sun," 136
"The 'Uncanny:'" aesthetics in, 159–60, 167–68; critical approaches to, 167–68, 189n8, 189n13; death in, 141, 151–52, 156, 164–65, 167; discursive style of, 145–47, 150, 153–54, 167–69, 176–77, 181; discussion of free will in, 151; discussion of Hoffmann in, 153–54; discussion of Jentsch in, 153–54, 156; the double in,

151–52, 154, 165, 181; dreaming in, 145–46, 147, 181; epilepsy and madness in, 153–56, 162; fiction in, 168; Italian anecdote, 135, 145–47, 150, 154, 157, 167–69, 176; living dolls in, 152–54, 158, 181; omnipotence of thoughts in, 141, 147, 161–62, 164; prompt fulfilment of wishes in, 141, 147, 164; repetition in, 145, 150; repression in, 140, 161, 164–65; Schelling in, 159; subjectivity implied in, 147, 150–52, 154, 158, 161, 176–77, 180; the sublime in, 159–60; similarities to "Circe," 135, 145–47, 154, 169; surmounting in, 140, 161–69 passim, 177. *See also* Freud, Sigmund

uncanny, the: relationship to the sublime, 134, 158–61, 166, 179, 181; in "Circe," 136–45 passim, 171–72, 175; *See also* "The 'Uncanny'"

unconscious, the, 139, 141, 148, 152, 157, 159, 161–62, 176, 188n1; as basis for all thought, 149–50; collective, 157; as heteronomous force, 152–54, 163–66, 169

understanding: Kantian faculty, 72–74, 173

Unheimliche, 136, 153, 160, 167

Ussher, James, 75

utopia, 17, 81, 87

violence, 23, 46, 97, 106, 171

volcanoes, 23, 46, 65

volition, feeling of, 42, 61–62, 121–22, 128, 151, 156, 168

waterfalls, 16, 23, 32. *See also* Niagara Falls

Wells, G. P., 69

Wells, H. G.: *Anticipations*, 83, 90–92; *The Discovery of the Future*, 91; *First and Last Things*, 77, 89; *The First Men in the Moon*, 82, 186n2; *The Future in America*, 58; *God, the Invisible King*, 71, 186n2; interest in scale, 68–70, 72–75, 187n7; interest in technology, 58; and Kant, 70–71, 186n2; mentioned, 16, 95, 181; philosophical views of, 77–81, 84–85, 88–93, 180; political views of, 82–83; "The Rediscovery of the Unique," 77–81; and science, 60, 77–78; *The Science of Life*, 69–70, 72, 74–75, 82–83, 86; *The Secret Agent* dedicated to, 120; *A Short History of the World*, 68–70; *The Sleeper Awakes*, 70; social ascent, 84; *The Work, Wealth and Happiness of Mankind*, 77. *See also The Time Machine*

will, Schopenhauerian, 99–110 passim, 113, 115–19, 123, 126–27, 158, 161

Wittgenstein, Ludwig, 182

Wollstonecraft, Mary, 173

Wordsworth, William, 2

working class. *See* proletariat

www.ingramcontent.com/pod-product-compliance
Lightning Source LLC
Chambersburg PA
CBHW070804230426
43665CB00017B/2482